NES

E

TO

HENLEY

REGATTA

&

REACH

Other JLB Publishing Services books

Michael Jones Guide to Rowing

MICHAEL JONES GUIDE TO

HENLEY

REGATTA & REACH

Michael CN Jones

Published by
JLB Publishing Services

This edition published in Great Britain by
JLB Publishing Services
PO Box 3336
Wokingham RG40 3FY
April 2001

A CIP Cataloguing Record for this book is available from the British Library

ISBN 0-9539365-1-1

Cover artwork by JLB Services
Cover photographs by Sue Milton
Book photographs by Michael Jones
unless stated

Printed by
Bath Press CPI

For
John, George, Charles, Norman and Simon

FOREWORD

I was appointed Secretary of Henley Royal Regatta in the autumn of 1975. On my arrival I knew little about the Royal Regatta and even less about the sport of rowing. Friends remind me than it took half a decade before I could, with confidence, describe which way the river flowed! In those early days I made all the common mistakes of the uninitiated and, in retrospect, I marvel at the tolerance shown me by those who had spent a lifetime immersed in the arcane mysteries of the sport.

I once read an article by a well-known journalist who had visited the Regatta when researching a series of stories on minor sports. He was unable to enjoy his day at Henley to the full because he felt excluded and isolated by the language used by the knowledgeable rowing folk who surrounded and, apparently, ignored him.

Both he and I would have benefited from this informative little book in which such terminology is clearly and succinctly explained. Happily for me, I have also been helped to a growing understanding by a host of friends who have been born and bred to the river and the Regatta. This book mentions some and the connecting factor is one of continuity. The Gartons, the Hobbs, the Lukers and the Fenns are representative of generations of knowledge and experience.

Michael Jones, the author, is similarly heir to long family connections with the Royal Regatta and the town of Henley. For those coming fresh to either, this book will be an invaluable guide and for those who think they know all there is to know - well - they should read it anyway - afterwards they may be no wiser but perhaps they will be better informed.

Richard S Goddard
Secretary
Henley Royal Regatta **April 2001**

INTRODUCTION

My original intention was to write a book on Rowing and Henley Royal Regatta for those new to both.

The outcome was two books. One on Rowing, which was published in February 2001, intended for the parents of the large number of youngsters coming into the sport and the friends and loved ones of older 'youngsters' taking it up for the first time; and this one written principally for those who want to know more about the Royal Regatta and River at Henley.

So to introduce this book, I will break with convention and, as with the Rowing Book, set out the four things the book isn't.

- First of all it's not a guidebook to the town, although if the reader has not been to Henley, he might be surprised to find out what is on the Reach and what else happens on the other 51 'non-Henley Royal Regatta' weeks of the year.
- Secondly, it's not intended to replace anything official such as the 'Constitution and Rules of Henley Royal Regatta'.
- Neither is it a history of the Regatta although inevitably details as to when and why things happened have been included. Contrary to general belief, Henley does change each year, as I hope my book will reveal.
- Finally, it's not intended for those who have spent a lifetime living in Henley or attending the Regatta, or those who have won a Henley medal and who should know it all - although I would like to think that even they might find some of it of interest.

So if that's what it's not, what in fact is it?

For many people, certainly those reading the tabloid press, Henley Royal Regatta means ladies being turned away because they are showing their knees, men wandering around in small caps and brightly coloured blazers, and people living it up on strawberries and *Pimm's* - and no one watching the racing.

People who haven't been to the Regatta before may not appreciate that many people enjoy the Regatta *because* it has its standards, its traditions and its dress code for those in the Stewards' Enclosure - elsewhere people can, and do, wear what they like.

Most people come to the Regatta to meet friends and, contrary to popular belief, to watch the races - or at least the races where they might have an interest, with perhaps a son or daughter or a friend competing. Some come to cheer their club or college and many come to watch reigning British Olympic Champions in action, something few British sports were able to offer spectators in the 1990s.

But most of all I believe people enjoy Henley because it is quintessentially English - picnics in the country, a day on the river, green lawns, blue skies, sunshine and the pleasure of seeing English amateur sportsmen beating the best in the world - sometimes.

Henley is still the Mecca for world rowing, as Ascot is for horse racing, Cowes for sailing and Wimbledon for tennis. Henley is an international Regatta although its head-to-head, knockout racing is very different to the multi-lane, repêchage, regattas of the Olympic Games and World Championships. In soccer parlance, Henley might be compared to the FA Cup, with multi lane Regattas being compared to the Football League. Whilst the latter might well produce the overall champion, it's the atmosphere and tension of the underdog meeting and possibly beating the favourite in a one-to-one encounter, that makes the FA Cup so exciting, and makes Henley unique in international rowing.

Visitors to the Regatta are usually baffled by the 'Hole in the Wall', the 'Barrier' and the 'Pink Palace'. They don't understand why the stations are called Berks after Berkshire and Bucks after Buckinghamshire when Henley is in Oxfordshire, and why FE Weatherly who wrote 'Danny Boy' and the 'Roses of Picardy' is so famous in the World of Rowing. In fairness there is no reason why they should understand. All sports have their own vocabulary and jargon, and rowing and Henley are no exception.

Many also come to Henley during the other 51 weeks of the year - and are often surprised to discover that the Henley Reach does have a life outside the Regatta. Few realise that rowing takes place on the river at Henley every day of the year - weather permitting. In addition to rowers and scullers, ranging from ten-year old novices to Olympic champions, training from the three clubs on the Reach, there are four other regattas in the summer, the Henley Boat Races in the spring and four head of the river races during the winter.

Others come to Henley simply to enjoy the river and the countryside and the historic and beautiful houses between Marsh and Hambleden locks.

So this book is intended to provide information about the Regatta and the stretch of River Thames at Henley for those who would like to know more about both. It's not meant to be a history book but as there are reasons for all developments at the Regatta and as most thinking people naturally ask 'why' when told about something, I have tried where possible to incorporate background details in the explanation.

I have purposely tried to avoid mentioning too many Henley personalities although naturally have made an exception in the case of Sir Steven Redgrave, CBE and listed all his Henley wins. For the record, and for the aspiring newcomer to show he is human after all, I have also listed the few occasions when he didn't win.

And to answer the question as to why I have called it the 'Michael Jones Guide to Henley - Regatta & Reach'; it is mainly to emphasise that it is not an official Regatta or Town publication. This is my book and, as with my Guide to Rowing, it gives me the opportunity to include references to items that I think are fascinating and informative and which I would like to pass onto others.

Finally I have arranged for the book to be the size it is so that it will slip easily into the pocket or handbag.

If, by being a ready source of information, it goes someway towards helping the reader understand and enjoy Henley, the Regatta and the beautiful Reach, all the work will have been worthwhile.

Michael CN Jones Henley-on-Thames - 9 April 2001

Acknowledgements

John Allen
Jill Butcher
John Fenn
Hilary Fisher
Henley Rowing Club
Tony Hobbs
Richard Goddard and Daniel Grist together with
Pam, Tessa, and Amelia in the Royal Regatta Office
Nicola Jones
Simon Jones
Leander Club and members of the Lensday Group
John Luker
Ivan Pratt
EG (Teddy) Selwyn
Mike Sweeney and the Stewards of Henley Royal
Regatta
John Waters
Susan Winter

and my many other friends, too numerous to mention, who have been gracious enough to answer my questions during the preparation of this book.

HENLEY

REGATTA
&
REACH

The Royal Regatta Course and Plan of the Enclosures, as shown overleaf, can also be found in the Regatta Programme. They are reproduced in this book with the kind permission of the Stewards of Henley Royal Regatta.

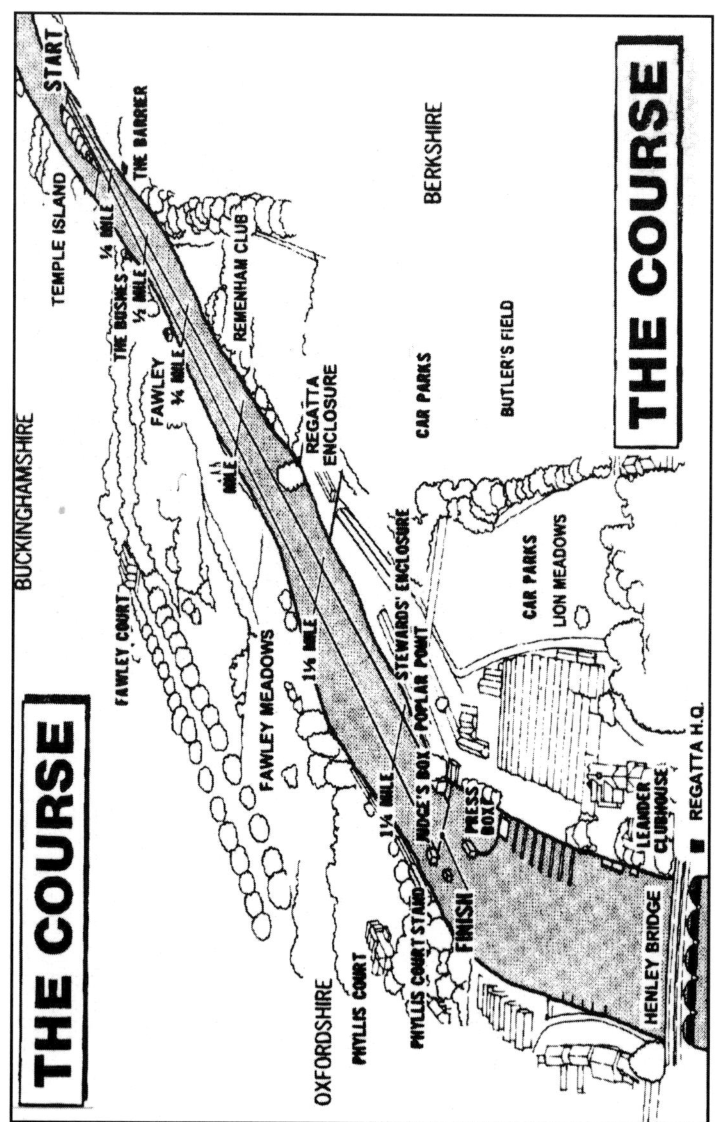
THE COURSE
START
THE BARRIER
TEMPLE ISLAND
BERKSHIRE
¼ MILE
THE BUSHES
½ MILE
REMENHAM CLUB
FAWLEY
¾ MILE
BUCKINGHAMSHIRE
MILE
REGATTA ENCLOSURE
CAR PARKS
BUTLER'S FIELD
STEWARDS' ENCLOSURE
CAR PARKS
LION MEADOWS
FAWLEY COURT
FAWLEY MEADOWS
1¼ MILE
POPLAR POINT
JUDGE'S BOX
1½ MILE
PRESS BOX
LEANDER CLUBHOUSE
REGATTA H.Q.
HENLEY BRIDGE
FINISH
PHYLLIS COURT STAND
PHYLLIS COURT
OXFORDSHIRE
THE COURSE

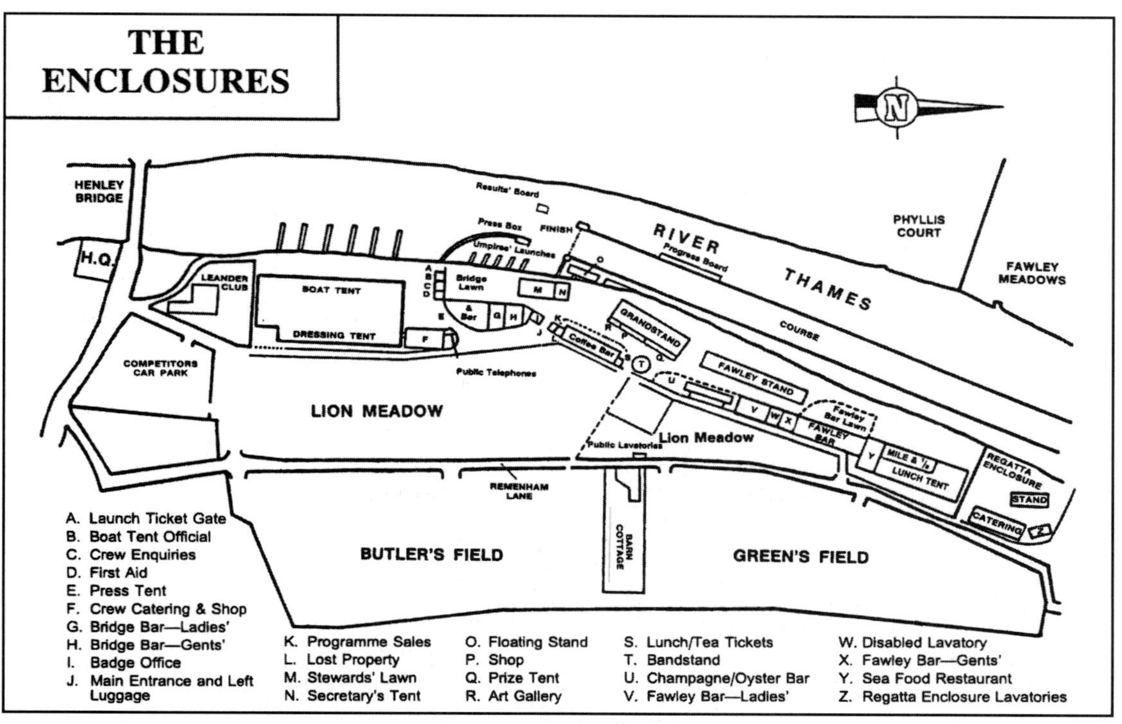
THE ENCLOSURES
HENLEY BRIDGE
H.Q.
LEANDER CLUB
COMPETITORS CAR PARK
BOAT TENT
DRESSING TENT
LION MEADOW
BUTLER'S FIELD
REMENHAM LANE
GREEN'S FIELD
BARN COTTAGE
Results' Board
Press Box
Umpires' Launches
FINISH
Bridge Lawn
& Bar
Public Telephones
Coffee Bar
GRANDSTAND
Public Lavatories
Lion Meadow
RIVER THAMES
Progress Board
COURSE
FAWLEY STAND
Fawley Bar Lawn
FAWLEY BAR
MILE & ⅞ LUNCH TENT
REGATTA ENCLOSURE
STAND
CATERING
PHYLLIS COURT
FAWLEY MEADOWS
N
A. Launch Ticket Gate
B. Boat Tent Official
C. Crew Enquiries
D. First Aid
E. Press Tent
F. Crew Catering & Shop
G. Bridge Bar—Ladies'
H. Bridge Bar—Gents'
I. Badge Office
J. Main Entrance and Left Luggage
K. Programme Sales
L. Lost Property
M. Stewards' Lawn
N. Secretary's Tent
O. Floating Stand
P. Shop
Q. Prize Tent
R. Art Gallery
S. Lunch/Tea Tickets
T. Bandstand
U. Champagne/Oyster Bar
V. Fawley Bar—Ladies'
W. Disabled Lavatory
X. Fawley Bar—Gents'
Y. Sea Food Restaurant
Z. Regatta Enclosure Lavatories

HENLEY
REGATTA
&
REACH

NOTES:

· Words which have been used in descriptions but which have been explained elsewhere have been printed in ***italics*** (and emphasised in **bold** to avoid confusion with boat names, quotations, etc).

· Rowing and Henley are inter-related but there is too much information for one 'pocket book'. So, having included some references to 'Henley' in my 'Guide to Rowing', I have explained some rowing jargon in this book, but only where there is a close Henley connection.

· 'Regatta' refers to Henley Royal Regatta unless stated.

· The names of the Regatta trophies and events are also inter-related, the abbreviated name of a trophy often being used to describe an event eg. it is acceptable to say that the Grand (the Grand Challenge Cup) is the senior event at the Regatta, and an entry in the Diamonds (the Diamond Challenge Sculls) means an entry in the men's single sculling event.

· All references to the masculine refer also to the feminine unless stated.

· For metric equivalents of British measurements and weights, and vice versa, see WEIGHTS AND MEASURES.

ADMINISTRATIVE STAFF COLLEGE

See - HENLEY MANAGEMENT COLLEGE

ADVERTISING

The Regatta does not allow advertising on Regatta property, and advertising on ***boats*** and ***oars*** on the ***River Thames*** is unlawful. To help competitors who rely on sponsorship the Regatta has rules, similar to ***ARA*** and ***FISA*** Rules, which govern the amount of information about sponsors that can be shown on boats, oars and ***clothing***.

ALIGNING

This is the procedure of ensuring the ***bows*** of ***boats*** are level at the start of a race.

Since 1967, the Aligner at Henley, referred to as the ***Start Judge***, has aligned the boats by instructing the officials on the ***start floats*** to pull back or push out the sterns of the boats until the ***bows*** are level with the starting line. When the Start Judge is satisfied that the bows are level he will indicate to the ***Umpire*** by switching his 'traffic lights' from red to green.

See - REGATTA COURSE and STARTING A RACE AT HENLEY

AMARYLLIS

Amaryllis is one of the six 50ft ***launches*** used for ***umpiring*** at the Regatta. Built by Messrs ***Hobbs & Sons*** in 1928 and subsequently purchased by Cambridge University Boat Club, *Amaryllis* was used until 1995 when it was sold to a local resident. It was then taken out of service and restored and is now being used again for umpiring at the Regatta.

Before *Amaryllis* was sold the Regatta arranged for a mould to be taken from the lines of the hull for the new launches ***Ariadne***, ***Argonaut*** and ***Ulysses***.

AMATEUR ROWING ASSOCIATION

The ARA was established in 1881 (although some records indicate 1882). It is the governing body of the sport in England except for ***Henley Royal Regatta*** and the ***University Boat Race***.

Based at The Priory, 6 Lower Mall, Hammersmith, London W6 9DJ, the Association uses the old clubhouse of the National Provincial Bank RC which it purchased from National Westminster Bank in 1990. The brick gatepost carries a small plaque 'This was part of the original stonework of the tower of the church of Henley-on-Thames'.

See - REGATTA AFFILIATION

AMATEUR STATUS

Only amateurs have been allowed to race at Henley. The controversial entry of a coxless four of French-Canadian lumberjacks in 1878 contributed much to the discussion as to what constituted an amateur.

In 1879 the ***Stewards of the Regatta***, in defining an amateur, decided that, to quote from the Rules of 1880:-

No person shall be considered as an Amateur Oarsman or Sculler or Coxswain:

1 Who has ever competed in any open competition for a stake, money, or entrance fee. (This does not apply to Foreign entries).

2 Who has ever competed with or against a professional for any prize.

3 Who has ever taught, pursued, or assisted in the practice of Athletic Exercises of any kind as a means of gaining a livelihood.

4 Who has been employed in or about boats for money or wages.

5 Who is or has been, by trade or employment for wages, a mechanic, artisan, or labourer.

This was similar to the definition of an amateur used by the ***Amateur Rowing Association***. Nevertheless, as a result of problems encountered in the 1920s and 1930s because of the more liberal definition of an amateur used by some other countries, the Stewards redefined an amateur in 1938.

Two significant instances helped to bring this about.

In 1920 the entry from JB Kelly Snr, a member of the Vesper BC, USA and who at one time had been an apprentice bricklayer, was refused by the ***Committee of Management***. The decision was taken principally because the Regatta had barred Vesper since 1906 following reports that their 1905 Henley crew had accepted money. Nevertheless the Committee of Management in 1920 recorded that Kelly was also not qualified under General Rule 1(e) of 1920 viz. no person shall be considered an amateur - *Who is or has been by trade or employment for wages, a mechanic, artisan, or labourer, or engaged in any menial duty*. Nevertheless Kelly was allowed to enter the ***Olympic Games*** in 1920 where he won the single sculls.

Then in 1936 the Regatta refused an entry from the Australian Olympic Eight because it consisted of policemen who were not considered to be amateurs.

The final step came in December 1997 when, to bring Henley into line with rules controlling international rowing, the ***Stewards*** removed all references in the rules of the Regatta to the word 'amateur', replacing it with the concept of ***eligibility***.

See - ENTRIES and ROYALTY

THE ANGEL ON THE BRIDGE

The Angel on the Bridge is believed to have been built in the early 18th century and is one of two ***Brakspear's*** public houses that face the river (the other is the ***Little White Hart***).

It is leased to Brakspear's, being owned by the Trustees of the Henley Municipal Charities, having been built on land given to the town in 1547 as part of the Longlands Charity.

Situated next to ***Henley Bridge*** with ***St Mary's Church*** in the background, the Angel on the Bridge is probably one of the most photographed public houses on the river. Like ***Regatta Headquarters*** across the river, the Angel on the Bridge has in it's basement, one of the stone arches of the original Henley Bridge believed to date from 1170.

The 'Angel' as it was originally known, became the 'Angel on the Bridge' relatively recently to avoid confusion with the nearby 'Angel' public house and restaurant at the bottom of ***White Hill***, which also changed its name and is now the 'Little Angel'.

ANGLING

The Remenham Angling Society has fishing rights off Regatta land (except ***Temple Island***) on both sides of the river. The RAS Bailiff also collects mooring fees from boats moored on Regatta land outside the Regatta period.

ANNIVERSARIES

There have been three significant anniversaries of the Regatta.

The Centenary in 1939 took place with the clouds of war looming over Europe. The ***Stewards*** organised a concert on the ***Floating Stand*** to celebrate the occasion and established a ***Double Sculling*** Race. There were eight entries for this new event and the final was a race between J Beresford Jnr and LF Southwood of Thames Rowing Club, who were also the British Double Sculls Gold Medallists at the 1936 Berlin ***Olympic Games***, and G Scherli and E Broschi of Societa Canottieri 'Nettuno' Di Trieste, Italy. Beresford and Southwood led by ½ length at the ***Barrier*** but Scherli and Broschi led by ½ length at ***Fawley*** and the milepost. At the $1^1/_8$ miles ***signal*** the doubles were level - and stayed level, the result being a ***dead heat***. The Stewards decided, for the first time in the history of the Regatta, to award goblets to both finalists rather than ask them to race again.

The sesquicentennial (150th) anniversary in 1989 took place when the Regatta had reached its peak in terms of financial success and record levels of ***entries***. A dinner, held in the Henley Town Hall on Saturday 25th March, spilled over to the 26th, the anniversary of the meeting which founded the Regatta. On 18th May 1989 a Dinner at Guildhall in the City of London was organised by ***Payne and Gunter*** the Regatta's Official Hospitality Caterers in 1989; income from the Regatta's ***Fawley Meadows Hospitality Village*** having led the improvement in the Regatta's finances over the previous 10 years. An evening of celebrations took place on 14th June the anniversary of the first Regatta and, immediately before the 1989 Regatta, a garden party was held at Stonor Park the home of Lord Camoys. At the Regatta every competitor was presented with a bronze commemorative medal. On the Saturday, all but three of the 28 living winners of the ***Diamond Challenge Sculls*** attended a reception and were presented with a presentation medal in recognition of the occasion - and 20 sculled over the latter half of the ***Regatta Course*** during the luncheon interval.

But the event that all those present on finals day will remember, apart from the spectacular Ball in the ***Stewards' Enclosure*** and extra ***firework*** display on ***Fawley Meadows***, was the final at 5.15pm of the ***Ladies Challenge Plate*** between Harvard University USA and Nottinghamshire County Rowing Association. NCRA, who averaged over two stones per man lighter than Harvard, led all the way and crossed the line five lengths ahead of Harvard. They broke the ***Barrier***, ***Fawley*** and Course records - the Fawley and full Course records having been set the previous day by Harvard. Immediately Harvard finished rowing the ***cox*** put his hand under the boat and pulled out a piece of wood that had been caught in the fin and dragged by the ***crew*** over most of the Course. Harvard did not appeal and NCRA were announced as the winner. When the Harvard coach was told about the incident he appealed on the grounds of outside interference, and this was upheld by the Committee. Both crews had disembarked and the ***Presentation of the Prizes*** was by then less than half an hour away so it was decided that the re-row would take place after the ceremony at 8pm.

Then, in front of an estimated crowd of 10,000 rowing

enthusiasts who had remained in the ***Enclosures*** and elsewhere along the Course to watch the event, they raced again. NCRA again led all the way and won by $^2/_3$ length, equalling their Fawley record and breaking their earlier Barrier and Course records.

The 150th Regatta in 1999 was a far more low key event, the main celebration being the presentation of a plaque by the Stewards to the Henley Town Council to commemorate the occasion; and a larger than usual firework display commensurate with the anniversary.

ARA

See - AMATEUR ROWING ASSOCIATION

ARGONAUT

Argonaut is one of the three 50ft ***umpire launches*** owned by the Regatta. The other two are ***Ariadne*** and ***Ulysses***. *Argonaut* was built by The Steam & Electric Launch Company of Ludham, Norfolk, using the mould taken from the lines of the hull of the umpire launch ***Amaryllis***.

Argonaut, together with the umpire launch *Ulysses*, was launched on 7th May 1993 by the ***Chairman*** of the ***Committee of Management***, Mike Sweeney, and the two past Chairmen, John Garton, CBE and Peter Coni, OBE, QC.

MA Sweeney. JL Garton, CBE. PRC Coni, OBE, QC.

ARIADNE

Ariadne is one of the three 50ft **umpire launches** owned by the Regatta. The other two are ***Argonaut*** and ***Ulysses***. *Ariadne* was built by The Steam & Electric Launch Company of Ludham, Norfolk, at a cost of £69,000, using the mould taken from the lines of the hull of the umpire launch ***Amaryllis***.

Ariadne was launched on 19th May 1992 by the then ***Chairman of the Committee of Management***, Peter Coni, OBE, QC. Ariadne replaced ***Bosporos***, which was then sold and shipped to Holland.

ART GALLERY

This gallery was established in 1994 under the auspices of ***Henley Royal Regatta Limited***, the Regatta's trading arm. It provides an exhibition of original works of art on the themes of the Regatta, the sport of rowing and the ***Henley Reach*** of the river.

The Gallery is situated in the ***Stewards' Enclosure***, next to the Regatta Shop behind the ***Grandstand***, and is open for viewing daily during the five days of the Regatta when the items are available for sale to Members and their Guests.

See - REGATTA MERCHANDISE

ASSENDON SPRING

This is the name of the watercourse (sometimes spelt Assenden) which rises in the ***Chiltern Hills*** in a field of farmer Maurice Hunt near the Henley to Watlington road, ½mile south of the village of Stonor; the field being part of the Stonor Estate of Lord Camoys.

The stream flows four miles along the side of the road through the villages of Middle and Lower Assendon, along the Fair Mile and into Henley where it flows underground ('culverted') and eventually flows into the river. The precise point has been the subject of debate but it is generally believed to have flowed into the river at the bottom of ***New Street***, where it joins ***Riverside***, at a point close to the finish of the ***Regatta Course***. Following flooding problems in the winter of 2000/2001, it was reported in the ***Henley Standard*** that in 1934 the stream had been diverted to ***Phyllis Court Club***.

There is a story that on 27th April 1774, when the spring was in full flow, a two-year old girl fell in and was carried underground the length of New Street and was discharged into the river where she was rescued without injury. This was one of the earliest cases to be reported to the Royal Humane Society, which was founded in 1774.

The Assendon Spring, which can be dated back over 300 years, does not flow continuously and is often dry for years. According to local folklore, although this has as many believers as disbelievers the latter claiming that often floodwater is mistaken for the spring, the flowing of the Assendon Spring is an omen for war having flowed in 1914 before the first World War and next in 1939 before the second World War. The last two occasions that it is reported to have flowed, before the winter of 2000/2001 when houses along the route particularly at Northfield End were badly flooded, were in 1950 before the Korean War and in 1981 shortly before the Falklands War.

ATHLETES

There is a general tendency in the administration of the sport to use the all-embracing term 'rowers' to describe all participants in the sport including scullers.

Nevertheless, it is incorrect to refer to ***rowers*** or rowing when describing ***scullers*** or ***sculling*** and vice versa.

To avoid the terminology problems of distinguishing between rowers and scullers, oarsmen and oarswomen, junior boys and junior girls, many prefer the all-embracing description 'athlete' when describing members of a ***crew***, including, whenever possible, the ***cox***.

(Note: The sport considers the cox, who is in charge of the boat, to be part of a ***crew*** and therefore justifies being referred to as an athlete. The cox is not included in the average weight of a crew)

For convenience the description 'athlete' has been used in this book wherever possible.

AWESOME FOURSOME

The popular name given to the Great Britain ***Olympic*** and World Champion ***Coxless Four*** of James Cracknell at ***Bow***, ***Steven Redgrave*** at two, Tim Foster at three and Matthew Pinsent at ***Stroke***. The ***crew***, also referred to as the 'Redgrave Four', was based at ***Leander Club*** in Henley and coached by Jürgen Grobler, Chief Coach of the Great Britain Men's ***Heavyweight*** Rowing Squad.

The crew won the Coxless Fours World Championship in 1997 at their first attempt and the ***Stewards' Challenge Cup*** at Henley

In 1998, in addition to retaining their World Championship title, they beat the Australian 1996 Olympic Coxless Fours Gold Medallists, the ***Oarsome Foursome***, (which also included three members of the victorious 1992 Australian Olympic Gold medal winning coxless four) in the semi final of the Stewards' Challenge Cup at Henley and went on to win the Cup for the second year.

In 1999, with Ed Coode replacing Tim Foster who was out of the crew for a year after sustaining a serious hand injury in

1998 and then an operation on his back, the crew were again World Champions and won the World Cup - and the Stewards' at Henley.

Finally, with Tim Foster back in the crew, they won the World Cup in 2000 and the Stewards' Challenge Cup making it four wins in the Stewards' in a row. In 2000 they became media personalities following the BBC programme 'Gold Fever' which monitored their progress from 1997 leading up to the Olympic Games. Their win in Sydney gave James Cracknell and Tim Foster their first Olympic Gold medals, Matthew Pinsent his third and Steven Redgrave his fifth.
See - INDOOR ROWING

BADGE OFFICE

Although primarily concerned with the issue of ***badges***, the Badge Office is the financial department of the Regatta and the office of the Regatta's Financial Manager - known informally, though wrongly, as the Regatta Treasurer.

On the Thursday before the Regatta the Badge Office staff move, with their desks and equipment, from their base in ***Regatta Headquarters*** to temporary premises at the entrance to the ***Stewards' Enclosure*** and remain there for the duration of the Regatta.

Whilst in the Stewards' Enclosure, the Badge Office is open to the public on the Friday and Saturday before the Regatta, and then throughout Regatta week, reopening in Regatta Headquarters after the Regatta.

BADGES

Regatta literature normally differentiates between badges, ***labels***, ***passes*** and ***tickets***.

At Henley, badges identify the wearer and thus the areas/enclosures where he/she may be permitted to enter eg.

badges worn by ***Stewards of the Regatta*** and ***Chairman's Assistants*** allow access to any part of the Regatta site, badges worn by ***Members of the Stewards' Enclosure*** allow access to the Stewards' Enclosure, ***Regatta Enclosure*** and ***Boat Tent Area***, Regatta Enclosure badges allowing entry to that Enclosure and to the Boat Tent Area.

BANDSTAND

Situated in the ***Stewards' Enclosure*** behind the ***Grandstand***.

A band, usually a regimental band, plays a selection of music throughout each day of racing until after the last race has finished when the National Anthem is played - apart from the last day of the Regatta when the National Anthem is played after the Presentation of the ***Prizes***.

The Programme of Music, which is submitted in advance to the Regatta for approval, is listed on the last page of the daily ***Regatta Programme***.

BANKING FACILITIES

Since 1972 Lloyds TSB (formerly Lloyds Bank) has provided banking facilities at the Regatta by means of a mobile banking unit. This is established on the edge of ***Little Lion*** by the ***Bandstand*** Entrance of the ***Stewards' Enclosure***, facing the road that crosses to ***Remenham Lane***. The Bank is open to the public during the five days of the Regatta

BARN COTTAGE

This house, built circa 1870, is situated in ***Remenham Lane*** between ***Butler's Field*** and ***Green's Field***.

Before 1949, when it became the home of the Selwyn family, it had been the groundsman's cottage belonging to ***Henley Cricket Club*** before the club moved to its present location at the end of Remenham Lane at the bottom of ***White Hill***. The cricket field was adjacent to the house on land later used by Henley Tennis Club and known as ***Selwyn's Meadow***. The cricket pavilion is still standing and is attached to Barn Cottage.

Barn Cottage was bought by the Regatta in 1983.
See - BARN COTTAGE BOAT CLUB

BARN COTTAGE BOAT CLUB

In the middle 1950s, ***Leander Club*** became the training base for a number of the country's top rowing athletes. As some were not eligible to join Leander under the rules that existed at that time, Barn Cottage Boat Club was established to enable the group to race together as one club. This was effectively the beginning of the squad training system.

The Club took its name from the house, ***Barn Cottage***, situated in ***Remenham Lane*** between ***Butler's Field*** and ***Green's Field***, the home of EG (Teddy) Selwyn, rowing coach and one of the founder members of the Club.

Barn Cottage BC quickly became the most successful rowing club in the country, its most notable achievement being to win the ***Head of the River Race*** (for eights over the reverse of the ***University Boat Race*** course of 4¼miles/6.84km, on the Tideway in London) on five consecutive occasions 1958 - 1962, and coming second in 1963, 1964 and 1965 - an achievement only surpassed by London RC who won from 1926 to 1935.

Barn Cottage won the ***Stewards' Challenge Cup*** in 1958 after which club members moved to Molesey BC and competed for both clubs. In 1960 Barn Cottage again won the Stewards' and club members made significant contributions to the Molesey crews that won the ***Grand Challenge Cup*** in

1960 the Stewards' in 1963 and the ***Prince Philip*** in 1964.

Barn Cottage Boat Club was wound up in 1966. Barn Cottage was bought by the Regatta in 1983.

See - SELWYN'S MEADOW

BARN ELMS

Barn Elms is the name of the house situated on land immediately ***upstream*** of ***Remenham Club*** on the Berkshire side of the river.

BARRIER

The Remenham Barrier, situated 2,089ft (636.7m) from the starting line, is the first official timing point on the ***Regatta Course***.

The only 'barrier' on the ***towpath*** at this point, is a cattle

grid. The reason for the name is not known - but on early maps it is referred to as a 'horse barrier' which may have meant a fence or gate, which would have been a barrier for horses towing boats.

The Official in the box at the Barrier, situated on the ***Buckinghamshire*** side of the Course, drops a flag as the ***bow*** of the leading boat crosses the Barrier line. As the Barrier box is also a ***signal box*** he will then raise the number board of the leading competitor to the top of the frame and position the other board against it relative to the distance the second competitor is behind the first. The Timekeeper and Race Recorder standing at the back of the ***umpire's launch*** are then able to record the time taken to reach the Barrier and the position of the race at that point.

Statistically, 86% of competitors ahead at the Barrier stay ahead and win the race.

See - RACE REPORTS and REGATTA RECORDS

THE BARRIER CUP

See - ROYAL HENLEY REGATTA

BERKS

Berks is the abbreviation for ***Berkshire*** and the name of the ***station*** on the ***Enclosures*** side of the ***Regatta Course***.

BERKSHIRE

All the land on the ***Henley Reach*** on the ***Enclosures*** side of the river from ***Marsh lock downstream*** to ***Hambleden lock*** is situated in the Royal County of Berkshire.

Wokingham District Council is the unitary authority responsible for this stretch of riverbank, the Berkshire County Council having been abolished in 1998.

For parliamentary purposes the Berkshire side of the Henley Reach is part of the Maidenhead constituency.

BIBLE

Organisers of regattas and ***head of the river races*** keep a record of the problems experienced during the lead-up to the event and on the day, which need attention before the following year. The meeting held after the event usually has a title such as the 'post mortem' or 'wash-up' meeting. The Royal

Regatta is no exception and used to record the problems in a book known as the 'Bible' so that the post Regatta meeting was always referred to the 'Bible Reading'. This meeting has now been replaced with a number of meetings each autumn between the ***Chairman*** and ***Secretary*** and the various people and organisations involved eg. the ***Chairman's Assistants***, ***Contractors***, ***Environment Agency***, ***Police***.

BIRDS

A wide range of birds can be seen on the ***Henley Reach*** including buzzards, ***Canada geese***, ducks, great crested grebe, heron, kingfishers, mallards, moorhens, the occasional red kite and, of course, ***swans***.

BLACK & EDGINGTON

Black and Edgington is the official tentage company of the Regatta. It supplies approximately 19,000 sq.m of tentage which is brought to the Regatta site during the three months leading up to the Regatta, and removed by the end of August each year.

The company, under various names, eg. John Edgington, Benjamin Edgington and now Black and Edgington, has been used by the Regatta since early in the 20th century. Since December 2000 Black & Edgington has been part of the Arena Event Services Division of Telecast Limited.

In addition to being the major tentage contractor at Wimbledon, the company has held a Royal warrant since 1863 and has supplied marquees and tentage for Royal and State occasions in London including Buckingham Palace garden parties.

BLACK PIGLET

This is the name of the workboat owned by the Regatta.

Other boats not owned by the Regatta but used during the event, primarily for Regatta Officials, include *Impey*, *Crossbill* and *L'Amazon*.
See - UMPIRE LAUNCHES

BLADE

The word 'blade' is often used in place of the words '***oar***' or '***scull***'. (Note: In this book 'blade' has been used when referring to oars and sculls together)

'Blade' is also the name of the flattened, curved part of an oar or scull which enters the water, also known as the 'spoon'.

BLANDY MEADOW

This is the name of the Enclosures 'field' next to ***Lion Meadow***. It was leased by the Regatta in 1926 and purchased in 1939.

This land was once owned by the family of Henley's most infamous resident, Mary Blandy. In 1751 Mary poisoned her father, Francis Blandy, a solicitor and Henley's Town Clerk. Francis Blandy had objected to her relationship with Captain William H Cranstoun, the son of a Scottish nobleman because Cranstoun had been previously married. Cranstoun, who was 13 years older than Mary, had supplied her with the arsenic claiming that it was a potion that would make her father look more kindly on their friendship.

Mary was hanged at Oxford gaol on 6 April 1752 at the age of 32 protesting her innocence claiming that she did not realise the potion was poisonous. Her body was brought back to Henley the same day and she was buried beside her father and mother in the chancel of ***St Mary's Church***. Cranstoun is reported to have suffered an agonising death in France less than a year later.

BLAZERS

Lightweight coloured jackets worn by sportsmen particularly oarsmen.

A variety of blazers are worn at Henley, the colours usually indicating the club or the ***crew*** of the wearer.

The name ‘ blazer’ has two origins.

1 That the name is derived from the ‘red’ (blazing) jackets worn by members of Lady Margaret BC, a college boat club of Cambridge University, founded in 1825, and

2 That in 1845, before blue jackets were standard British naval wear, the Captain of HMS Blazer purchased smart dress jackets with multi-coloured vertical stripes for the crew of his gig. As a result the jackets became known as ‘blazers’.

BOAT AUCTION

See - PHILLIPS TRADITIONAL RIVERCRAFT AND EPHEMERA AUCTION

BOAT DOCK

See - STEWARDS’ BOAT DOCK

BOAT NUMBER PLATE

See - IDENTIFICATION NUMBER

BOAT REPAIRERS’ COMPOUND

See - COMPETITORS’ CAR PARK

BOAT TENT AREA

The area between the ***Stewards’ Enclosure*** and ***Leander Club***.

Competitors’ ***boats*** have been kept on this land since 1873 when the wooden boathouse, situated where ***Regatta Headquarters*** now stands, became too crowded. There is a record of boats also being kept by ***Temple Island*** in 1888.

The Regatta purchased the site, known then as Regatta Meadow, in 1926. Individual tents were erected each year until 1963, since when the Boat Tent has been a single, pur-

pose built, framed tent. The design was modified in 1999 and now comprises 16 bays capable of holding up to 335 boats. Despite this it has not been possible for many years to provide storage racks for every boat entered for the Regatta.

There are six floating rafts, referred to as '***crew*** rafts' or

'embarkation stages', which protrude from the bank along the front of the Boat Tent. These had been fixed rafts until the early 1970s when they started to present problems with the timbers lifting whenever the river level rose. So between 1973 and 1976 they were all replaced by floating rafts. Competitors are expected to put their boats into the water on the ***downstream*** side of a raft so that the ***stream*** will help them keep clear as they move out into the river. Boats return on the ***upstream*** side where the stream helps the boat to come alongside the raft.

Since 1986 entry to the Boat Tent Area frontage has been restricted during the Regatta to those with a Boat Tent Area ***badge*** (which can be obtained free of charge from the Regatta) or those with any other Enclosure badge. This is to exclude picknickers who get in the way of competitors going on to or coming off of the water.

Admission to the Boat Tent Area is via either the main entrance by the side of the ***Crews' Catering Tent*** or the gate on the ***towpath*** at the end of the ***Leander*** Wall. Entry to the Boat Tent and the Competitors' ***Dressing Tents***, the Sports Council Dope Testing Unit, the ***Ergo Room*** and ***Crews' Lounge***, situated at the rear of the Boat Tent is restricted to competitors, ***coaches*** and Regatta officials.

Other tents, all at the downstream end of the Boat Tent Area next to the Stewards' Enclosure, include the Boat Tent

Officials and Crews' Enquiries Tent where competitors attend to be ***weighed*** before the Regatta. There is also a ***Press Tent***, a ***First Aid*** Tent manned by members of ***St John Ambulance*** and a tent used by the Sports Injury Clinic.

The Boat Tent Officials, who allocate boat racks to competitors and sell ***Lists of Entries***, are responsible for the area from the Monday, sixteen days before the Regatta, when the tentage is taken over from ***Black & Edgington***, until after the Regatta has finished.

BOAT TRAILER

Boats are often transported on trailers towed by cars or mini buses. ***Pairs***, ***doubles*** and single ***sculling*** boats and usually ***fours*** can be loaded in one piece. ***Eights*** are normally 'sectional' (and some fours) so that they can be dismantled into two parts for easy transportation.

Occasionally it is possible to transport a boat with the ***riggers*** attached but usually they are removed and placed in the base of the trailer together with the other items of equipment including ***blades***, stools and bicycles.

Those Regatta competitors required to race in the ***Qualifying Races*** on the Friday before the Regatta, are normally expected to park their boat trailer in ***Lion Meadow*** and 'boat' (take their boat to the water and embark) direct from there. Competitors who qualify are usually then allocated a rack in the Boat Tent and their trailer moved to the official Boat Trailer Park round the hedge line of ***Butler's Field***.

Those who do not qualify are required to remove their boat and trailer as soon as possible.

BOATER

A straw hat with a hard flat brim traditionally worn when boating, sometimes incorporating a ribbon/band in the club colours of the wearer.

BOATS

Racing boats are referred to simply as boats - and definitely not '***canoes***'.

Racing boats were traditionally made of wood but now most are made of carbon fibre and plastic in a variety of colours.

Sliding ***riggers***, permitted between 1981 and 1983, have been banned since 1984 and it is prohibited to use any substance on a boat capable of modifying the natural properties of water to improve performance nor to use any substance such as prefabricated plastic film on the outer skin of the boat to improve performance.

For safety reason the Henley Rules specify that:-

- every boat shall carry securely affixed to the ***bow*** a white protective ball, 4cm in diameter, of hardened rubber or similar material unless the bow is so constructed as to afford equivalent protection and visibility,
- all boats must be equipped with stretchers (a board fitted in the boat usually with shoes attached) or shoes which allow the competitors to get clear of the boat without using their hands and with the least possible delay, and
- the opening of an enclosed ***coxswain's*** seat must be at least 70cm long and it must be as wide as the boat for at least 50cm. The inner surface of the enclosed part must be smooth and no structure of any sort shall restrict the inner width of the coxswain's section.

There are seven types of racing boat used at the Regatta:-

Rowing

· ***Eights*** - (***Grand***, ***Ladies'***, ***Thames***, ***Temple***, ***Princess Elizabeth*** and ***Henley Prize***)

· ***Coxless Fours*** - (***Stewards'***, ***Visitors'*** and ***Wyfold***)

· ***Coxed Fours*** - (***Prince Philip*** and ***Britannia***)

· ***Coxless pairs*** - (***Silver Goblets***)

Sculling

· ***Quadruple Sculls*** - (***Queen Mother***, ***Fawley***, ***Men's Quadruple Sculls*** and ***Women's Quadruple Sculls***)

· ***Double Sculls*** - (***Double Sculls***)

· ***Single Sculls*** - (***Diamonds*** and ***Princess Royal***)

See - OFFICIAL REGATTA BOATS, PLEASURE BOATS and UMPIRE LAUNCHES

BOOK OF HONOUR

The ***Grand*** and the ***Prince Philip Challenge Cups*** are the only two ***Regatta trophies*** that have a Book of Honour where the names, weights, times, etc of winners are recorded. The names are written by hand in the book for the Prince Philip but printed in the book for the Grand.

BOOM SHED

Between 1934 and 1955 the ***booms*** used in the construction of the ***Regatta Course***, were floated along a specially built channel from the river when the Course was dismantled and stored in a shed next to ***Remenham Club***, leased by the Regatta.

In 1955, having failed to move the shed to Fawley Meadows, despite having received planning permission, the ***Stewards*** did not renew the lease and stored the booms in the open on the ***downstream*** end of ***Blandy Meadow***, next to the present site of the ***Regatta Enclosure***.

The booms are now stored either side of the wet dock in

Regatta Headquarters.

Since 1962 the Boom Shed has been used as a boathouse by ***Upper Thames Rowing Club***.
See - WAR YEARS

BOOMS

Approximately 220 booms are used in the construction of the ***Regatta Course***. They are 60ft lengths of timber (Douglas fir) and float between ***piles*** thereby marking the boundaries of the straight Course.

The booms, first used at the end of the 19th century, were originally intended to help prevent ***pleasure boats*** interfering with the races by keeping them off the Course. In later years booms also helped to alleviate the effect of wash (waves caused by the passage of a boat) on those racing.

Consideration has been given to using materials other than wood for the booms but only wood floats with the correct profile to deal with the wash from pleasure boats.

When not being used for the Course the booms and piles are stored either side of the wet dock at ***Regatta Headquarters***.
See - BOOM SHED

BOOZIER OF EPERNAY

The name of the house producing the Regatta's own label champagne introduced at the Regatta in 2000.

BOSPOROS

Bosporos, built by The Steam & Electric Launch Company of Ludham, Norfolk, in 1994 and owned by Oxford University Boat Club, is one of the six 50ft launches used for umpiring at the Regatta.

Its predecessor, also named *Bosporos*, was built by Messrs ***Hobbs & Sons*** in 1952 and purchased by Lord Nuffield for OUBC. It was subsequently bought by the Regatta in 1980 and continued to be used for umpiring until ***Ariadne*** replaced it in 1992. *Bosporos* was then sold and shipped to Holland.

There is an interesting story connected with the name of the first *Bosporos*. It seems it was intended to be named 'Bosporus' after the Straits of Bosporus - Bosporus being the Greek word for Oxford and because of the close proximity of the Straits to the site of the deaths of Hero and Leander. As there was already a boat registered with that name, the spelling was changed to *Bosporos* to keep within the regulations. The story continues that, in 1952, OUBC already owned two boats, *Olive* and *Umbridge*, so it was expected that *Bosporos* would be followed by the purchase of a fourth boat which would have a name beginning with the letter 'C' - but this did not materialise.

In 1992 OUBC re-registered the name of *Bosporos* after the original boat had left the country enabling it to be used for their new launch.

See - UMPIRE LAUNCHES

BOW

(Bow pronounced as in bough of a tree)

Bow has two meanings in ***rowing***.

- The bow of a ***boat*** , being the front/forward end (the point) - the opposite end to the stern (the rear/back end), and
- The name given to the ***athlete*** (not the ***cox***) who is seated nearest to the bow of the boat.

The athlete '***rowing***' at bow usually has his ***oar*** on the starboard side of the boat (starboard = right-hand side looking towards the ***bow***). Because of this athletes who row with their oar on the starboard side of the boat are referred to as rowing on 'bow side'.

BOW LOADER

A ***coxed boat*** where the ***cox*** is positioned sitting/lying on his back in the front (***bow***) of the boat immediately behind the bow ***athlete*** eg. between the bow athlete and the bow of the boat.

Bow Loaders are also referred to as ***Front Loaders***.

BOW NUMBER

See - IDENTIFICATION NUMBER

BOW STEERS

The ***bow athlete*** is usually given the task of ***steering*** a ***coxless boat*** because by turning his head he can see ahead more easily than others in the boat. The reference 'bow steers' is used to denote this responsibility.

BRAKSPEAR'S HENLEY BREWERY

WH Brakspear & Son, is the oldest and largest of the three remaining independent breweries in ***Oxfordshire*** and one of the smallest traditional family brewers in the country.

In 1779 Robert Brakspear began working for his Uncle Richard Hayward in the Brewery in Bell Street. Following the death of Hayward in 1797, Brakspear bought out the remaining partner in 1803 and in 1812, shortly before his death, he amalgamated his brewery with Appleton and Shaw and the brewery moved to ***New Street***.

Robert's son William Brakspear became a partner in the company in 1825 and, by 1848, he was sole proprietor. He then took his sons Archibald and George into partnership.

William died in 1882 but the business continued to prosper and, after becoming a limited company, bought and closed down the local Grey's Brewery in Henley in 1896.

The company expanded for most of the 20th century although in the final two decades went through a period of rationalisation, disposing of the more unprofitable pubs and boosting the business of the rest. It also entered into trading arrangements with Whitbread and Scottish Courage enabling Brakspear's ales to be sold throughout southern England.

The brewery's brick chimney and the two white cowled kiln stacks are a feature of the Henley skyline at the finish of the ***Regatta Course***. The cowls made of fibreglass with plastic on a timber and metal frame were put in place in November 1988 being replicas of the 1903 original wooden cowls.

In the past ***coxswains*** have been known to attend at the brewery and shovel hops in the heat in an effort to lose weight before a race.

The brewery has over 90 public houses, 16 of which are in Henley. The ***Angel on the Bridge*** on ***Thames Side*** and the ***Little White Hart Hotel*** on ***Riverside*** face the river. The Anchor in Friday Street, the Little Angel at the bottom of ***White Hill***, the Two Brewers at the junction of ***White Hill*** and the Wargrave Road, and the Rose and Crown in New Street, are within 200m or so of the river.

Brakspear's also own the ***Henley Cricket Club*** ground at the bottom of White Hill and the old brewery stables next to the Little White Hart Hotel, which had been the home of

Henley Rowing Club from 1903 to 1986 and which is now the Brewery's Conference Centre. The Brewery also owns much of the river frontage and moorings along Riverside.

BRIDGE BAR

The Bridge Bar is situated at the ***upstream*** end of the ***Stewards' Enclosure***. Bar and table service is available providing a wide range of beers, champagnes and spirits, including ***Pimm's***.

The Bridge Bar opens at 10am each day (11am on Sunday).

BRIDGE BAR LAWN

The area immediately in front of the ***Bridge Bar***

THE BRITANNIA CHALLENGE CUP

The Britannia Challenge Cup was presented to the Regatta in 1969 by Nottingham Britannia Rowing Club to mark the Club's centenary.

The event, usually referred to as the 'Britannia' or even more simply as 'The Brit', was introduced in 1968, when it was referred to as the ***Henley Prize***, and was for ***coxed fours*** below ***Prince Philip*** standard. Entries were restricted to crews from the UK and Republic of Ireland until 1989 when it was opened to crews from any country. Current ***heavyweight*** and lightweight national squad oarsmen are not allowed to compete in the Britannia; neither is any oarsman who has ***rowed*** 'or ***sculled***' in the ***Olympic Games*** or a similar high-ranking event. (Note: The sport generally treats rowing and sculling as separate disciplines, an ***athlete's*** status in one not influencing the other) Neither is a 'Blue (meaning he has represented Oxford or Cambridge in the Boat Race) or a 'Purple' (meaning he has rowed with distinction for London

University) or one who has rowed at a similar level at university in the USA, allowed to enter.

No athlete may compete in the Britannia if he has previously won an event at the Regatta - other than the ***Temple***, the ***Princess Elizabeth*** or the ***Fawley***.

Athletes, other than ***coxswains***, competing in this event are not permitted to compete in any other event at the same Regatta.

The entrance fee for this event is £50 and the Stewards have limited the number of entries to 32.
See - REGATTA TROPHIES

BUCKINGHAMSHIRE

The land on the ***Fawley Meadows***, ***Henley Management College*** side of the river from the county boundary, which is opposite ***Remenham Club***, ***downstream*** to ***Hambleden Lock***, is situated in the county of Buckinghamshire.

The county ***upstream*** of Buckinghamshire is ***Oxfordshire*** (viz. ***Henley-on-Thames*** is in Oxfordshire).

For parliamentary purposes the Buckinghamshire side of the ***Henley Reach*** is part of the Wycombe constituency.
See - BUCKS

BUCKS

Bucks is the abbreviation for ***Buckinghamshire*** and the name of the ***station*** on the ***Fawley Meadows*** side of the ***Regatta Course***.

BUOYS

An anchored, floating, marker, usually brightly coloured to make it easily visible, used to indicate a hazard or the edge of a ***navigation*** channel or racing lane/***station***.

The Regatta uses coloured plasticised rubber floating buoys from the start of the ***Regatta Course*** to the beginning of the ***booms*** at the top of ***Temple Island*** and then in some of the gaps between the booms along the side of the Course. Buoys are also used ***downstream*** of the Start to determine the ***navigation*** channel and ***warm-up area***.

On the ***Henley Reach*** the Environment Agency buoys with the green triangle 'topmark', as seen by the site of the old ***Fawley Boathouse***, warn of the existence of submerged concrete near to the river-bank.

BUSHES

The area of trees and bushes on the ***Buckinghamshire*** bank on ***Park Farm Meadows***, owned by the Regatta since 1955, is known as the Bushes.

It has been claimed that these give an advantage to competitors on the ***Bucks station*** when there is a westerly cross-wind, referred to as a 'bushes wind'.

See - REGATTA COURSE

BUTLER'S FIELD

Butler's Field is so named because it had been owned by the Butler family, landlords/tenants 1864-1950 of the Little Angel public house at the end of ***Remenham Lane***. Butler's Field is situated on the opposite side of the lane from ***Lion Meadow*** and is one of the three main official Regatta ***car parks***.

It was purchased by the Regatta in 1951 and includes the 3½ acres of ***Selwyn's Meadow*** purchased from the Selwyn family in 1948.

Car park ***labels*** for car parking can be purchased for all five days on the same basis as Lion Meadow and the same space will be allocated as in the previous year provided the application is received before the end of March. Unreserved daily labels can also be purchased in advance of the Regatta and at the gate on each day of the Regatta, subject to availability.

A public ***footpath*** crosses Butler's Field from Remenham Lane to the bottom of Sham Hill, the hill to the east of Butler's Field and ***Green's Field***.

Butler's Field is linked to Green's Field by a road behind ***Barn Cottage***.

See - CAR PARKS

THE CABLE

An electricity cable crosses the ***Regatta Course***, buried in the bed of the river, at a point near to the inlet to ***Fawley Court***. It was laid down in the early 1930s to supply power to Remenham.

CAFÉ REGATTA

See - CREWS' CATERING TENT

CAMP-SHEDDING

Camp-shedding (also known as camp-sheading & camp-

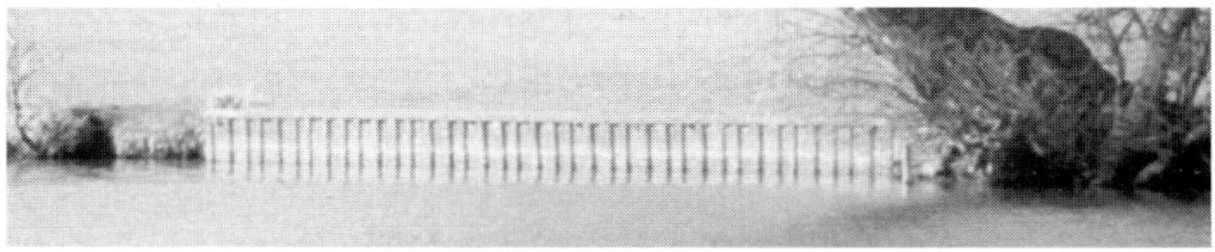

sheeting) is the reinforced wall built to replace the natural riverbank to reduce further erosion.

CAMPING PUNT/SKIFF

See - PUNT and SKIFF

CANADA GEESE

Canada Geese (Branta canadensis) are native of North America. They are approximately the same size and weight as a ***swan*** and were originally established in England as an ornamental fowl on private lakes. They subsequently moved to the rivers where they have been allowed to multiply and now outnumber native geese and are far more of a hazard to river users than swans. Because they foul the river-bank and damage crops, Canada geese are considered a nuisance by many and a pest by most farmers.

Although the Regatta co-operates with HM The Queen's Swan Marker in removing the swans from the ***Henley Reach*** before the Regatta, it has found that the most successful way of coping with the Canada geese has been to operate a 'Goose Patrol' during the days of the Regatta. This involves a member of the ***casual staff*** based in a small fast boat in radio contact with Regatta ***Umpires*** and the ***Environment Agency*** staff, herding the geese off the ***Regatta Course*** whenever they are a threat to themselves and to those racing.

CANOES

A narrow open boat, with a pointed ***bow*** and ***stern***, propelled with a ***paddle*** (or with an engine eg. motorised canoes).

Such is the lack of information about rowing that ***rowing*** and ***sculling boats*** are occasionally referred to as 'canoes' by non-rowing people.

In 1867 the Regatta programme included a canoe-chase over land and water - for the first and last time.

CANVAS

The bow deck (foredeck) between the ***bow*** of the boat and the breakwater immediately behind the bow ***athlete***/single ***sculler***

- so named because when ***boats*** were made of wood this was covered in canvas.

The length of the 'canvas' varies from approximately 2.4m (8ft) on an ***eight*** to 3m (10ft) on a ***sculling*** boat.

The distance of 'a canvas' can be used to describe the winning margin in a race at the Regatta.

See - FINISHING A RACE

CAR PARKS

There are three main official Regatta car parks - ***Lion Meadow***, ***Butler's Field*** and ***Green's Field***. The other two official car parks are the ***Competitors' Car Park*** and ***Fawley Meadows Car Park***.

Except for the Competitors' Car Park, car park ***labels*** can be purchased in advance subject to availability at ***Regatta Headquarters*** or at the car park entrance. In this regard Lion Meadow is only available for 5 days reserved parking and the incumbent from the previous year is normally given first refusal such that there is now an unofficial waiting list for places. Labels for 5 day reserved parking can be purchased for Butler's Field and labels for daily parking places can be purchased in advance for Butler's Field, Green's Field and Fawley Meadows.

Labels are of different shapes to assist police and others directing traffic to the Regatta car parks.

There are other car parks opened just for the Regatta but

which are not owned by the Regatta eg. the ***Henley Cricket Club*** and ***Henley Rowing Club*** car parks.

CARPENTERS ARMS

This inn/public house stood on the site of the ***Regatta Headquarters*** by ***Henley Bridge*** from the beginning of the 18th century (the plaque on the wall records 1714).

The Carpenters Arms closed in September 1973 and the building appeared derelict until purchased by the Royal Regatta in 1983 and demolished in 1984 to make way for the new building.

CASUAL STAFF

Up to 150 casual staff are recruited by the Regatta from May. Tentage, catering, security, car parking and other ***contractors*** also recruit casual staff making the total over 1,500 during the five days of the Regatta.

The Regatta has always employed additional casual staff over the Regatta period. Until the 1950s the town celebrated the Regatta as a holiday with companies and schools closing for the Regatta period. This enabled many local men (very few women worked at the Regatta until the 1970s) to earn extra money by working at the Regatta.

Students, on holiday from college or university, now undertake most of the casual work and some continuing to work at the Regatta for many years after finishing their education.

CATWALK

The name given to the platform walkways that lead from:-

· the ***downstream*** end of the ***Boat Tent Area*** to the ***Press Box*** situated in the middle of the river at the finish of the ***Regatta Course***, and

· the ***Stewards' Lawn*** to the ***Stewards' Box*** on the finish line.

CHAIRMAN

The Chairman of the ***Committee of Management***, known simply as 'Chairman', is responsible for all aspects of the Regatta. The Committee of Management, which is elected annually from the body of the Stewards, elects its own Chairman each year. The Chairman, with the Committee of Management, 'manages' the Regatta through the Regatta ***Secretary*** and the staff based in ***Regatta Headquarters***.

There have been ten Chairmen since a Committee of Management was first established in 1881:-

· JF Hodges 1881 - 1894,
· HT Steward 1894 - 1915,
· C Gurdon 1915 -1919,
· WAL Fletcher (four days) 1919, (died from pneumonia after being gassed during the war)
· FI Pitman 1919 - 1942,
· HG Gold, OBE 1945 - 1951,
· HRN Rickett, CBE 1952 - 1965,
· JL Garton, CBE 1965 - 1977,
· PRC Coni, OBE, QC 1977 - 1993, and
· the present Chairman, Mike A Sweeney who was first elected in 1993.

CHAIRMAN'S ASSISTANTS

In 1975, John Garton, then Chairman, decided that each year the 15 or so people who assisted the Regatta in positions of responsibility, would be appointed 'Chairman's Assistants' to recognise their status.

Chairman's Assistants are each issued with a silver ***badge*** in the shape of a shield giving them the same access as

Stewards of the Regatta to go anywhere on the Regatta site.

CHALLENGE CUPS

The Cups were called Challenge Cups because, until 1871, competitors would 'challenge' the winner from the previous year. The challengers would then race in heats to decide who should race against the holder for the Cup.

CHAMPAGNE & PIMM'S BAR

This Bar is situated in the ***Stewards' Enclosure*** next to the ***Bandstand*** behind the ***Fawley Stand***.

Bar and table service is available providing vintage and non-vintage champagne together with ***Pimm's*** and fresh orange juice.

The Oyster Bar, located within the garden area of the Champagne & Pimm's Bar, serves fresh oysters and other shellfish together with champagne and draught stout.

CHANTRY HOUSE

The Chantry House, which belongs to ***St Mary's Church***, is a Grade One listed, timber-framed building, constructed in the early 15th century. It is so named because it is believed chantry priests from the church may have used the building.

Because of the difference in the height of the land, the middle floor of the three floors is the ground floor on the churchyard side giving the appearance from that side of a two-story building.

The first and second floors (the ground and first floors as seen from the churchyard) are used for parish purposes and the ground floor on the side that faces the ***Red Lion Hotel*** car park is leased to the Hotel.

The ground floor was a granary and the rest of the building was a schoolhouse from before 1553 until the early 19th century, apart from when it was closed during the period of the plague in 1666.

The building, joined to the Red Lion Hotel, is believed to be the last remaining structure of the original Henley Wharf.

CHARITY RAFT RACES

An event on the river at Henley which takes place ***upstream*** of ***Henley Bridge*** and is organised by the Henley Lions Club in aid of charity.

CHILDREN

Since 1980, children under the age of 10 have not been allowed in the ***Stewards' Enclosure***. Children under the age of 14 have free access to the ***Regatta Enclosure***.

CHILTERN HILLS

The hills that can be seen in the distance looking ***downstream***

towards ***Temple Island*** and the start of the ***Regatta Course***, are the southern edge of the Chiltern Hills which run from Reading, round the north of Henley and north east towards Luton.

CHIT BOOKS

For many years all ***Members of the Stewards' Enclosure*** were issued with Chit (order form) Books. Chits can be used to purchase food and drink in the Enclosure and pay for car parking, members settling their account after the Regatta. No interest is incurred on this credit facility but users pay a handling charge of 10%+VAT to offset the administration cost.

As only approximately 10% of members used the books, and with an increasing risk of books being lost and then used fraudulently, the Stewards decided to issue Chit Books from 2000 only to those who were expected to use them.

CHURCH SERVICE

See - REGATTA SERVICE.

CLOTHING

The Rules of the Regatta state that 'Every competitor's clothing must consist of a vest and shorts as a minimum'.

The sport refers to the clothing worn by competing ***athletes*** as racing strip - often referred to by the athletes as rowing kit. The ***ARA*** Rules require every athlete in a ***crew***, except for the ***cox***, to wear the uniform racing strip of the club when competing and for athletes in ***composite crews*** to wear the racing strip of the club they represent.

Rowing vests and shorts are usually manufactured from lycra. Before the introduction of lycra, athletes wore cotton vests usually with short sleeves, and cotton shorts although there was a period in the 1960s and 70s when woollen shorts were popular.

Crews in the first ***Henley Regatta*** in 1839 wore 'rowing costumes' comprising 'guernseys' (a type of woollen jersey), together with caps and rosettes, in the colours of their clubs.
See - DRESS

COACH

The coach is responsible for teaching and training the ***athletes***. At Henley a coach will accompany a competitor by cycling along the ***towpath*** although this is becoming increasingly difficult because of the large number of spectators.

Coaching during a race is forbidden.
(Although 'coach' is not a term exclusive to ***rowing*** I recall a friend wondering how a 64-seater coach could travel along the towpath at Henley, let alone follow the instructions on the signposts 'Coaches Keep to the Right' - MCNJ)

COFFEE & LIQUEUR BAR

The Coffee and Liqueur Bar is situated in the ***Stewards' Enclosure*** behind the ***Grandstand*** next to the ***Luncheon and Tea Tickets Kiosk***.

It is open from 9.30am each day and serves coffee, tea and iced coffee together with a range of liqueurs and ice creams. Strawberries and cream and French patisseries are also served throughout the day.
Continental breakfast is available between 9.30am and 11am.

COLOURS

The colours of the club, or the colours and national emblem of the country in the case of international events, are normally painted on the 'spoon' of the ***oar*** or ***scull*** (***blades***).

The ***clothing*** (vest, shorts, etc) worn by ***athletes*** is usually in a uniform style and colour to associate the athlete with his club.

At Henley details of the colours on the blades are shown on the ***Entry Form*** and recorded on the reverse of the ***List of Entries*** and in the ***Regatta Programme***.

COMMENTARY AT HENLEY

Commentary on races at Henley is restricted to factual information about the race and is delivered in a prescribed format.

Information on the progress of a race is passed from the officials manning the ***signal boxes*** along the ***Regatta Course*** to the Official Timekeeper and Race Recorder who stand at the back of the ***Umpire's launch***. A Race Reporter, who is a member of the commentary team, also standing in the back of the launch, then conveys this information by a radio link to the main commentary point based on the top floor (***upstream*** end) of the ***Floating Stand*** and to the officials on the ***Progress Board***.

A public address system was first used at Henley in 1946, the same year the BBC started a radio commentary on the Regatta. Before 1965, when radios were first used on umpire launches, the commentary on races was given from 'transmission boxes' situated by the side of the Course at the ***Barrier***, ***Fawley*** and milepost.

Since 1960 a microphone has been positioned on a pile (post) by the Umpire's launch at the start of the Course so that the starting instructions given by the Umpire to the competitors can be broadcast to those in the ***Enclosures*** over the public address system.

See - RACE REPORTS & STARTING A RACE AT HENLEY

COMMITTEE

See - COMMITTEE OF MANAGEMENT

COMMITTEE LAWN

See - STEWARDS' LAWN

COMMITTEE OF MANAGEMENT

A Committee of Management was first established in 1881 and is elected by the ***Stewards*** each year from their own number. The Committee, which has a maximum number of 12, then elects its own ***Chairman*** and meets some eight times each year to 'manage' the Regatta.

The Henley Rules state that:- 'All questions of eligibility, qualifications, interpretation of the rules or other matters not specifically provided for shall be referred to the Committee, whose decision shall be final. In case of exceptional emergency the Committee shall have power to abrogate, alter or suspend any rule at the instance of any competitor, provided it is satisfied that no other competitor is thereby placed in a less favourable position than he would have been in if such an emergency had not occurred.'

The Committee is also responsible for appointing the ***Umpires*** and the ***Start*** and ***Finish Judges***.

COMPETITORS' BADGES

Each ***athlete*** who qualifies to race at the Regatta receives a Competitors' Badge, which gives him access to the ***Boat Tent Area*** and ***Regatta Enclosure*** throughout the Regatta.

COMPETITORS' CAR PARK

This is situated behind ***Leander Club*** and part is reserved as a Boat Repairers' Compound.

The land, originally known as 'The Nook', was purchased by the Royal Regatta in 1938. Outside the Regatta period part is now leased for use by Leander Club.

See - CAR PARKS

COMPOSITE CREWS

When ***athletes*** from two or more clubs compete in the same ***crew*** the crew is referred to as a composite. Irrespective of how many clubs combine to make up an entry, only two club names are shown on the ***List of Entries*** and in the ***Regatta Programme***.

CONSTITUTION AND RULES OF HENLEY ROYAL REGATTA

In 1849, 33 years before the ***ARA*** was established, the first published 'Laws of Boat Racing' were drawn up by representatives of Oxford and Cambridge Universities and the principal London clubs. These were incorporated into the Henley Rules in 1850 by the ***Stewards*** of ***Henley Royal Regatta***.

Thirty-five years later, when the majority of the Stewards were men with rowing experience, the present Constitution and Rules of the Regatta were established. The Constitution commences with the words *On the 9th April, 1885, at a meeting of the Stewards, certain resolutions were agreed to, and, as subsequently amended, are as follows:-.* There then follows fifteen very brief, mainly one sentence, paragraphs setting out how the Stewards should conduct themselves with regard to meetings, etc.

This Constitution is followed by three Bye-Laws, two of which determine how new Stewards should be elected and the third deals with how a Steward can bring forward any matter for discussion.

The Bye-Laws are followed by the ***Qualification Rules*** for each event and then the 'General Rules' applicable to entries, competitors and races.

CONTRACTORS

The main contractors at the Regatta are:-

- ***Black & Edgington*** - tentage,
- ***Freeboom*** - river work,
- ***Henley Contracting*** - lawns and all the groundwork during the Regatta and throughout the year, and
- ***Higgs & Co*** - printing

The three main catering contractors are:-

- ***Letheby & Christopher***, responsible for the bars and

restaurants in the ***Stewards' Enclosure***,

· ***London Catering Services***, responsible for the bar and restaurant in the ***Regatta Enclosure***, and

· ***Sodexho Prestige*** (previously known as Town & County) - responsible for the ***Fawley Meadows Hospitality Village***.

Other contractors include

· Cook's Nurseries - flowers and gardens in the Enclosures,

· Onsite Communications - all the radios and communications,

· Parking Promotions - day to day organisation of the ***car parks*** and the sale of ***Regatta Programmes***,

· Special Events Security - security and guard duties, and

· Simon Jones - recruiting and organising the casual staff.

Between 1982 and 1999 many of the contractors' staff, particularly those working for Black and Edgington and Freeboom (Hobbs until 1990), together with the ***Chairman*** and ***Secretary*** and staff in the ***Secretary's Office***, competed annually for the 'Contractors Skittles Trophy Plate' cup presented by Darbyshire Security Services in 1982.

There were occasions in the 1980s when the game was 'Aunt Sally' - a contest where the competitors throw sticks at a small wooden dummy. However in most years the contest, which took place on the Monday before the Regatta, was conventional nine-pin skittles. In later years, from 1991, this was played on a specially constructed skittle alley at ***Henley Rowing Club***.

The trophy is now on display at ***Regatta Headquarters***.

COPAS LAND

The local name for most of the land on the ***Berkshire*** side of the river, from a point opposite the ***Fawley Box*** to the Flower Pot landing stage, ***downstream*** from ***Hambleden Lock***.

The land is part of ***Remenham Farm***, which is owned by the Copas Partnership.

Since the 1980s the land downstream from the ***Barrier***, has been used for corporate hospitality marquees. Outside the Regatta period it provides an ideal setting for river related events, one of the largest held there in recent years being the British Waterways Festival of 1997 organised by the Inland Waterways Association.

See - TEMPLE ISLAND ENCLOSURE

CORPORATE HOSPITALITY

See - FAWLEY MEADOWS HOSPITALITY VILLAGE

COURSE

See - REGATTA COURSE

COX/COXSWAINS

In ***coxed crews*** the cox is in charge of the ***boat*** being the only member of the ***crew*** facing forward and able to see ahead.

A coxswain (pronounced ‘cox’n’ or ‘coxen’) is generally referred to as ‘cox’. **This abbreviation has been used in this book where appropriate**.

The cox is responsible for the safe navigation of the boat and for keeping the crew informed as to their progress when racing.

All coxswains must wear an approved life-jacket or buoyancy aid and be able to escape easily from the boat should it capsize.

A cox ***steers*** a boat by lines along the side of the boat to the rudder. Coxswains are positioned either sitting in the stern of the boat facing the ***stroke athlete***, or lying in the ***bows*** of the boat immediately behind the bow athlete.

The infamous happenings of the ***Stewards' Challenge Cup*** of 1868 resulted in rules being introduced at Henley regarding coxswains specifying:-

· that coxswains 'shall not steer for more than one crew for the same prize',

· that the cox must be in the boat at the end of a race, even though any other member of the crew need not,

· ***minimum weights*** for coxswains relative to the average weight of the crew, and

· a minimum weight for coxswains generally, below which they were prohibited from competing in the Regatta.

The first two of these rules are still in force.

The third rule, imposed in 1869, involved relating the weight of the cox to the average weight of the crew on a sliding scale so that heavier crews carried a heavier cox. This was dropped after the 1962 Regatta.

With regard to the fourth rule, the Stewards decided at their December 2000 meeting, 131 years after the rule was introduced, that the minimum weight requirement should also be dropped thereby bringing Henley Rules on this into line with ***ARA*** Rules. This means that coxswains at Henley can again be of any weight, although ***dead-weight*** will still need to be carried if they weigh below the minimum specified for their event. With regard to the latter, the rules on coxswains specify that, apart from those competing for the ***Henley Prize***, a crew must carry a minimum weight of 55kg (8st 9lb). The minimum weight to be carried in the Henley Prize is 50kg (7st 12lb).

Since 1974 ***women*** have been permitted to cox men's crews at the Regatta.

See - COXED/COXLESS, FRONT LOADER, SUBSTITUTIONS and WEIGHING-IN

COXED/COXLESS

These definitions refer to whether the ***crew*** includes a ***cox***.

At Henley, unlike other regattas, the definitions are not added to the name of the ***boat*** or the event in the ***Regatta Programme*** to describe whether it is coxed or coxless. Instead the ***boat*** is usually referred to by the event for which it is competing eg. a spectator would be expected to know that a Brit four or a heat of the ***Britannia Challenge Cup*** is for ***coxed fours***; a Visitors' four or a heat for the ***Visitors' Challenge Cup*** is for ***coxless fours***.

See - STEWARDS' CHALLENGE CUP

A COXED FOUR

This describes ***four athletes 'rowing' a boat'*** with a ***coxswain***. The ***cox*** of a four can be positioned either lying on his back in the ***bow*** or sitting in the stern.

(Note: Four athletes ***sculling*** a boat with a coxswain is referred to as a 'coxed quad' ie. a quadruple scull with a coxswain) However there are no events for coxed quads at Henley.

At Henley, coxed fours compete for the ***Prince Philip*** and ***Britannia Challenge Cups***.

The ***fastest recorded time*** at the Regatta taken by a coxed four over the ***Regatta Course***, (1mile 550yds), (***Leander Club*** for the Prince Philip Challenge Cup in 1995) is 6min 44sec - a speed of 10.16knots or 11.7mph (18.82kph).

A COXLESS FOUR

This describes ***four athletes 'rowing' a boat'*** without a ***coxswain***.

(Note: Four athletes ***sculling*** a boat without a coxswain is referred to simply as a 'quad' ie. a ***quadruple scull***)

At Henley, coxless fours compete for the ***Stewards'***, ***Visitors'*** and ***Wyfold Challenge Cups***.

The ***fastest recorded time*** at the Regatta taken by a coxless four over the ***Regatta Course***, (1mile 550yds), (Cambridge University & 'Mladost', Croatia for the Stewards' Challenge Cup in 1995) is 6min 22sec - a speed of 10.74knots or 12.37mph (19.9kph).

A COXLESS PAIR

See - PAIR

CREWS

Spectators, unfamiliar with ***rowing***, often, incorrectly, refer to a crew as a team.

Although the ***ARA*** defines single ***scullers*** as crews, the description 'crew' is usually reserved for ***boats*** of four or eight ***athletes***. ***Pairs***, ***doubles*** and scullers are generally referred to simply as pairs, doubles or scullers.

Where there is more than one athlete in a boat the ***seats*** and athletes are numbered, excluding the ***cox***, from the ***bows*** of the boat, starting with the number 1 seat - the athlete occupying this is always referred to as 'bow'. The seats and athletes are then numbered consecutively towards the stern of the boat, each athlete being referred to by his seat number. The last athlete, irrespective of the number of athletes in the boat or whether it is a sculling or rowing boat, is always called the ***stroke***.

In rowing boats (not sculling boats) odd numbered seats are generally referred to as being on bow side and even numbered seats ***stroke*** side.

See - REGATTA PROGRAMME

CREWS' CATERING TENT

The ***Crews'*** Catering Tent (also known as Café Regatta, the Crews' Cafeteria or the Crews' Amenities Area), is situated next to the Boat Tent by the main entrance to the ***Boat Tent Area***. The facility was originally divided between ***athletes*** and boatmen, but is now open to all including the public.

CREWS' ENQUIRIES OFFICE

See - BOAT TENT AREA and REGATTA HEADQUARTERS

CREWS' LOUNGE

The ***Crews'*** Lounge, first used in the middle 1980s, is a room where competitors can relax before or after racing.

Also called by its original name of the Crews' Rest Tent, the Crews' Lounge is situated at the rear of the Boat Tent next to the ***Crews' Catering Tent*** and has a television and drinks facility and an official in attendance at all times.

CROSSING POINTS

The two official crossing points for ***crews*** and ***scullers*** to cross the ***Regatta Course*** are at:-

· the $1^1/_8$ miles ***signal***, normally for crossing from the ***Buckinghamshire***, ***navigation***, channel to the ***Berkshire*** side, and

· the ***Barrier*** for crossing from the Berkshire side to the Buckinghamshire navigation channel.

Both crossings are marked with green ***flags*** on ***piles***.

THE DANESFIELD CUP

See - ROYAL HENLEY REGATTA

DATE OF THE REGATTA

See - GARTON CALENDAR

DEAD HEATS

The ***rules*** refer to a dead heat as two ***boats*** reaching the finishing line simultaneously.

Only 29 races have resulted in dead heats since the Regatta started in 1839 (up to the 2000 Regatta).

The first dead heat was in a heat of the ***Stewards' Challenge Cup*** in 1846 between Guy's Club, London and Dreadnought Club Henley. The Dreadnought Club disputed the decision and refused to row again so the race was awarded to Guy's Club.

There were three dead heats, including the 1846 race, up to 1902; three between 1903 and 1914; six between 1920 and 1938, two at the centenary Regatta of 1939 including the most famous dead heat in the history of the Regatta in the final of the ***Double Sculls*** between J Beresford Jnr and LF Southwood of Thames Rowing Club and G Scherli and E Broschi of Societa Canottieri 'Nettuno' Di Trieste, Italy; and 15 between 1946 and 2000.

See- ANNIVERSARIES and REGATTA COURSE

DEAD-WEIGHT

This is the name of the additional weight to be carried by a ***crew*** in order to bring the weight of the ***cox*** up to the minimum required under Henley ***Rules***. A Regatta Official under the direct control of a ***Steward***, will place the dead-weight in the boat as close as possible to the position of the cox, and will retrieve it after the race. The dead-weight used at Henley was in the form of slabs of lead until 1970 since when sealed bags of sand have been used.

See - WEIGHING-IN

THE DIAMOND CHALLENGE SCULLS

This event for ***single sculls***, usually referred to simply as the

'Diamonds' was established in 1844 and the prize was a Diamond Scarf Pin. The six inch crossed silver sculls were not instituted until 1850 at which time the Scarf Pin was replaced by a silver-gilt ***'pineapple' presentation cup***, originally hand made, which, like the pin, is presented to the winner to keep.

The crossed sculls are set in a case surrounded by silver plaques recording the names of the winners, a new case being presented in 1957 to ensure there was room to record future winners.

The presentation of the cup to the winner was stopped after 1973 for cost reasons and winners were given small crossed sculls instead. In 1994 the Regatta recommenced the practice and, at a special ceremony in 1994, all except three of the 1974 - 1993 winners were able to attend a special ceremony and presented with ' their' pineapple cup.

In 1845, the second year of the event, JW Conant of St John's College, Oxford, who had lost in the 1844 final, used ***outriggers*** and won his first race easily. He led the previous year's winner, TB Bumpsted of the Scullers Club, London, by over a length within a few ***strokes*** of the start, Bumpsted, it being recorded in *Bell's Life*, 'fairly turned round on his thwart (seat) to see what had become of Mr Conant'. Despite this, Conant was beaten in the final by S Wallace of Leander Club. The third sculler in the race, H Chapman of Crescent Club, London, who had been challenging Wallace more closely at the finish than Conant, was disqualified. It has never been clarified as to whether Wallace and Chapman also used outriggers.

The Diamond Challenge Sculls was the first major ***Regatta trophy*** to be taken abroad when JJK Ooms of Amsterdam won in 1892. Notable winners include Stuart A Mackenzie (SAM) who won six times between 1957 and

1962 - his six pineapple cups are now on display at the ***River and Rowing Museum*** in Henley.

The Diamonds was part of the ***FISA*** World Cup group of races in 1993, 1994 and 1995.

Entry was unrestricted until 1999 since when, in order to maintain a high quality and to reduce the number of ***entries*** which required the majority to '***qualify***', those entering have been required to be of not less than ***ARA Senior*** 1 status, or the international equivalent status, in ***sculling***.

The entrance fee for this event is £30 and the Stewards have limited the number of entries to 16.

DISTRICT CHALLENGE CUP

This was an event introduced at the Regatta in 1840 for ***coxed fours*** limited to crews and clubs from Maidenhead, Marlow, Reading, Wallingford and Henley, members having to reside with four miles of their town club. In 1842 Oxford and Windsor were included but not Oxford University.

Due to lack of interest the event was discontinued after 1846 and in 1847 the trophy became the ***Visitors' Challenge Cup***.

DISTRICT GOBLETS

This event was introduced at the Regatta in 1858 for ***pairs*** residing within 25 miles of Henley. Public schools and universities were excluded until 1861.

This event was withdrawn after 1867 due to lack of interest.

DOUBLE

See - DOUBLE SCULLING

DOUBLE SCULLING

This describes two persons in a ***boat***, each with two ***sculls***, one in each hand (a pair of sculls). Two ***athletes*** double sculling and a double sculling ***boat*** are usually referred to simply as a 'Double'.

At Henley the only double sculling event is for the ***Double Sculls Challenge Cup***.

The ***fastest recorded time*** at the Regatta taken by a double scull over the ***Regatta Course***, (1mile 550yds), (B Jamieson & DJ Gleeson, Augusta Training Centre, USA in 1995) is 6min 55sec - a speed of 9.89knots or 11.39mph (18.32kph).

Note:-

· doubles are not ***coxed***,

· it is incorrect to refer to two scullers in a boat as 'rowing', and

· two athletes '***rowing*** ' a boat is referred to as a '***pair***' or 'pair-oar''.

THE DOUBLE SCULLS CHALLENGE CUP

A ***Double Sculling*** race was introduced in 1939 to mark the centenary of the Regatta. The 1939 event was memorable for the ***dead heat*** between the English double of J Beresford Jnr and LF Southwood of Thames RC who had won the gold in the 1936 Berlin Olympic Games, and the Italian European Champions G Scherli and E Broschi.

Double Sculling was included as a permanent event in 1946 at the first Regatta after the War. The Double Sculls Challenge Cup was first presented in 1946 and the silver base was added in 1987.

The entry qualifications are unrestricted other than that, at the date of entry, the double shall be at least ***ARA Senior*** 1 status, or equivalent international status, in sculling.

The entrance fee for this event is £40 and the Stewards have limited the number of entries to 16.

See - ANNIVERSARIES and REGATTA TROPHIES

DOWNSTREAM

The ***stream*** on the ***Henley Reach*** flows from ***Marsh Lock*** through ***Henley Bridge*** towards ***Temple Island*** and on to ***Hambleden Lock***. Thus competitors on the ***Regatta Course*** race ***upstream*** ie. against the stream.

It is acceptable to refer to a place that is downstream of another as being 'below' it eg. the finish of the Regatta Course is below ***Henley Bridge***.

See - RIVER THAMES and UPSTREAM

DRAGON BOATS

Dragon Boats originated in China 2000 years ago and are still in use in that country. They are long, shallow, flat-bottomed boats, rather like an enlarged ***punt***, with a large dragon's head on the ***bow*** and a dragon's tail on the stern. They are propelled by a crew of up to 100 paddlers kneeling along the side of the boat. A drummer is positioned high up in the bows and the crew keeps time to the beats of the drum. A helmsman stands in the stern and steers the boat with an oar fixed to the stern, which acts as a ***rudder***.

The modern racing version of a dragon boat is approximately 25ft long and has a crew of up to two dozen paddlers.

See - EYOT BOAT CENTRE and HENLEY DRAGON BOAT CLUB

THE DRAW

Racing at Henley is on a knockout basis over five days and the Draw takes place in the Henley Town Hall on the Saturday afternoon preceding the Regatta.

The ***Grand Challenge Cup*** (the replica presented to the Regatta in 1964 by the 1914 Harvard Crew) is used to hold the slips with the names of the competitors.

The Draw, made by the ***Chairman*** of the ***Committee of Management***, identifies competitors in the first rounds of each event and the ***stations*** on which they will race. Competitors can see from the Draw their path to the final and the ***stations*** on which they will race in each round.

Since 1969 certain competitors have been ***selected*** (not seeded) to avoid their meeting in the early rounds eg. competitors from the same part of the world and those of a high calibre. This ***selection*** system was adjusted in 1993 and scullers in the ***Diamond Sculls*** and the special event created that year for women scullers, were also 'seeded' so that the two events could be included as part of the ***FISA*** World Cup.

The Draw for the selected competitors in each event takes place immediately before the full Draw for that event.

A standard Draw Chart was introduced in 1969 to assist members of the public who attend the Draw.

Full details of the Draw, which shows the names of selected crews in *italics* and which is updated as appropriate with the results of the previous days racing, are shown in the ***Regatta Programme***.

See - QUALIFYING RACES

DRESS

Contrary to the annual comments in the tabloid press, there are no dress requirements for the majority of people attending Henley Royal Regatta ie. those viewing the racing along the banks of the river, or in boats, or in the ***Regatta Enclosure***.

The ***Stewards of the Regatta*** have laid down regulations for ***Members*** and their Guests in the ***Stewards' Enclosure*** which, as indicated in the Membership Survey of October 1999, have the support of 75% of the membership.

There are also dress regulations (different to those for the

Stewards' Enclosure) for those in the ***Fawley Meadows Hospitality Village*** - as there are for those entering other establishments on the ***Henley Reach*** during the Regatta eg. ***Leander Club***, ***Phyllis Court Club*** and ***Remenham Club***.
See - CLOTHING and MEMBERSHIP SURVEY

DRESSING TENTS

The Men's Dressing Tent (see picture above) and Women's Dressing Tent, famous for their very cold showers, are situated at the back of the Boat Tent. They are still referred to as 'tents' even though the Men's Dressing Tent has been inside the main Boat Tent since 1963.

Women were allowed to compete at Henley as ***coxswains*** in 1975 and, in 1978, a Women's Dressing Tent was established between the Boat Tent and the ***Leander Club*** Wall. The Women's Dressing Tent was subsequently moved inside the Boat Tent next to the Men's Dressing Tent.
See - BOAT TENT AREA

DRINK

See - FOOD AND DRINK

DRUGS

Rowing, like most modern sports, is concerned about the

harmful effects of drugs on ***athletes***. In 1972 the Regatta introduced rules relating to drugs and requires that no competitor shall infringe the provisions of the Olympic Movement Anti-Doping Code, as adopted and supplemented by the ***FISA*** Anti-Doping Regulations. Since 1991 the Sports Council's Dope Testing Unit has carried out random testing of competitors at the Regatta - all of which have proved to be negative.

The Unit was based in a tent at the ***downstream*** end of the ***Boat Tent Area*** until it was moved into the Boat Tent next to the Men's Dressing Tent in 2000.

EAST EYOT

East ***Eyot*** (the phonetic pronunciation is usually 'eye-ot') is

the first ***island upstream*** from ***Henley Bridge***. There are no buildings on the island, which is used solely by wildlife

AN EIGHT

This describes eight ***athletes*** '***rowing***' a ***boat*** - it is also the name of the boat. (Note: Eight athletes '***sculling***' a boat is called an octuple although there are no events for octuples at Henley)

At Henley, eights compete for the ***Grand Challenge Cup***, the ***Ladies' Challenge Plate***, the ***Thames***, ***Temple*** and ***Princess Elizabeth Challenge Cups*** and the ***Henley Prize***.

The ***fastest recorded time*** at the Regatta taken by a men's eight over the ***Regatta Course***, (1mile 550yds), (R-C Hansa Dortmund. Germany for the Grand Challenge Cup in 1989) is 5min 58sec - a speed of 11.46knots or 13.2mph (21.24kph).

The ***fastest recorded time*** at the Regatta taken by a women's eight over the Regatta Course, (Marlow RC & Thames RC in the ***Women's Invitation Eights*** in 1998) is 6min 47sec - a speed of 10.08knots or 11.61mph (18.68kph).

ELIGIBILITY TO COMPETE AT HENLEY

In December 1997 the Regatta deleted all references to the word 'amateur' from the rules and introduced the concept of 'Eligibility':-

· Entries for events at the Regatta are accepted only from clubs that have been continuously affiliated to the ***ARA*** or an appropriate national association or federation for at least one year before the closing date for entries. In this regard the Henley Rules also require any such national association or federation outside the United Kingdom to have entered into an Agreement in the prescribed form with the ***Committee of Management*** of the Regatta, and

· Each ***athlete*** competing in the Regatta must have been a member of the club he/she is representing for at least two months before the closing date for entries.

SEE - under name of individual ***Regatta trophy*** for details of event entry requirements.

ELIMINATING RACES

See - QUALIFYING RACES

THE ELSENHAM CUP

See - ROYAL HENLEY PEACE REGATTA

ENCHANTRESS

Enchantress, built in 1913 by Messrs ***Hobbs and Sons*** and still owned by the company, is one of the six 50ft ***umpire launches*** used at the Regatta.

HRH The Princess Elizabeth (HM Queen Elizabeth) and HRH Princess Margaret used *Enchantress* when they visited the Regatta in 1946.

ENCLOSURE ATTENDANTS

Over the years these duties have been undertaken by a range of organisations and groups including ***Oxford College Servants***, sixth formers from local schools and colleges, Army Apprentices and the Army.

The present Enclosure attendants, also referred to affectionately as the 'bowler hatters', undertake similar work at Ascot and other race meetings.

ENCLOSURES

(See plan on page 17)

There are two official Enclosures at the Regatta - the ***Stewards' Enclosure*** and the ***Regatta Enclosure***.

The times of opening the Enclosures each day depends on the time of the first race but is likely to be 8am on Wednesday, Thursday and Friday, 8.30 on Saturday and 11am on Sunday.

Attendants are on duty in the Enclosures to ensure Regatta regulations are observed.

ENTRANCE FEES

All clubs entering events at the Regatta are required to pay an entrance fee. ***Entry*** in any of the ***eights*** events in 2001 was £80, the fours and ***quads*** events £50 and ***single sculling*** events £30. The entrance fee for the ***Goblets*** and the ***Double Sculls*** was £40.

ENTRIES

Each club entering an event at Henley is required to complete a form showing:-

· the full name with all initials, date of birth and weight of each ***athlete*** including ***coxswains***,

· the steersman in the case of entries in ***coxless fours*** events,

· the colours that will be on the ***blades***,

· the names of each club with regard to a ***composite crews***, and

· the status level and number of points of each athlete with regard to entries for small boat events ie. the ***Silver Goblets and Nickalls' Challenge Cup***, the ***Double Sculls Challenge Cup***, the ***Diamond Challenge Sculls*** and the ***Princess Royal Challenge Cup***.

The form must also be accompanied by the ***entrance fee***.

Since 1989 athletes, except coxswains, have not been allowed to enter more than two events at the same Regatta. (Note: In 1931 HRA (Jumbo) Edwards won the ***Grand Challenge Cup*** at noon rowing in the London RC eight, the ***Stewards' Challenge Cup*** at 3.30 also rowing for London, and the Silver Goblets and Nickalls' Challenge Cup at 5.45 rowing for Christ Church College, Oxford)

The entry form is required to be signed by a 'duly authorised official' of the club or each club in the case of ***composite crews***. Entries from clubs not affiliated in the United Kingdom ie. not affiliated to the ***Amateur Rowing Association***, the Scottish ARA, the Welsh ARA and the Irish

Amateur Rowing Union in respect of entries from Northern Ireland, need the countersignature of an authorised official of the Association or Federation to which they are affiliated.

Entries start to arrive at ***Regatta Headquarters*** from the beginning of April although over half arrive during the three days immediately before the closing date - and in most years a few arrive too late to be included - some missing the deadline by minutes as the Regatta is notoriously strict in applying the 2pm deadline - see below.

(I never cease to be amazed that, even though some clubs will have had athletes in training for many months specifically for Henley, they will leave submitting their entry to the last minute, thereby running the risk that a delay, possibly caused by a traffic hold-up on the M4 or on the approach roads to Henley or even when parking, could result in their entry being refused; thus wasting months, even years, of preparation, even to the extent of ruining the ambitions and aspirations of the young athletes involved - MCNJ).

Entries close at 2pm on the Tuesday fifteen days before the Regatta - before this time and for two days afterwards, the Regatta does not disclose details of who has entered or how many are on the list. Late entries or entries by telephone, telegram or telex are not accepted. Facsimile transmitted entries are only permitted for entries in the Grand, Stewards', ***Prince Philip and Queen Mother Challenge Cups***, the Silver Goblets and Nickalls' Challenge Cup, the Double Sculls and ***Princess Royal Challenge Cups***, the ***Henley Prize***, the ***Women's Quadruple Sculls*** and the Diamond Challenge Sculls from outside the UK, and only if they are on the prescribed entry form.

The day after the closing date for Entries the ***Committee of Management*** meets to accept the entries, which are officially released the following day at 2pm. The Committee meets again the following Sunday to decide which competitors, in those events where the entries have exceeded the predetermined limit, will be required to Qualify

From earliest times the Henley ***Rules*** have been kept under review to prevent competitors entering events that are inappropriate for their status and ability. After the record entry of 552 in 1998 when 324 competitors were required to race in the ***Qualifying Races*** for 96 places, changes were made to the entry qualifications in the small boat events to raise the standard of competition and reduce the size of the entry. This resulted in an entry of 428 in 1999 - the lowest entry since the 400 of 1991.

The rules require that any objections to any club or crew on the List must be made in writing to the ***Secretary*** 'at least four clear days before the Regatta' and any objections to the qualification of a competitor must be made in writing 'at the earliest moment practicable'. No protest will be accepted after the Prizes have been presented.

One final point with regard to the strict 2pm entry deadline. Many delivering their entry form to Regatta Headquarters will have noticed a small black and white print of Admiral John Byng on the desk of the Steward responsible for entries in the Crews' Enquiry Office. Although the reason for it being on display is personal, those with knowledge of naval history may believe it to be no coincidence that reference is made to Admiral Byng at this time given that the Regatta makes no allowance for mitigating circumstances regarding any late entries.

(Admiral Byng , a British naval hero, was found guilty of negligence by way of not doing enough to assist other ships when the British Fleet was in battle with the French Fleet in

May 1756. Byng's case was that to lose his ship would have weakened the British influence in the Mediterranean and possibly resulted in the loss of Gibraltar. The 12th Article of War allowed no mitigating circumstances to be taken into consideration and, as an example to others, despite pleas by his friends and even by the Court-Martial, he was 'shot to death'. The execution took place on Monday 14 March 1757 on board the 'Man-of-War' *Monarque* at Spithead.)

See - AMATEUR STATUS, ELIGIBILITY, LIST OF ENTRIES AND COLOURS OF THE CREWS and OVERSEAS ENTRIES

ENVIRONMENT AGENCY - THAMES REGION

The Agency acts as guardian of the environment, protecting and improving it for future generations. During the Royal Regatta the *Windrush*, flagship of the Thames Region of the Environment Agency, and the five patrol boats, *Chess*, *Mole*, *Tillingbourne*, *Whitewater* and *Wye* are based on the ***upstream*** end of ***Fawley Meadows*** next to ***Phyllis Court Club***.

Before 1963 the boats of the ***Thames Conservancy***, which was then the river authority, were moored at the upstream end of the ***Boat Tent Area***. The move to Fawley Meadows followed the disruption caused when the new *Windrush* (not the present boat of that name), which was larger than its predecessor, moored at the ***Press Box*** and in the ***Umpires Launch Bay*** rather than at the TC moorings.

The Agency took over responsibility for rivers in England and Wales in 1996 when it succeeded the ***National Rivers Authority*** and incorporated the work of HM Inspectorate of

Pollution and the Waste Regulation Authorities.

The NRA had been responsible for the ***River Thames*** since 1989 when it took over from the ***Thames Water Authority*** who succeeded the ***Thames Conservancy*** in 1974. The TC as it was often referred to (and occasionally still is), was established in 1857. It succeeded the Thames Navigation Commissioners in 1866, the TNC having had general authority for the whole river upstream of Staines since 1751.

Before 1751 there had been a number of commissioners responsible for different parts of the Thames. These included the Oxford - Burcot Commissioners in 1624, the Navigation Commissioners in 1695 and the City of London, who had been responsible for the whole river but hadn't concerned itself with anything upstream of Staines.

The duties of the Environment Agency include the control/registration, by way of issuing some 25,000 licences, of all craft using the river. All racing boats need to be registered by the Environment Agency and special arrangements are made for those boats at the Regatta eg. boats from overseas and those from other parts of the United Kingdom, that do not normally use the ***River Thames***. The Agency also registers ***umpire launches***.

The Agency also ensure the enforcement of the river bylaws which govern the erection of landing stages on the river and holding regattas, ***head of the river races*** and other waterborne events. In this regard the Agency 'consents' to the ***Stewards*** holding the Regatta and charges an 'accommodation' fee for the creation of the ***Regatta Course***.

The Thames Region of the Agency is also responsible for the 44 ***locks*** on the non-tidal Thames and Blake's Lock on the River Kennet at Reading. All the bylaws are on display at each of the Thames locks.

The Agency operates a flood defence and flood warning service, which provides a 24-hour monitor of rainfalls and river levels. Coloured boards displayed at locks caution river users about the strength of the ***stream*** - Yellow boards when the stream is increasing and Red boards when the stream is so strong the Agency recommend boats do not use the river.

Thames Region deals with the maintenance of the 135.18miles (217.55km) of navigable non-tidal freshwater river, from the town bridge at Cricklade to the boundary obelisk 425yds (390m) ***downstream*** of Teddington Lock (the Port of London Authority being responsible for the tidal river downstream of this point). The Region is also responsible for the River Kennet from where it joins the Thames at Reading to a point 64m (70yds) east of the High Bridge in Reading.

Among its less well known activities, the Environment Agency supports otters through the Thames Otter Project, water voles through the BBOWT (***Berks***, ***Bucks*** and ***Oxon*** Wildlife Trust) Water Vole Recovery Project, native crayfish, Desmoulin's Whorle Snail and the Depressed River Mussel. It also needs to be consulted in the event of a sponsored walk along the river-bank.

See - NAVIGATION, SPEED LIMIT ON THE RIVER and SWIMMING

ERGO ROOM

The Ergo Room is situated next to the ***Dressing Tent*** at the back of the Boat Tent

An Ergometer, referred to in the sport as an Ergo, is a ***row-***

ing machine. It consists of a seat that moves along a rail and an '***oar***' handle attached to a chain, which is fixed to a fly-wheel, which provides resistance. The basic machine has a digital display, which shows various criteria including the amount of energy and calories used during the exercise and the number of metres 'rowed'.

At Henley in recent years, heavy river traffic during the Regatta has prevented competitors from warming up properly before a race and winding down afterwards. So, since 1997, the Regatta has provided the Ergo Room which has 18

Concept II ergometers to deal with this problem. Similar arrangements have been made for competitors at the World Rowing Championships and the ***Olympic Games*** Regattas.
See - INDOOR ROWING

EVENTS

The names of the Henley Royal ***Regatta trophies*** and events are interrelated, the abbreviated name of a trophy often being used to describe an event eg. it is acceptable to say that the Grand (the ***Grand Challenge Cup***) is the senior event at the Regatta, and an entry in the Diamonds (the ***Diamond Challenge Sculls***) means an entry in the men's single sculling event.

In the sport 'event' can also be the all-embracing definition of any 'race, series of races or timed event' that determine the winner in a particular class of competition eg. ***head of the river races*** and regattas.

EXPERIMENTAL COURSE

This was the Course used at the Regatta in 1924.
See - REGATTA COURSE

EYOT

Eyot or Ait is a small ***island***, particularly one in a river (rather than at sea). The reason for highlighting the word 'eyot' is because of its pronunciation - the phonetic pronunciation is either 'eye-ot' or 'eight'.

The large island ***downstream*** of ***Marsh Lock*** is ***Rod Eyot*** and the first ***upstream*** of ***Henley Bridge*** is ***East Eyot***. There is also the ***Eyot Boat Centre*** on the ***Berkshire*** bank about quarter of a mile upstream of ***Henley Bridge***. In all of these the pronunciation is usually 'eye-ot'. In London the island on the Middlesex side of the ***University Boat Race*** Course at the 2½ miles mark, referred to as Chiswick Eyot on many maps and Chiswick Ait on Port of London Authority official charts, is usually pronounced 'eight'.

EYOT BOAT CENTRE

The ***Eyot*** Boat Centre (the phonetic pronunciation is 'eye-ot') is one of the Thamesfield Youth Association Charity organisations and is for young persons involved with canoeing on the river. The Centre is based on the ***Berkshire*** bank of the river immediately ***upstream*** of the ***Thamesfield Nursing Home*** (The Nursing Home has no connection now with the Thamesfield Charity other than the name - the Henley Youth

Centre, which is also one of the Thamesfield Youth Association Charity organisations, had been based in the building before the building was sold).

The Eyot Boat Centre is also the base for the ***Henley Dragon Boat Club***.

FAIRGROUND

From 1920 until 1966, a funfair was built each year on the ***downstream*** end of ***Blandy Meadow***, the land which is now the ***Regatta Enclosure***. In the early days the fair extended into ***Lion Meadow***. Because of a need for more car parking space, coupled with an increase in vandalism of Regatta tents attributed to those visiting the funfair, the contract for the use of Blandy Meadow was not renewed in 1966. There was no funfair at the Regatta in 1967 but it is now established each year on land in Wargrave Road.

FASTEST RECORDED TIMES

The list of the ***fastest recorded time***s in races to the ***Barrier***, ***Fawley*** and Finish are shown as the penultimate entry in the ***Regatta Programme***.

The ***stream*** and the ***weather***, particularly the wind, can influence the times - as in 1965 when every record was equalled or broken with the exception of the ***Ladies'*** (Fawley and Finish times) and the ***Visitors'*** (Barrier and Fawley times).

Competitors that equal a record or set a new record receive a Certificate signed by the Regatta ***Secretary***.

See - EIGHT, COXED FOUR, COXLESS FOUR, PAIR, QUADRUPLE SCULL, DOUBLE SCULL and SINGLE SCULL

FAWLEY

'Fawley' or 'The Fawley' can cover a range of items and

places at Henley, all of which take their name from the nearby village of Fawley.
See - FAWLEY BAR, FAWLEY BOATHOUSE, FAWLEY BOX, FAWLEY CHALLENGE CUP, FAWLEY MEADOWS, FAWLEY NARROWS, and FAWLEY STAND.

FAWLEY BAR

The Fawley Bar is situated approximately halfway down the ***Stewards' Enclosure*** in the same way that the ***Fawley Box*** is the halfway point on the ***Regatta Course***.

Bar and table service is available providing a wide range of beers, champagnes and spirits, including ***Pimm's***.
The Bar opens at 10am each day (11am on Sunday).

FAWLEY BOATHOUSE

A boathouse existed at Fawley in 1874 but it is not clear whether this was on the ***island*** which is set in the ***Buckinghamshire*** bank at the halfway point on the ***Regatta Course***.

Early in the 20th century, a boathouse was constructed on the island and was still standing in 1969 - but had collapsed and been removed by 1992 when the Regatta purchased the island. All that can be seen now is the wet dock.

Despite this, the location is still often referred to as the

Fawley Boathouse.

The water channel on the non-river-side of the island has almost disappeared.

FAWLEY BOX

Fawley is the name of the halfway point on the ***Regatta Course*** although technically the Fawley post, 3,435ft from the starting line, is 3,495ft from the finish line (see REGATTA COURSE for explanation)

The Official on the Fawley Box, situated of the ***Buckinghamshire*** side of the Course, drops a flag as the ***bow*** of the leading boat crosses the Fawley line. The time taken to reach Fawley, the second official timing point on the Course, is then recorded by the ***Timekeeper/Race Recorder*** standing in the stern (back) of the ***Umpire's launch***. It is also advised to the Official on the Fawley Box so that it can be shown on boards on the ***upstream*** side of the Box.

As the Fawley Box is not a '***signal box***' the distance the leading competitor is ahead of the other competitor is advised by the official on the Box to the Timekeeper/Race Recorder for recording on the ***Race Report*** sheet.

Statistically, 90% of competitors ahead at Fawley stay ahead and win the race.

See - REGATTA RECORDS

THE FAWLEY CHALLENGE CUP

The Fawley Challenge cup is competed for by ***quadruple sculls***. The event, referred to simply as the 'Fawley', was established in 1992 and has the same age entry requirements as the ***Princess Elizabeth*** in that ***athletes*** must not be aged 19 before the last day of the Regatta. Unlike the Princess Elizabeth, which is for schools only, the Fawley is open to any club.

Athletes competing in this event are not permitted to compete in any other event at the same Regatta.

The Fawley Challenge Cup trophy was presented to the Regatta in 1985 in memory of Nicholas Young who rowed for Westminster School and St Catherine's College Oxford. Before 1992, ***crews*** in the ***Special Race for Schools*** competed for the trophy.

The entrance fee for this event is £50 and the Stewards have limited the number of entries to 16.

See - REGATTA TROPHIES

FAWLEY COURT

The large 17th century building on the ***Buckinghamshire*** bank that stands back from the river just down ***downstream*** of the site of the ***Fawley Boathouse***.

After the Norman Conquest in 1066 William I gave Fawley manor to his brother-in-law Walter Gifford, one of the leading compilers of the Doomsday Book. Sir William de Sakeville, then occupied Fawley in 1079 and built a fortified manor house in the early part of the 12th century.

In the 1470s the manor was acquired, through marriage, by Thomas Rokes, created Sheriff of Buckinghamshire by Henry IV.

In 1616 Fawley, owned then by Sir William Alford, was sold to Judge Sir James Whitelock (sometimes spelt Whitelocke and sometimes Whitlock) who subsequently bought ***Phyllis Court*** and Henley Park. His son, Judge and Parliamentarian, Sir Bulstrode Whitelock, inherited the property.

Because of Sir Bulstrode's support for Parliament, Fawley Court, like Phyllis Court, was attacked at the beginning of the Civil War by Royalist troops under Prince Rupert. Fawley Court was badly damaged such that when Sir Bulstrode returned to Henley and was made Governor of the Phyllis Court garrison he had to live there while Fawley Court was made habitable.

In 1651 Sir Bulstrode bought the ruined house at ***Greenland*** but after the restoration of the monarchy he was fined heavily for his support of Cromwell and sold Greenland in 1660. He also made over Phyllis Court to William, his eldest surviving son from his second marriage.

Sir Bulstrode retained Fawley which then passed into the hands of his son by his first marriage, Sir James Whitelock. Sir James then sold the property to Colonel William Freeman circa 1680 who began the rebuilding.

The new house is said to have been designed by Sir Christopher Wren in 1683/4 and the carved ceilings of the drawing room, which date from 169(Grinling Gibbons. William Freeman die leaving Fawley to his nephew John Coc name of Freeman. Cook (Freeman) start with a Gothic Chapel in 1732 and a Mau 1769 the ownership of Fawley had passed to Sambrook Freeman, son of John Cook (Freeman) and great nephew of Colonel William Freeman. The work continued and James Wyatt, surveyor of Westminster Abbey, undertook various additions including the fireplace and many of the ceilings as well as the Temple on ***Temple Island***. During his time Lancelot 'Capability' Brown was commissioned to design the park and gardens including planting many of the great trees that exist today on the estate.

Over the years Fawley Court has received many Royal visits. In December 1688, William of Orange and his wife Mary stayed at Fawley Court and at Phyllis Court on their way to London for their coronation. Later George III, George IV and William IV stayed there, William later appointing Peter Freeman Williams, Admiral of the Fleet.

In 1853 Fawley Court was sold to the Scottish banker Edward Mackenzie whose son, the surveyor and railway engineer William Mackenzie, was a colleague of the prominent engineer Thomas Telford. During the later part of the 19th and early 20th century the Mackenzie family enlarged the building, rebuilt the terrace, put up the wrought iron gates and created the ornamental waterway to the river.

The house was neglected during the Second World War having been requisitioned by the army; and was badly damaged by fire in 1973.

Since 1953 the house has been owned by the Congregation of Marian Fathers and a new church, founded by Prince

Radziwill, built in the grounds.

e house, used initially as a school for Polish boys, is w a religious and educational centre and incorporates a museum to Polish history and culture. It is open to the public from 2pm to 5pm every Wednesday, Thursday and Sunday (apart from Easter and Whit Sundays) from March to October. See - HENLEY BRIDGE

THE FAWLEY CUP

See - ROYAL HENLEY PEACE REGATTA

FAWLEY MEADOWS

Fawley is the name of the estate and lands, which stretch along the Buckinghamshire side of the river from ***Phyllis Court*** to ***Fawley Court***.

The Royal Regatta owns the land from Phyllis Court Club to the ***Fawley Boathouse*** island. Fawley Court owns the next 150m of river-bank and the remaining 18½ acres to a point just ***upstream*** of ***Temple Island*** and known originally as ***Park Farm Meadows***, were purchased by the Regatta in 1955.

The Fawley Meadows bank has always been used for mooring pleasure boats during Regatta week - originally these were ***houseboats*** and lately large ***pleasure boats***.

In 1973/4 the Stewards considered developing part of Fawley Meadows with houses and a marina in order to raise funds for the Regatta but this met considerable local resistance so the plans were deferred.

In 1976 the Regatta established an official Corporate Hospitality facility on Fawley Meadows and in 1977 added a temporary Regatta Office to deal with the increase usage of the meadows and the moorings during the Regatta.

Guests from the ***Fawley Meadows Hospitality Village*** are able to reach the ***Enclosures*** on the ***Berkshire*** bank by using the private ferryboat service that operates between Fawley Meadows and the ***Regatta Enclosure***.

Many organisations not connected with the Regatta use Fawley Meadows outside the Regatta period eg. the Henley Rugby Club uses the field next to the Marlow Road between October and April each year, the Asian Music Festival and the ***Thames Traditional Boat Rally*** are annual summer events and caravan rallies take place throughout the year. The part of Fawley Meadows next to ***Phyllis Court*** is the site of the ***firework*** display that takes place on the Saturday of the Regatta.

There is a public ***footpath*** which runs from a point on the Marlow Road by ***Phyllis Court***, along the river edge of Fawley Meadows, across the grounds of Fawley Court and ***Park Farm Meadows***, returning to the Marlow Road by the ***Henley Management College***.

In 1990 20 acres of Fawley Meadows was designated a site of special scientific interest by the Countryside Commission.

FAWLEY MEADOWS CAR PARK

The Fawley Meadows car park is situated on the ***Buckinghamshire*** side of the river and accessible from the Marlow Road. It is used mainly by those visiting the ***Fawley Meadows Hospitality Village*** or those with moorings.

Car park ***labels*** can be purchased on a daily basis although it is not possible for members of the public using the Fawley Meadows car park to reach the ***Berkshire*** bank, other than via ***Henley Bridge*** or ***Hambleden lock***. Nevertheless those coming from Oxford or from Marlow and the M40 who are not deterred by the walk of approximately a mile, find parking on

Fawley Meadows a convenient means of avoiding the traffic queues each side of Henley Bridge.
See - CAR PARKS

FAWLEY MEADOWS HOSPITALITY VILLAGE
The Regatta's Official Hospitality facility, managed by ***Sodexho Prestige***, is based on ***Fawley Meadows*** on the ***Buckinghamshire*** side of the river.

The Regatta first established this service in 1976 in order to provide additional income to counter the increasing costs of staging the Regatta. The first contract was awarded to Paynes of Shepherd's Bush, London (before the company became ***Payne & Gunter***).

Official and unofficial corporate hospitality expanded rapidly in the 1980s, reaching a peak in 1989 when the Regatta celebrated its sesquicentennial (150th) anniversary. At that time unofficial (non-HRR) hospitality tents were being erected on any available land adjacent to the river - and in some instances over a mile away from the Regatta.

During the general economic recession in the early 1990s, the hospitality business declined, although by the end of the decade a recovery was being experienced.

In 1997, after Payne & Gunter merged with ***Letheby and Christopher*** the official caterers in the ***Stewards' Enclosure***, the Regatta's hospitality contract on Fawley Meadows was awarded to Town & County plc of Alperton in Middlesex, a subsidiary of Gardner Merchant Leisure, Sodexho Alliance Group. On 21st February 2000 Gardner Merchant Leisure changed its name to Sodexho since when Town & County, being one of the four companies in the group responsible for the major events part of the business, has managed the Fawley Meadows Hospitality Village under the name of ***Sodexho Prestige***.

The service is mainly for corporate hospitality although smaller non-corporate parties can be accommodated as the village has a high-class restaurant where tables can be

reserved for parties of two or more. Bookings are for the whole day and include a complimentary bar including Champagne and ***Pimm's***, a five-course luncheon with wines and a traditional afternoon tea. Music is provided by a live jazz band.

Access to the Hospitality Village is via either the Marlow Road or by the Official ***ferry boats***, which are reserved for guests' use.

Special badges, referred to as swing badges, are issued to

those using the hospitality village, which also give access to the ferry and the ***Regatta Enclosure***.

FAWLEY NARROWS

This term is used by the ***Environment Agency*** to describe the navigation channel at ***Fawley*** where the ***Regatta Course*** is very close to the ***Buckinghamshire*** bank.

See picture on page 189.

FAWLEY STAND

The Fawley Stand is situated approximately halfway down the ***Stewards' Enclosure*** in the same way that the ***Fawley Box*** is the halfway point on the ***Regatta Course***.

The Fawley Stand, originally called the Open Stand, was built for the 1948 ***Olympic Games*** Regatta. In 1949 it was reduced in size for the Royal Regatta and was lengthened by 50ft in 1967. In 1981 it was renamed the Fawley Stand when it was again increased in size, covered, and fitted with seating. In 1990 the stand was further enlarged and now seats over 2000 spectators.

Seats cannot be reserved in the Fawley Stand - unlike the ***Grandstand***.

FAWLEY TEMPLE

See - TEMPLE ISLAND

FÉDÉRATION INTERNATIONALE DES SOCIÉTÉS D'AVIRON

Known in the sport simply as FISA, the International Federation of Rowing Associations (the English translation) is the international governing body of world ***rowing***.

FERRY BOATS

The Regatta in liaison with ***Sodexho Prestige***, the company managing the Regatta's official ***Fawley Meadows Hospitality Village*** operates a private ferry boat service between the village on ***Fawley Meadows*** on the ***Buckinghamshire*** bank, and the ***Regatta Enclosure*** on the ***Berkshire*** bank.

The six ferryboats operate between 11am and 7pm on each of the five days of the Regatta. To enable these boats to cross the ***Regatta Course*** safely, Ferryboat Course Marshals are situated in boats against the ***booms*** on either side of the crossing point.

FERRY COTTAGE

Situated on the ***Buckinghamshire*** bank approximately 250m

upstream of ***Hambleden Lock***.
See - PINK COTTAGE

FINISH JUDGE

See - FINISHING A RACE AT HENLEY

FINISHING A RACE AT HENLEY

A competitor has finished a race when the ***bow*** or any part of the ***boat*** crosses the finish line.

Whilst each competitor is required to start the race with the full complement of ***athletes*** in the boat the ***rules*** state that a ***crew*** *shall not be debarred from winning a race if a competitor other than a* ***coxswain*** *leaves the boat during the race.*

The rule has not been tested for the eventuality of two athletes other than the cox leaving the boat but it would seem reasonable to assume the crew could still be allowed to win the race. Reference to leaving the boat covers the situation of an athlete falling into the water as a result of catching a crab or hitting a pile. (Note: An ***athlete*** 'catches a crab' when he is unable to extract the spoon of the ***oar/scull*** from the water at the end of the ***stroke***) If the coxswain leaves the boat during the race *the crew shall be deemed not to have completed the Course.*

A Finish Judge will press a button as the bow of the leading boat crosses the finish line. This activates a light which indicates to the Timekeeper and Race Recorder in the ***Umpire's Launch*** that the race has finished. Pressing the button also activates an audible signal to tell competitors that they have reached the finish line.

When all the boats have crossed the finish line the ***Umpire***, after a brief pause to give the competitors time to appeal should they be unhappy about any incidents in the race, will raise a white ***flag***. This indicates to the Judges in the ***Judges' Box*** on the ***Buckinghamshire*** side of the ***Regatta Course***, that the race is in order.

If one of the competitors has not completed the Course eg. as a result of hitting the booms or because of equipment failure, the Umpire will delay raising the white flag until he has been able to inform the Finish Judges verbally that the verdict should be that the race was '***Not Rowed Out***'. In this regard the Umpire has the power to decide the winner of a race if it should be stopped before the competitors reach the finish line.

If there has been a disqualification during the race or if there has been an incident which the Umpire wishes to discuss with the Committee he will raise the red flag and advise the Finish Judges accordingly.

If the race is in order the Finish Judges determine the winning order and the margin and will take no account of anything that has happened in the race before the ***boats*** cross the finish line. In the event of a close finish, they will call for a photo-finish picture to be displayed in the Judges' Box. (The photo-finish equipment was first used at the Regatta in 1983. The camera is fixed to the Judges' Box and the recording equipment installed on the ***Floating Stand***.)

At Henley the winning margin is expressed in distances, as at most river regattas, rather than in time (seconds) as at multi-lane regattas. There is no minimum distance and the Judges may use photographic evidence to determine the winner. Distances are usually given in feet up to 6ft (although there is no rule specifying the maximum) and after this the measurements used are relative to the ***lengths*** of the boats in the race using lengths and fractions of a length - quarter, third, half, two thirds and three quarters of a length. The only exception is when the winning margin is the distance between the ***bow*** of the boat and the breakwater immediately behind the first (bow) ***athlete***, in which case it is described as a '***canvas***'. As a 'length' can vary according to type of boat in the race, an ***eight*** winning by one length will have won by approximately 18.3m (60ft) whereas a ***sculling*** boat will have won by approximately 8.2m (27ft). Beyond five lengths the verdict is usually given as '***easily***'.

In the event of a ***dead heat*** the race is re-rowed at a time arranged by the ***Committee of Management***. If a competitor refuses to re-row he is disqualified.

See - RACE REPORTS, STARTING A RACE AT HENLEY, STEWARDS CHALLENGE CUP and UMPIRING A RACE AT HENLEY

FIREWORKS

Since the end of the 19th century there has been a firework display on the Saturday night of the Regatta which, until 1974 when Sunday racing was introduced, was also the final day of the Regatta.

In the early days of the 20th century the event took place on ***Blandy's Meadow*** on the ***Berkshire*** side of the river. The present display, which involves approximately 3,200 fireworks containing nearly ¾ ton of explosives, takes place on ***Fawley Meadows*** on the ***Buckinghamshire*** side.

The display, which commences at 10pm, is financed by donations from the public and local businesses to the Henley Firework Fund. This fund was formed in 1910 and works under the authority of Henley Town Council to finance the display. The Organising Committee includes the Mayor of Henley and the ***Secretary of the Regatta*** (both ex-officio positions) two members of Henley Town Council, the President of Henley Lions Club, the Manager of the local branch of Barclays Bank and three local residents who are co-opted at the annual meeting.

Joseph Wells & Sons provided the fireworks and organised the displays from 1920 to 1972 when the Reverend Ron Lancaster of Kimbolton Fireworks, Huntingdon took over.

Boats start gathering in the middle of the river opposite the display area as soon as the last race has finished. The main public viewing area is on the Berkshire bank in the ***Regatta Enclosure***, which is opened on Saturday evening for the purpose.

FIRST AID

Members of St John Ambulance provide First Aid during the five days of the Regatta. Their main base is in the ***First Aid***

Tent in the ***Boat Tent Area*** but they also have first-aid stations on ***Fawley Meadows***, in ***Phyllis Court*** and at ***Remenham Farm*** on land opposite to ***Temple Island***.

FISA

See - FÉDÉRATION INTERNATIONALE DES SOCIÉTÉS D'AVIRON

FISH

There are reported to be over 115 species of fish and eels in the freshwater Thames (the river ***upstream*** of Teddington lock). This includes salmon mainly as a result of the scheme started in the late 1970s to introduce young salmon (smolts) into the Thames and to assist them to swim upstream by the installation of 'salmon ladders' at each of the weirs on the river.

Other fish in the ***Henley Reach*** include barbel, bleak, bream, carp, chub, dace, eels (although these are not as plentiful now as they were up to the end of the 19th century), flounders, grayling, gudgeon (considered in the past to be a favourite fish of lady anglers), loach, millers thumb, minnows, perch, pike or jack (small pike - the pike was a popular fish in Henley up to the end of the 19th century), pope, roach, rudd, ruff, stickleback, tench and trout, (golden and silver).

FIXED STAGE

The stage on piles immediately ***downstream*** of the ***Floating Stand*** in the ***Stewards' Enclosure***, first used in 1950, is referred to as the Fixed Stage. The entrance to the Enclosure from the ***Stewards' Boat Dock*** is situated at the downstream end of the Fixed Stage.

See pictures on pages 104 and 271.

FLAGS

Two flags are flown on Regatta land during the Regatta, both in the ***Stewards' Enclosure***. The Union Flag is flown from a flagpole by the ***Bandstand*** and the ***Henley Royal Regatta*** Flag in front of the ***Luncheon Tent***.

Official Regatta boats, eg. the slipper launch *L'Amazon* and the workboat ***Black Piglet***, fly a small blue flag with the initials 'HRR' in white from the stern.

The Official ***Ferryboats***, which operate between the ***Fawley Meadows Hospitality Village*** and the ***Regatta Enclosure***, fly a blue flag with the words 'HRR FERRY' in white.

Umpire launches fly a white flag with the word 'UMPIRE' in blue from a staff (pole) at the stern

The ***Environment Agency*** patrol boats fly blue flags from the stern with the words 'RIVER INSPECTOR' in white - apart from *Windrush* which flies a blue flag with the words 'HARBOUR MASTER' in white

If a member of the Royal family is in official attendance at the Regatta or on a boat, then the appropriate Royal Standard will be flown on the boat and/or in the Stewards' Enclosure in place of the Union flag.

Pleasure boats fly a variety of flags but the main one seen is the red ensign.

(Note: Ensign is another name for a flag which has a smaller flag, the union flag, in the top corner next to the flag pole/staff. The rest of the ensign is either white, ie. the White Ensign, as flown on naval ships and by the Royal Yacht Squadron; blue, ie. the Blue Ensign, as on government boats or boats owned by persons with naval connections such as members of the naval reserve; and red, ie. the Red Ensign, which is flown on merchant ships and boats owned by UK nationals)

(Note also: The union flag may only be flown from a boat with the permission of the Ministry of Defence. The union flag is often mistakenly referred to as the union jack. This is because on warships the flag that flies from the jackstaff (the flagpole on the bow of the ship), to denote nationality when in harbour, is known as the 'jack' and on British warships the jack is the union flag)

An ***umpire*** of a race at Henley will use red and white flags.

The white flag is used in a race to indicate when warnings/instructions are being given and the direction a competitor should take if out of his ***station***. The white flag is also used if the Umpire wishes to stop one of the competitors but not the race. It is also used when all the competitors have passed the finish line, to indicate that the Umpire has no reason to dispute the finishing order determined by the Finish Judges.

The red flag is used to start the race and if the Umpire wishes to stop the race before the competitors have reached the finish line, or if there is a problem at the finish.

On the ***Regatta Course*** the green flags on piles indicate the official ***crossing points*** for ***crews*** and ***scullers*** at the $1^1/_8$miles ***signal*** and the ***Barrier***; and the yellow pennants on the piles next to the signal boxes are used to identify the wind direction and to help estimate the wind force for the ***Race Reports***.

See - STARTING A RACE AT HENLEY, UMPIRING A RACE AT HENLEY and FINISHING A RACE AT HENLEY

FLOATER
See - FLOATING STAND

FLOATING STAND
Known originally as the 'Stewards' Barge', and now more popularly as the 'Floater', the Floating Stand is positioned off the ***Berkshire*** bank by the ***Secretary's Tent*** in the ***Stewards' Enclosure*** at the finish of the ***Regatta Course***.

Set at an angle to the bank it provides an excellent view of

the whole Course.

The upper deck is for ***Members*** of the Stewards' Enclosure and the lower part is reserved for Guests of the ***Stewards***.

The Regatta ***commentary*** team is based at the ***upstream*** end of the upper deck, as is the videotape equipment used for recording the finish of each race.

A Committee Barge was moored at Poplar Point from 1886 when the Finish of the Course was moved ***downstream*** from ***Henley Bridge***. A floating stand was used at the Regatta in 1939 and, between 1946 and 1948, it was also used for 'end of Regatta' concerts on the Saturday evening. The present Stand was built in 1958 and fully renovated, and the hull replated, in 1988.

The stand was used for many years as a concert platform for the ***Henley Festival*** and it is still used by the ***Henley Town and Visitors' Regatta*** at the end of July. After these events the canvas is removed and it is moored at the upstream end of ***Fawley Meadows*** on the ***Buckinghamshire*** bank for the winter - where at least one tourist has thought it to be a ferry for transporting cattle across the river!

FLOODING

Most of the land along each side of the river on the ***Henley Reach*** is referred to as being in the flood plain, meaning that it is liable to flooding in the winter and spring.

There have been four exceptionally high floods experienced on the Henley Reach in the last 200 years and which, as elsewhere on the river, have been recorded on houses by the river. Three are commemorated on plaques on the wall of the lock keeper's house on ***Marsh Lock*** showing the 1894 and 1947 levels which were about 2ft (61cm) higher than the 1875 flood. (picture shows two of these). A stone set in the wall

of No 11 Thames Side and another at the ***Angel on the Bridge*** record the flood of 28 January 1809 which was approximately 21inches (53cm) higher than the 1894 level.

The river levels reached in the winter of 2000/2001, whilst below those referred to above, were the highest experienced

Montage picture of Lion Meadow on Wednesday 13 December 2000

for 21 years, and the strong ***stream*** caused more than the usual number of rowing events to be cancelled.
See - REGATTA WEATHER

FOOD AND DRINK

For the record, approximately 30,000 pints of ***Pimm's***, 28,000 pints of draft beer and 4,500 bottles of champagne are sold in the bars and restaurants in the ***Stewards' Enclosure*** at each Regatta. In addition, even though Henley, unlike Wimbledon, is not known for its consumption of strawberries, approximately 1.75 tons of strawberries are eaten during the five days of the Regatta.

FOOTPATH

There are three public footpaths across Regatta land in addition to the ***towpath***.

One crosses ***Lion Meadow*** from ***Leander Way*** to a point on the ***Remenham Lane*** by the storage sheds. It used to be fenced on each side and known as 'Birdcage Walk'. The second crosses ***Butler's Field*** from Remenham Lane to the bottom of Sham Hill, the hill to the east of Butler's Field and Green's Field. The third is across ***Fawley Meadows*** from a point on the Marlow Road by ***Phyllis Court***, along the side of the river and back onto the Marlow Road by the ***Henley Management College***.

The path that runs along the edge of the river on the Berkshire bank is a '***towpath***', used in the past for those towing boats.

FOREIGN ENTRIES

See - OVERSEAS ENTRIES

A FOUR

This describes four ***athletes*** '***rowing***' a ***boat***. The boat is also called a four.

Four is also the name given to the fourth ***athlete*** numbering from the bows, in an ***eight***.

(Note: Four athletes '***sculling***' a boat is referred to as a 'quad' ie. a ***quadruple scull***)

See - COXED FOUR and COXLESS FOUR

FREEBOOM

Between 1920 and 1989 the ***Regatta Course*** was built by a small group of men employed by ***Hobbs and Sons Ltd***.

Since 1955 the team had included John Fenn who by 1989 was the Supervisor. On 1 January 1990, with the full co-operation of Hobbs and Sons, John Fenn established Freeboom Ltd and took over responsibility for all river construction work for the Regatta. The name 'Freeboom', although curiously apposite, was coincidental, being the name of the off-the-shelf company used at the time of formation of the company.

FRONT LOADER

This generally refers to a ***boat*** where the ***cox*** is positioned lying in the ***bows***. It is also referred to as a '***bow loader***'.

GARTON CALENDAR

From the early days there were problems fixing the date of the Regatta. Eventually, in 1881, the first ***Committee of Management*** established a rule that the Regatta was to be held not earlier than Thursday and Friday in the week in which July 1 falls. 1968 was an exception when the Regatta took place a week later than normal to accommodate schools taking examinations.

To deal with the increase in the number of other regattas on the Thames, many taking place on Sundays, a table was prepared to provide a means of stabilising as far as possible the dates on which annual regattas are held. Published in August 1972, it was known as the Garton Calendar because it was issued by John Garton, CBE, then President of the ***Amateur Rowing Association*** and ***Chairman*** of the Committee of Management of ***Henley Royal Regatta***.

The Garton Calendar shows the dates on which each successive Sunday falls year by year - the cycle being repeated every 28 years. Henley Royal Regatta is held in week 27, this being the week leading up to the 27th Sunday in the year. This effectively fixes the dates of many other regattas, particularly those on the Thames in May, June and July. For example Reading Amateur Regatta is always in week 24, three weeks before Henley, Marlow in week 25, two weeks before Henley, and the Henley Town & Visitors' Regatta in week 31, four weeks after the Royal Regatta.

Over the next 50 years, unless exceptional pressure is put on the ***Stewards*** to change the system, the Sunday, finals day, of the Regatta will be the first Sunday in July EXCEPT in 2001, 2007, 2018, 2029, 2035 and 2046 when it will be the second Sunday.

The Regatta takes place at the end of the English schools Summer Term and always follows Ascot as part of the Summer Season although it does not always clash with the same week of the Wimbledon fortnight. This is because Wimbledon currently starts on the 6th Monday before the 1st Monday in August!

GENERAL ENCLOSURE

In the early days of the Regatta there was an enclosure for the ***Stewards*** of the Regatta and their guests. In 1919, when the Stewards opened up 'their' Enclosure to ***Members*** of the Stewards' Enclosure 'Club', a separate Enclosure was established, immediately ***downstream*** from the ***Stewards' Enclosure***, mainly for competitors who were allowed free access.

Before the Second World War, in an effort to raise money, the Stewards allowed members of the public to have access to the second enclosure for a fee, thereby changing it from a ***Crews'*** Enclosure to a General Enclosure.

The ***Public Enclosure*** was established next to the General Enclosure in 1967. Pressure on the Stewards to increase the size of the Stewards' Enclosure resulted in the General and Public Enclosures being merged in 1971 and the establishment of the ***Regatta Enclosure***.

GIN PALACES

A description, usually made by rowing people, of the larger, often ocean going, type of cruiser seen on the river and which are popular at Henley

See - PLEASURE BOATS

THE GOBLETS

See - SILVER GOBLETS and NICKALLS' CHALLENGE CUP

GOOSE PATROL

See - CANADA GEESE

THE GRAND

See - GRAND CHALLENGE CUP

THE GRAND CHALLENGE CUP

Picture courtesy of Henley Stewards

The Grand Challenge Cup, competed for by ***eights***, the event being referred to simply as 'The Grand', is the only trophy from the first Regatta in 1839 that is still competed for annually at the Regatta. The other ***Regatta trophy*** from 1839, the ***Town Cup***, is now competed for at ***Henley Town & Visitors' Regatta***.

In 1839 the Grand Challenge Cup, made by Makepeace & Co of Lincoln's Inn, London, was valued at 100 guineas (£105.00). Additional bases were added in 1896, 1954 and 1986 to enable the full names of all the winning ***crews*** to be recorded. The names are also recorded (printed) in a ***Book of Honour***, which was added as part of the trophy in 1954.

In 1914 Harvard University, USA won the Grand Challenge Cup. It remained in the USA during the First World War years and was next competed for in 1920. In 1964 the nine members of the Harvard ***crew*** that had won in 1914 returned to the Regatta and presented the Regatta with a replacement trophy for the Grand which was beginning to show signs of wear. The full crew, including the cox, then weighed in before going onto the water to row past the ***Enclosures***. They were then presented to HM Queen Elizabeth the Queen Mother.

A limited edition book was written to commemorate the event edited by John William Middendorf Jnr who rowed at five in the 1914 crew. (From a personal point of view I was pleased that my father, Norman Jones, undertook the weighing-in in 1964, my grandfather, Charles Drewett, having been 'clerk to the scales' in 1914 - MCNJ)

The names of past winners have been engraved on the replica cup, which has been presented since 1964, and is used, with the full base, for the ***Draw***. The original Grand Challenge Cup remains on display in ***Regatta Headquarters***, other than when it is put onto a special silver base and placed in the centre of the table in front of the ***Chairman*** at all meetings of the ***Stewards*** and the ***Committee of Management***. This base, which was presented to the Regatta in 1965 by HRN Rickett, Chairman 1952-1965, incorporates a drawer for a pen for signing the Minutes.

Interestingly, Harvard also won the Grand in 1939 so that the Cup remained in the USA for the duration of the Second World War. Those who like to recall coincidental events remind us that in 1950, the third time that Harvard won the Grand, was immediately before the start of the Korean War, the third major war of the 20th century involving Great Britain and the USA. Harvard also won the Grand in 1959 and 1985.

The Grand is the senior event at the Regatta being for crews of international standard and has always been open to eights from any ***amateur*** club - other than in the ***Olympic Games*** year of 1908 when overseas crews were banned.

Leander Club has won the Grand more times than any

other club. Cambridge University BC last won the Grand in 1858 and Oxford in 1859. Oxford and Cambridge do not now enter representative crews in the Grand, and colleges from those universities that featured among the winners up until 1951, are now expected to enter the ***Ladies*** or ***Temple***.

In 1989 R-C Hansa Dortmund, Germany won the Grand Challenge Cup in a record time of 5 minutes 58 seconds thereby covering the ***Regatta Course*** at a speed of 11.47 knots or 13.2mph/21.24kph.

The entrance fee for this event is £80 and the Stewards have limited the number of entries to 16.

THE GRANDSTAND

The Grandstand, also known as the ***Members'*** Stand, is situated in the ***Stewards' Enclosure*** approximately 30m ***downstream*** of the finish of the ***Regatta Course***.

Although there are records of grandstands along ***Riverside*** in front of the ***Red Lion*** and ***Little White Hart*** hotels in the early days of the Regatta, the earliest report of a grandstand on the ***Berkshire*** bank was an unofficial stand erected in 1873 at ***Poplar Point***. This was wrecked by indignant oarsmen, allegedly led by WB Woodgate of the ***Stewards Challenge Cup*** 1868 fame, because it blocked the view of the Course from the Finish at the Red Lion/***Henley Bridge***. In 1889 an Official Grandstand was erected on the Berkshire bank to mark the jubilee of the Regatta.

The existing Grandstand was first used in 1954 and extended in 1962. Since 1970, Members have been able to reserve seats for themselves and their guests in the main part of the Grandstand. The ***upstream*** end of the Grandstand has an unreserved section for Members only.

The only other 'Regatta' stands are the ***Floating Stand*** and the ***Fawley Stand*** in the Stewards' Enclosure, and the stand in the ***Regatta Enclosure*** - although there are stands at ***Phyllis Court Club*** and ***Remenham Club***.

GREENLANDS

See - HENLEY MANAGEMENT COLLEGE

GREEN'S FIELD

Green's Field is situated on the opposite side of ***Remenham Lane*** from ***Lion Meadow***. Named after a tenant farmer, it was originally part of the ***Remenham Court*** estate and was purchased by the Regatta in 1958. It is now one of the three main official Regatta ***car parks*** and joined to ***Butler's Field*** by a road behind ***Barn Cottage***.

Car park ***labels*** can be purchased on a daily basis.

GUN

When the finish of the ***Regatta Course*** was at ***Henley Bridge*** the ***Stewards*** arranged for a gun to be fired when a race had started so that ***pleasure boats*** could move off the Course.

The Notice of the first Regatta in 1839 refers to signal guns being fired four times. The first at the bridge half an hour before the race was due to start and the second, also at the bridge, was to let officials at the Start know that the Course was clear. The third was at ***Temple Island*** to signal the start of the race and the fourth at the bridge announced the race had ended.

A maroon (rocket), based at ***Remenham Farm***, was used in later years and discontinued after the Second World War.

HALL OF FAME

See - ROWING HALL OF FAME

HAMBLEDEN

Hambleden is a picturesque village and parish in ***Buckinghamshire*** a mile north of ***Hambleden Lock*** on the south-western edge of the Chiltern Hills. The village, popular with the makers of films and television series, is very old and there is evidence of a Roman Villa on the road leading from the river at Mill End.

The name of the village is spelt Hambleden not Hambledon - the latter being the village in Hampshire famous as the birthplace of cricket.

HAMBLEDEN LOCK

Hambleden Lock marks the ***downstream*** end of the ***Henley Reach***. There has been a mill at this site since 1086 when it was mentioned in the Doomsday Book, although the present

picturesque building stopped working as a mill in 1952.

Because there was a Mill at this site in 1086 it is believed that there must have been a weir and thus, by law, a flash ***lock***. The Hambleden Manor records show the existence of a flash lock winch in 1338 and there is a record of an accident at the lock in the late 14th century when the winch rope broke and killed two people.

The first pound lock at Hambleden was built in January 1773, having been designed, like ***Marsh Lock*** and many others on the Thames in the late 18th century, by the Reverend Humphrey Gainsborough, minister at the Congregational Chapel in Henley and brother of Thomas Gainsborough the painter. It was subsequently rebuilt in 1873.

The present lock, built in 1994, is 50% larger than the 1873 lock. It cost approximately £1.9m and has the latest 36 nozzle rapid filling system which is able to discharge 679,000 litres of water in four minutes. The lock chamber is 61m (200ft 3in) long, 7.7m (25ft 3in) wide, 2.2m(7ft 3in) deep when full of water and has a 'dropfall' (the difference between the level of the water on the Henley Reach ***upstream*** of the lock and the level downstream of the lock) of 1.44m (4ft 9in)

Hambleden Lock is 70.34km (43.71miles) upstream of the Teddington Boundary Obelisk, beyond which the river is the responsibility of the Port of London Authority, and 147.21km (91.47miles) downstream of Cricklade Bridge, the generally accepted limit of navigation on the river. It is 3.69km (2.29miles) downstream of ***Henley Bridge*** and 5.21km (3.24miles) downstream of Marsh Lock at the other end of the Henley Reach.

Hambleden Lock has six weirs.

The lock is manned between 9am and 7pm, although during Regatta week this is changed to accommodate the increase in the number of boats on the river. It has a refuse disposal facility for boat users but no public toilets - yet.

The ***University Boat Race,*** held on the Henley Reach in 1829 for the first and only time, started at Hambleden Lock. See - ENVIRONMENT AGENCY - THAMES REGION and RIVER THAMES

THE HAMBLEDEN PAIRS
See - ROYAL HENLEY PEACE REGATTA

HEAD OF THE RIVER RACES
Head of the River Races are also known as Processional Races or simply as 'Heads'.

Competitors are usually divided into divisions according to ability, age, sex, etc, and, often starting in the order they finished in the same event the previous year, race over a prescribed distance, usually in excess of 2,500m (1½ miles). They normally start at intervals of 10 to 15 seconds and are timed over the course to determine the winner.

Four head of the river races take place on the ***Henley Reach*** - the ***Henley Fours and Eights***, the ***Henley Schools***, the ***Henley Sculls***, and the ***Upper Thames Fours and Small Boats***.

HEADQUARTERS
See - REGATTA HEADQUARTERS

HEAVYWEIGHT
In ***rowing*** and ***sculling*** it is generally accepted that a 'good big-un will beat a good little-un'.

Research has shown that where the average weights of the

two ***University Boat Race crews*** have varied by more than 7lbs the heavier ***crew*** has won 80% of the time.

Over the years the average weight of ***athletes*** has been increasing. The last time a crew averaging less than 11 stone competed in the Boat Race was 1862 - a crew averaging less than 11st has never won the Boat Race. The last time a crew won averaging under 12st was in 1946 and the last time an under 13st crew won was in 1963.

In 1966, following the lead of the USA and ***FISA***, Great Britain recognised lightweight rowing as a separate classification.

Heavyweight and lightweight national crews are specifically prohibited from entering the Ladies Challenge Plate, the Thames, Temple, Visitors', Wyfold and Britannia Challenge Cups and the Men's Quadruple Sculls Challenge Plate events.

THE HEDSOR CUP

See - ROYAL HENLEY REGATTA

HENLEY BOAT RACES

Five races take place each spring at Henley (except in 2001 for the reasons given below) between Oxford and Cambridge Universities and are known as the Henley Boat Races.

The Course is 2,000m (1mile 427yds) ***downstream*** from the finish point of the Royal ***Regatta Course*** to the ***Buckinghamshire*** side of ***Temple Island***.

The main race is the Women's Boat Race - the women's equivalent of the ***University Boat Race*** which takes place in London between the men's boat clubs. The first Women's Boat Race, or 'Ladies Race' as it was then known, took place on the ***Isis*** (the name of the ***River Thames*** at Oxford) in 1927. The competitors were the Oxford University Women's Boat

Club (OUWBC) and Newnham College representing Cambridge. The ***crews*** were judged on speed and on style each ***crew*** rowing separately over a ½mile course. The style aspect of the competition was dropped after three years and the speed comparisons were changed from 1936, after five contests, to a conventional side-by-side race.

The races took place most years between 1927 and 1952. In 1941, when Girton became the second Cambridge college to take up rowing, Cambridge University Women's Boat Club (CUWBC), established in 1895, took over the role of representing the University.

After 1952 there was a gap until 1964 following which it became an annual race held alternately on the ***Isis*** and the Cam until 1977 when the race moved to Henley. By the end of the 20th century, including the 2000 race, Cambridge had won 37 of the 55 races and Oxford 18.

The first race between the Women's Reserves Eights Osiris (Oxford) and Blondie (Cambridge) took place in 1966. The second race was in 1968 and the third in 1975 after which it became an annual event.

The average weight of the men's crews in the University Boat Race increased gradually over the years. The last time a crew in the Boat Race averaged under 11 stones was in 1862 and the last time an under 12st crew competed was in 1947. The last time an under 13st crew competed was in 1990 - although the last time an under 13st crew won was 1961. Because of this, lightweight oarsmen have found it increasingly difficult to be selected for the blue ***boats***. So when Great Britain officially recognised lightweight rowing in 1966 the two universities established their own lightweight rowing clubs and, on the instigation of Richard Bates of St John's College, Cambridge, started the annual Lightweight Boat

Race for men in 1975 at Henley.

In 1976 the race between the Osiris and Blondie and the race between the Lightweight Men's crews moved to Henley and were subsequently joined by the Lightweight Women's Race which was established in 1984 and the Men's Lightweight reserve crews race between Nephthys (Oxford) and Granta (Cambridge) established in 2000.

The 2001 races were moved to the National Water Sports Centre at Holme Pierrepont, Nottingham because of fears over the level of the river and the flooding of the towpath at Henley, and the countrywide restrictions imposed at that time in connection with the foot and mouth disease.

HENLEY BREWERY

See - BRAKSPEAR'S HENLEY BREWERY

HENLEY BRIDGE

Henley Bridge, which carries the A4130 road over the river, was the finish line for races at the first Regatta in 1839. The following year the Finish was moved about 30yds ***down-stream*** of the bridge for safety reasons - where it remained until the 'New Course', with the Finish at ***Poplar Point***, was established in 1886.

There has been a bridge at this point on the Thames almost continuously since 1170, indeed there are references to a bridge here in Roman times.

Before 1774 the bridge had a central wooden arch with stone arches extending out from each bank. It had been repaired in 1483 and the buildings on it repaired in 1514. It was damaged during the Civil War in 1642 and was declared so dangerous in 1754 that a ferryboat was used to enable people to cross the river. The remains of this bridge were swept away in the floods of 1774.

The present Henley Bridge, authorised by an Act of Parliament, was designed by William Hayward of Shrewsbury and built in 1786/8, although Hayward died in January 1782 before building commenced. It was built of Headington stone approximately five metres downstream of the earlier bridge. The bases of the wooden piles of the earlier bridge still exist on the riverbed. The stone arches of the original 1170 bridge can be seen under ***Regatta Headquarters***, on the ***Berkshire*** side of the river, having been discovered in 1984 during excavation work for the new building; and under the ***Angel on the Bridge*** on the ***Oxfordshire***/town side.

The bridge has five arches. The keystone of the centre arch has a carved relief of the head of Tamesis or 'Old Father Thames' (see picture on left). The head, adorned with bulrushes, faces downstream towards the ***Regatta Course*** and ultimately the estuary of the river.

A carved relief of the head of ***Isis*** (see picture on right) adorned with water plants, is on the other side of the arch facing ***upstream*** towards ***Marsh Lock*** and the source of the river. Both were put in place in 1786 and are the work of the Honourable Mrs Anne Damer, the daughter of General Conway, who lived in Park Place - the large house at the top of ***White Hill*** on the Berkshire side of the river. It is believed she used the face of Sarah Freeman of

Fawley Court as a model for Isis.

The bridge has a normal headway of approximately 4.34m (14ft 3in), this being the distance between the water level and the centre of the centre arch - the water level being the standard head water level of ***Hambleden Lock***, the next lock downstream. As a result, allowance must be made for the ***stream*** and gradient of the water at any time, as this will reduce the headway.

The bridge is 74.03km (46miles) upstream of the Teddington Boundary Obelisk, beyond which the river is the responsibility of the Port of London Authority, and 143.52km (89.18miles) downstream of Cricklade Bridge, the generally accepted limit of navigation on the river. It is 1.52km (.95mile) downstream of ***Marsh Lock*** and 3.69km (2.29miles) upstream of Hambleden Lock.

The bridge cost £10,000 to build. To recover this, and the £3,000 that it cost to improve the approaches, tolls were imposed on all people and animals using it until 1873 by which time the cost had been recouped. The Toll Gate Cottage that existed by the original toll gate on the Berkshire side of the bridge was demolished soon after 1873. The new Toll Gate Cottage, built in its place but back from the road next to ***Leander Club***, was sold in 1963 and subsequently demolished.

See - ENVIRONMENT AGENCY - THAMES REGION, SWIMMING and THIRD BRIDGE

HENLEY CHURCH

See - ST MARY'S CHURCH

HENLEY CONTRACTING

The company responsible for maintaining the Regatta land throughout the year.

HENLEY CORPORATION SWIMMING BATHS

The Henley Baths was the local, and misleading, name for the area of river designated for swimming situated ½mile upstream of ***Henley Bridge*** on the ***Berkshire*** side.

The Baths comprised an area of the river enclosed with ***booms*** and chains, and with lawns and a semi circle of changing cubicles on the land. The facility was accessed via the Wargrave Road.

The Henley Baths were opened in 1875, substantially refurbished in 1919 and 1934 and closed in 1978 after the indoor pool at Gillotts, a mile from the centre of Henley, had opened in February 1977 - and after swimming in the river had become unacceptable.

In 1979 the site was leased by Henley Town Council to ***Henley Rowing Club*** who moved there from their ***Riverside*** premises on 1 June 1986.

HENLEY CRICKET CLUB

Situated off the ***Remenham Lane*** at the bottom of ***White Hill***, the Cricket Club ground, owned by ***Brakspear's Henley Brewery***, is used for car parking during the Regatta.

This had previously been the ground of Henley Brewery Cricket Club, which closed in 1973.

Henley Cricket Club was founded in 1869 and dissolved in 1915. It had been based further along the ***Remenham Lane*** at ***Barn Cottage*** - the pavilion is still standing on that site, attached to Barn Cottage.

Henley Town Cricket Club was formed in 1886 and closed in 1908. Both clubs started up again later in the 20th century and merged in 1976.

During the Regatta the edges of the cricket field are used for car parking. This is organised by the Brewery, Henley

Cricket Club and Henley Rowing Club. Early in 2001 plans were being put forward by the Brewery to move the cricket field approximately 50m to the east of the site, replacing some of the allotments, to make way for a full time car park.

HENLEY DISABLED REGATTA

Disabled ***athletes*** are encouraged to take up the sport and events are organised specifically for them.

The Henley Disabled Regatta was established in 1989 and takes place three weeks after the Royal Regatta each July.

HENLEY DRAGON BOAT CLUB

Established in 1991 and based at the ***Eyot Boat Centre***, the club has some 35 members and three ***dragon boats***.

Dragon Boat racing on the ***Henley Reach***, in aid of the Imperial Cancer Research Fund, takes place in July two weeks after the Royal Regatta.

HENLEY EVENTS

This can relate to:-

- the organisation, Henley Open Events which organises the ***Henley Fours and Eights Head of the River*** and the ***Henley Sculls***, or
- events at ***Henley Royal Regatta***.

(Note: The names of the Henley Royal ***Regatta trophies*** and events are interrelated, the abbreviated name of a trophy often being used to describe an event eg. it is acceptable to say that the Grand (the ***Grand Challenge Cup***) is the senior event at the Regatta, and an entry in the Diamonds (the ***Diamond Challenge Sculls***) means an entry in the men's ***single sculling*** event)

HENLEY FESTIVAL

Established in 1983 the Henley Festival of Music & the Arts takes place on Regatta land, principally the ***Stewards' Enclosure***, on the evenings of Wednesday through to Sunday in the week immediately following the Regatta.

Although the Festival also uses much of the Regatta tentage, which is suitably adapted for the purpose by ***Black & Edgington***, it is financed and organised independently from the Regatta.

HENLEY FIREWORK FUND

See - FIREWORKS

HENLEY FOURS AND EIGHTS HEAD OF THE RIVER

Established in 1975 this ***head of the river race***, which was originally for ***fours*** but now includes ***eights***, takes place each February, river conditions permitting, and is organised by the Henley Open Events Committee based at ***Henley Rowing Club***.

Competitors race over a course 3,000m (1.86miles) ***upstream*** from '***Pink Cottage***' (***Ferry Cottage***) to the finish of the ***Regatta Course***.

HENLEY MANAGEMENT COLLEGE

Situated in 30 acres of parkland on the ***Buckinghamshire*** bank, ½ mile ***downstream*** of ***Temple Island***, the Henley Management College, previously known as the Administrative Staff College, is based in Greenlands House and enjoys about a ¼ mile of river-bank. (Note: The 's' on the end of Greenland is believed to be a 19th century addition)

Local history books indicate that Greenland was owned by Thomas Chaucer, Speaker of the House of Commons in 1407 who was probably the son of Geoffrey Chaucer author of the Canterbury Tales. If this is correct it is possible that it subsequently came into the ownership of Sir William Stonor by inheritance, Sir William being related to the Chaucer family through his mother.

In 1480 Sir William Stonor sold Greenland House to John D'Oyley whose ancestors had come to England with William the Conqueror.

Greenland stayed in the D'Oyley family until the Civil War in 1642. At that time Greenland voluntarily became a Royalist garrison unlike ***Phyllis Court*** and ***Fawley Court***, that were owned by Parliamentarian Sir Bulstrode Whitelock, (sometimes spelt Whitelocke and sometimes Whitlock) and which were taken by force. Parliamentary forces occupied Henley in January 1643 and retook Phyllis Court and Fawley Court. The Phyllis Court garrison was then strengthened and battles took place for the Royalist Greenland garrison including bombarding the house by cannon fire from the opposite side of the river. Eventually, on 11 July 1644, Greenland surrendered and the building was subsequently demolished.

In 1651 Sir Bulstrode bought Greenland but after the restoration of the monarchy and in order to pay the heavy fines imposed on him for supporting Cromwell, he sold it to Penning Alstone in 1660 without rebuilding it,

Greenland then changed hands four times until John Greene purchased it in 1685. On his death in 1687 it passed to his daughter Elizabeth and was then sold in 1719 to the Stevens family. They held the estate and the ruins of the house for around 100 years until it was sold to Thomas Darby-Coventry in the early 19th century. Thomas then started building the present house.

Greenlands House was sold in 1853 to Edward

Marjoribanks, MP for Berwick and, following his death, was bought by the wealthy newsagent WH Smith, MP, in 1871. In 1874 Smith became Secretary to the Treasury, in 1877 First Lord of the Admiralty and later Leader of the House of Commons. On his death in 1891, in recognition of his service to the country, Queen Victoria offered his widow, Emily, a Viscountacy, which she accepted and became Viscountess ***Hambleden***.

The Hambledens continued to live at Greenlands until after the Second World War, removing the tower on the building in 1934.

Over the years Greenland House has received many Royal visits. Robert D'Oyley is believed to have entertained Queen Elizabeth I at Greenland before being knighted in 1576 when he became Sheriff of Oxfordshire. King George V with Queen Mary and Princess Mary visited in 1912 and Queen Elizabeth the Queen Mother visited Greenlands when, with Princess Margaret and Lord Snowdon, she visited the Regatta in 1964.

The Administrative Staff College leased Greenlands in July 1946 and purchased it in December 1952.

In addition to its own management training courses, the College, which has 112 en-suite bedrooms, also offers bed and breakfast accommodation as well as facilities for private conferences and meetings.

HENLEY-ON-THAMES

Henley-on-Thames, population 10,527 (1991 Census), is reputed to be one of the oldest settlements in Oxfordshire. It is 36 miles west of London and has been the focus of river and road links with the capital since 1150, being for some time the highest point ***upstream*** of the navigable Thames. Goods were brought to Henley by river for onward transportation by road.

As such Henley, with its bridge, was strategically important in the Civil War and the scene of battles between 1642 and 1644 with ammunition being brought up the river by barge and then taken overland to Oxford.

Henley has its great houses of ***Fawley Court***, Friar Park the home of Beatle George Harrison, ***Greenlands***, Park Place, ***Phyllis Court*** and Stonor Park

George Ravenscroft pioneered glass making in Henley in 1674; ***Brakspear*** has had a brewery in Henley since 1779; ***Hobbs*** has made boats and been engaged on the river at Henley since 1870 and ***Higgs*** has printed in Henley since 1877 and printed the ***Henley Standard***, Henley's only newspaper, since 1892. Stuart Turner, Henley's leading engineering company has made a range of pumps and engines since 1906; Sports cars were manufactured by Adrian Squire in the 1930s and Perpetual, one of the country's leading and most successful financial services companies and Henley's largest employer, started in the town in 1974.

Henley has a number of churches and chapels including the parish churches of ***St Mary's*** and Holy Trinity, and has over 300 listed buildings of many styles and covering many periods. Henley also has its fair share of award winning new buildings including ***Regatta Headquarters*** completed in 1986 and the ***River and Rowing Museum*** completed in 1998, both of which were opened by Her Majesty The Queen.

The town has had a ***railway*** since 1857 and seems to have had road traffic problems forever and which will probably not be resolved until the matter of the ***third bridge*** has been resolved

Henley has a wide range of sports clubs and three very successful rowing clubs - ***Henley Rowing Club***, ***Leander Club*** and ***Upper Thames Rowing Club***. It has its Royal and

Town and Visitors' Regattas and, a little further ***downstream***, its ***Disabled***, ***Veteran*** and ***Women's*** Regattas.

Henley Royal Regatta, the most famous organisation linked with Henley, was established in Henley in 1839, 10 years after the first Oxford and Cambridge ***University Boat Race*** took place on the ***Henley Reach*** in 1829.

It is estimated that Henley receives 337,000 visitors a year, 13,000 of whom arrive by boat.

HENLEY PHOTOGRAPHS

See - PHOTOGRAPHERS

HENLEY PRIZE

The Henley Prize is a name usually given by the ***Stewards*** to a new event when it is introduced. When the Stewards are satisfied that the event should be adopted on a permanent basis it is then given a name and a trophy. In recent times this has included the ***Britannia*** which started out in 1968 as an event for the Henley Prize, and the ***Fawley*** which was called the Henley Prize in 1990 and 1991.

The event for ***Women's eights*** is currently referred to as the Henley Prize and has the same unrestricted entry qualifications as the ***Grand***, the ***Stewards'*** the ***Queen Mother***, the ***Prince Philip*** and the ***Women's Quadruple Sculls***, being for any club ***crew*** of international standard.

The entrance fee for this event is £80 and the Stewards have limited the number of entries to eight.

At present there is no trophy for this event.

See - REGATTA TROPHIES

HENLEY RAFT REGATTA

This event is organised by Henley Lions Club in conjunction with the annual duck derby in aid of local charities.

HENLEY REACH

This is the 3.24miles (5.21km) of ***River Thames*** between ***Marsh lock*** at the ***upstream*** end, and ***Hambleden lock*** at the ***downstream*** end.

HENLEY RECTORY

Built in second half of the 18th century, the Rectory on ***Thames Side***, now known as the 'Old Rectory' was the home of the incumbent of ***St Mary's Church***. It was also used as the temporary home for many clubs visiting Henley for the Regatta, their flags being hung from the windows of the building.

The building was sold to Perpetual plc in 1978/1979, Perpetual having started in Henley in 1974. Perpetual was bought in 2000 by Invesco, whose parent company is Amvescap based in the USA.

The present Rectory, built in the grounds of the old Rectory, is situated behind the high wall in Hart Street, across the road from the church.

HENLEY REGATTAS AND OTHER ROWING EVENTS

There are four regattas held on the ***Henley Reach*** each year in addition to the Royal Regatta. The ***Henley Disabled Regatta***, ***Henley Town & Visitors' Regatta***, ***Henley Veteran Regatta*** and ***Henley Women's Regatta***.

There are also four ***head of the river races*** (long distance processional races where the competitors are timed to determine the winner), the ***Henley Fours and Eights***, ***Henley Schools***, ***Henley Sculls*** and ***Upper Thames Fours and Small Boats***. There are also the ***Henley Boat Races***.

The Henley Reach is also used by many other organisations for a wide range of events including dragon boat racing, raft racing and even plastic duck racing.

HENLEY REGATTAS ELSEWHERE

In Australia there are three 'Henley' Regattas, the Henley on Yarra in Melbourne, the Henley on Torrens in Adelaide and in Alice Springs, where there is no water, there is the Henley on Todd. This latter regatta, which has taken place annually since 1961, consists of ***crews*** racing with bottomless boats and running along a dry river bed!

The Royal Canadian Henley Regatta was established in 1880 and, since 1903 has taken place on Port Dalhousie's Martindale Pond, St Catherines, Ontario.

HENLEY ROWING CLUB

Henley Rowing Club is one of the oldest rowing clubs in the country. It was established in 1839 but some records show an earlier date of 1830. The Club was originally based in various river-side buildings until 1903 when it moved into the old brewery stables owned by ***Brakspear's Henley Brewery***, next to the ***Little White Hart Hotel*** on ***Riverside***.

On 1 June 1986, with the assistance of a Sports Council

grant, the Club moved to its present premises along the Wargrave Road, ½mile ***upstream*** from ***Henley Bridge*** on the ***Berkshire*** bank. The Wargrave Road site, which had been leased by the Club since 1979, had previously been the ***Henley Corporation Swimming Baths*** when swimming in the river was acceptable. In 1995 the Club received a Lottery Sports Fund grant to enable the premises to be extended.

Henley Rowing Cub provides full boating facilities for men and women from juniors to veterans. Since 1989 the Club has specialised in junior rowing and is now one of the country's most successful clubs for juniors; the junior girls in particular helping to take the Club to the top of the Women's Premier Division of the National Rowing League in 2000, with the Henley men topping the First Division of the League.

Henley RC was one of the pilot clubs in ***Project Oarsome***, a scheme for attracting into rowing young persons from state schools with no previous experience of the sport.

HENLEY ROYAL REGATTA

The Regatta was established for the benefit of the town at a public meeting on 26 March 1839 in the ***Henley-on-Thames*** Town Hall. This is not the same Town Hall that is standing today where the Regatta ***Draw*** takes place and which was built to celebrate Queen Victoria's Diamond Jubilee in 1900. It was the Grade II, colonnaded, Georgian building which had been built in 1795. This building was dismantled in 1900 and moved to nearby Crazies Hill where it was rebuilt and named Summerfield House.

The meeting took place after there had been a number of races on the ***Henley Reach*** including the first University Boat Race in 1829 and the race between Oxford University and

Leander Club in 1831 - both being referred to Henley Regattas.

The meeting resolved to establish an annual Regatta which *under judicious and respectable management would not only be productive of the most beneficial results to the town of Henley, but from its peculiar attractions would also be a source of amusement and gratification to the neighbourhood and to the public in general.*

The first Regatta was on a single afternoon on Friday 14 June 1839. There were six entries for the ***Grand Challenge Cup*** (although two withdrew before the day) and three entries for the ***Town Cup***. It was a success despite the heavy thunderstorm during the morning, and in 1840 was extended to two days.

Its popularity continued as evidenced by a letter to the ***Stewards*** from 222 townspeople dated 15 June 1849 congratulating them on their achievement. Two years later in 1851, despite the Regatta being reduced to one day in 1850 because only 15 entries were received, the Regatta received its 'Royal' prefix when His Royal Highness Prince Albert became the first Royal Patron. On the death of Prince Albert, Queen Victoria confirmed Henley's Royal Patronage and this has been renewed by each succeeding Monarch.

The early Regattas were held on a Monday and Tuesday but with the increase in popularity following the opening of the ***railway*** in 1857, the days were changed to Friday and Saturday. This change went ahead despite the worry of some that it would be a problem for vicars who normally spent Saturdays writing their sermons for Sunday church services!

In 1867 the programme included a '***canoe***-chase' over land and water - for the first and last time.

For the first 30 years local people ran the Regatta and it wasn't until 1868 that the first rowing person was elected a

Steward. By 1883 the Stewards were predominantly rowing men and in 1885 a major reorganisation took place since when the Constitution and Rules of the Regatta have retained a reference to the resolutions agreed at the meeting on the 9th April of that year. In 1886 the Regatta became a three-day event with racing on Thursday, Friday and Saturday.

The Regatta remained popular with the public throughout Victorian and Edwardian eras and in 1906 Wednesday was added to make it a four-day event. Finals day was moved to Sunday in 1974 and Wednesday was dropped from the racing programme until 1986 when, because of the increase in entries, the Regatta moved from a four-day event to five days and Wednesday again became the first day.

Throughout the 1980s and 1990s the number of entries regularly broke records resulting in more competitors having to enter the ***Qualifying Races*** on the Friday before the Regatta. The large number of entries also meant that, despite adding the extra day in 1986, racing before Saturday often started at 8.30am and finished around 7.30pm. In 1998 the number of entries reached a record 552 following which the Stewards changed some of the entry requirements causing the 1999 entry to fall to 428, the lowest level since 1991.

The Regatta gained considerable benefit from the improved economic position of the country and the surge of interest in the Regatta in the late 1970s and throughout the 1980s and 1990s. As a result the financial position changed drastically from a loss of £2,756 incurred in 1972 and rumours in the local press in 1975 that it might even close down, to an upsurge in popularity in the 1980s and a profit of £327,701 before tax in 2000.

By the beginning of the 21st century the event was costing over £1.6m to stage and producing a gross income approaching £2 million with assets valued at over £3m. This improvement was brought about by the Stewards without resorting to sponsorship or advertising, no mean achievement for the premier event of an amateur sport.

Apart from the storage sheds at the back of ***Lion Meadow*** there are no permanent structures on the Regatta land.

Erecting the tentage and constructing the Course takes three months and starts in April. The land and river are clear by the middle of August apart from the components of the ***Grandstand***, which are stored under a tarpaulin on the site during the winter.

The Regatta now has its own ***Regatta Headquarters*** and a permanent staff of six.

See - ROWING HALL OF FAME and ROYALTY

HENLEY ROYAL REGATTA LIMITED

This is the trading company of the Royal Regatta. It was establishment in 1988 primarily to protect the name of the Regatta and its reputation against unauthorised use following an attempted registration of the name Henley Royal Regatta in Japan.

The company is also used for the generation of income from the sale of merchandise particularly through the ***Regatta Shop***. In addition it receives income from letting ***Temple Island*** and other parts of the Regatta site.

The company is also responsible for the franchise of the Regatta's logo.

The trading business has expanded over the years and now produces an annual pre tax profit in the region of £200,000 of which approximately £160,000 is donated to the ***Stewards' Charitable Trust***.

HENLEY SAILING CLUB

Henley has its own sailing club, established in August 1896, based on the reach ***upstream*** of ***Marsh lock*** near to Wargrave.

HENLEY SCHOOLS HEAD OF THE RIVER

Established in 1985 this ***head of the river race*** takes place each February, river conditions permitting, and is based at ***Upper Thames Rowing Club***. Competitors race over a course 3,000m (1.86miles) ***upstream*** from '***Pink Cottage***' (***Ferry Cottage***) to the finish of the Royal ***Regatta Course***.

HENLEY SCULLS

Established in 1971 this ***head of the river race*** takes place each October, river conditions permitting, and is organised by the Henley Open Events Committee based at ***Henley Rowing Club***. Competitors race over a course 3,000m (1.86miles) ***upstream*** from '***Pink Cottage***' (***Ferry Cottage***) to the finish of the Royal ***Regatta Course***.

HENLEY STANDARD

The *Henley Standard* is the only local newspaper published in the town. At the beginning of the 20th century there were two other newspapers in Henley, (Kinch's) *Henley Advertiser* and the *Henley Chronicle*, but both ceased publication before the First World War.

The *Henley Standard* started as the *Henley Free Press* in 1885. The name was changed to the *Henley and South Oxfordshire Standard* on 2 September 1892 when Thomas Octavius Higgs of ***Higgs & Co*** first undertook the printing, and to the *Henley Standard* in 1956. Although still published in Henley it was last printed locally in 1984 and is now printed by Newbury Weekly News Ltd in Newbury.

Some consider the most famous contributor to the *Henley Standard* to have been the local Shiplake resident Eric Blair, who in 1914 at the age of eleven, had a poem published in the newspaper encouraging men to join the Forces at the time of the Great War. Under the pseudonym George Orwell, Blair later wrote *Animal Farm* and *1984*.

HENLEY SWIMMING BATHS

See - HENLEY CORPORATION SWIMMING BATHS

HENLEY TOWN & VISITORS' REGATTA

The Henley Town & Visitors' Regatta, often simply referred to as the T&V, is one of the largest one-day Regattas on the Thames. Racing is usually three abreast, on a course ***upstream*** from a point opposite the inlet to ***Fawley Court*** to a finish line in front of the site of the ***Fawley Stand*** (the stand usually has been dismantled by the end of July), opposite the ***Hole in the Wall***. (Note: Before moving to its present position in 1968, the Town & Visitors' Regatta's Course finished at ***Poplar Point***, the finish of the Royal ***Regatta Course***)

The earliest records show that the Henley Town & Visitors' Regatta was originally known as the ***Henley Rowing Club*** Boat Races. It changed to The Town Regatta during the latter part of the 19th century and the word 'Visitors' was added when it was decided to extend invitations to row at the Regatta to oarsmen and clubs from outside the immediate locality.

From 1928 the Regatta was divided into skiffing and rowing sections, each holding its own Regatta on different days on the ***Henley Reach***. Initially the ***Skiff*** Regatta was the more popular of the two but by the mid 1930s interest had fallen off and in 1938 skiffing was discontinued.

Following the success of multi lane racing on the Henley

Reach at the 1948 ***Olympic Games***, the Regatta offered three abreast racing in all events.

The Town & Visitors' Regatta is one of the few, if not the only, 'one day' Regatta, that produces a Regatta Programme recording the names of all the ***athletes*** competing at the Regatta set out in race order.

The Regatta has always had a President who, since 1928, has been elected to serve for one year only. Because of the close relationship with the Royal Regatta, many ***Stewards*** including the ***President*** and ***Chairman***, as well as the ***Secretary of the Royal Regatta***, have served as President of the Town & Visitors' Regatta.

The Regatta, which uses some of the ***Stewards' Enclosure***, is 'sponsored' (not financially) by the Royal Regatta, and thus is permitted to close the ***towpath***.

The Town and Visitors' Regatta offers 30 trophies for competition. The most famous is the ***Town Cup*** which was one of the two trophies competed for at the first Henley 'Royal' Regatta in 1839 and which, since 1884, has been held in Trust by the T&V for the Royal Regatta.

When the Government changed the August Bank holiday from the beginning to the end of August in 1965, the Regatta, which for many years had been held on the Bank Holiday Monday and was at that time the last Thames regatta of the season, had to move date. It now takes place on the Saturday of week 31 of the ***Garton Calendar***, being the week leading up the 31st Sunday of the year, and the fourth Saturday after the Royal Regatta.

HENLEY UNITED ROWING CLUB

This club was established in 1886 'to provide facilities for working men and youths'. It became affiliated to the National Amateur Rowing Association at the end of the 19th century when the ***ARA***'s definition of an ***amateur*** split the sport.

HURC was based between the Little White Hart Hotel and the ***Brakspear's Henley Brewery*** stables, which from 1903 was the boathouse of ***Henley Rowing Club***. The club subsequently merged with ***Henley RC*** in 1946 after the manual worker aspect of the amateur definition was abolished.

HENLEY VETERAN REGATTA

Established in 1994 this Regatta takes place a week after the Royal Regatta each July and is based at ***Upper Thames Rowing Club***. Competitors race over a 1,000m course ***upstream*** from ***Temple Island*** to ***Remenham Club***.

HENLEY WOMEN'S REGATTA

This regatta was established in 1988 to provide an event for women on the ***Henley Reach***. At that time women, other than as coxswains, were barred from competing at the Royal Regatta.

Henley Women's Regatta is based at ***Remenham Farm*** by the ***Barrier*** and takes place in June two weeks before the Royal Regatta. Various courses have been tried over the years but the most successful seems to be the present distance 1,500m ***upstream*** from the start of the Royal ***Regatta Course*** to ***Remenham Club***.

The Henley Women's Regatta takes place on the Saturday and Sunday of week 25 of the ***Garton Calendar***, the Sunday being the 25th Sunday of the year, and two weeks before the finals day of the Royal Regatta.

It should be noted that Henley Women's Regatta does not enjoy being called 'Women's Henley'

HIGGS & CO

Higgs & Co was established in Henley in 1877 and has published the ***Henley Standard***, originally the *Henley and South Oxfordshire Standard*, since 1892. This independent, family owned, company, which has offices at Caxton House on the corner of Station Road and Reading Road, has printed the ***Regatta Programme*** since 1886.

John Luker, present Chairman of Higgs & Co is a ***Steward of the Regatta***, as were his father, Tom Luker, and Grandfather Charles Luker who acquired the business as sole proprietor in 1900 before purchasing the property in 1919.

HOBBS & SONS

Hobbs and Sons Ltd is the only chandlery (supplier of equipment for boats) on the reach as well as being the only boat repairer and supplier of petrol & diesel.

Established in 1870 by HE (Harry) Hobbs, a member of a long established Henley family, the company first had premises in Wharf Lane, Henley at the bottom of ***New Street*** before moving to its present site in 1898 at the bottom of Station Road.

During the first half of the 20th century the company, managed by the six sons of Harry Hobbs, expanded and took over other boat premises along the river. They also built a number of 50ft ***umpire launches*** which were used extensively on the river at regattas and, being referred to as 'Hobbs Launches', became a feature of the Royal Regatta.

Between 1920 and 1989 the Company also built the ***Regatta Course*** and dealt with all the river construction work for the Regatta.

ARB (Dick) Hobbs took over the business from his father in 1953 and continued with the post war changes into the hire cruiser trade. He was followed by his son Tony Hobbs, who became a Queen's Waterman in 1981, and subsequently his grandson Jonathan, the fifth generation and great, great, grandson of the founder.

The company now has a fleet of large boats for hire including two 50 seater all-weather river buses for sightseeing trips and the Edwardian styled 'umpire launch' ***Enchantress***.

In 1991 the company commissioned the design and construction of the 115ft Mississippi style, 125 passenger, riverboat, the *New Orleans*. The *New Orleans*, built at Greenwich, is the largest boat on the ***Henley Reach***, and is available for corporate and private functions, weddings, seminars and conferences.

In April 2001 the 75ft *Hibernia*, built in South Wales and available for parties of up to 50 people, became the latest addition to the Hobbs fleet. The *Hibernia* is named after a steam-powered umpire launch used at the Regatta in the late 19th and early 20th centuries.

See - SALTERS STEAMERS

HOLE IN THE WALL

The popular name given to the gap in the ***Phyllis Court*** embankment wall, 200m from the finish of the ***Regatta Course***,

The inlet, under a small bridge, is for members of Phyllis Court Club to access the Club moorings.

The name 'Hole in

the Wall' is completely unofficial although widely used. A few consider, quite erroneously in the opinion of the large majority, that the 'hole' relates to the hole in the ***camp-shedding*** on the opposite (***Berkshire***) bank, where the ***stream*** by the side of ***Remenham lane***, flows under the ***Stewards' Enclosure*** into the river.

HOOPER'S

Hooper's boat hire business is based on ***Riverside*** at the bottom of ***New Street*** on the opposite side of the river to the Regatta's ***Boat Tent Area***. Established in the 17th century to build barges and large sailing boats near to the present site, the business, which has remained in the Hooper family for over 300 years, changed to hiring out pleasure boats during the 19th century.

HOSPITALITY

See - FAWLEY MEADOWS HOSPITALITY VILLAGE

HOUSEBOATS

When referring to past Regattas, particularly those of the Victorian and Edwardian eras, the existence of houseboats is usually mentioned. These were large decorated barges up to 75ft long and 14ft beam (width), with two decks, one above the other with sleeping accommodation and rooms for dining and entertaining. Houseboats usually had no self-propulsion and travelled the length of the river during the summer, towed by a tug or by a horse along the bank (along the ***towpath***) and would stop at various regattas including Henley.

Houseboats were most popular at Henley towards the end of the 19th century - with reports of around ninety being moored along the ***Fawley*** (***Buckinghamshire***) bank of the river at the Regatta of 1888. In later years there were reports of waiting lists for the limited number of moorings.

The popularity of houseboats diminished after the First World War being replaced by the smaller cabin cruisers.
See - PLEASURE BOATS

IDENTIFICATION NUMBER

The number shown on the ***bows*** of ***boats*** at the Regatta relates to the number of the competitor on the ***List of Entries***.

Before 1959 the number had been printed on a label and glued to the side of the boat. After 1959 various methods were used to attach the number to the boat including the use of wooden holders that clipped to the bow deck. The present system involves the number being shown on a small plastic plate which is fixed into a slot, called an ‘Empacher slot’ which is a standard fitting on the bow deck of modern racing boats, hence reference to it also as a ‘bow number’.

Since 1960 the competitor’s number has been shown in the ***Regatta Programme*** in brackets after the name of the competitor.

INDOOR ROWING

Indoor rowing, using ergos, is very popular in most gymnasiums and among ***athletes*** from many disciplines other than rowing including Formula 1 motor racing drivers, volleyball players and footballers. There are many competitions world wide including a World Indoor Rowing Championship event. The first British Indoor Rowing Championship took place in Henley in 1991 with over 250 entries - by 2000 the event had moved to Reading and had 1900 entries, the ages ranging from nine to ninety, making it the largest indoor rowing event in the world.

On 24 February 1999 at the ***River and Rowing Museum*** at Henley, as part of the fund-raising efforts for Comic Relief, a ten man team from ***Leander Club***, coached by Jürgen Grobler, set a new World ergo 100,000 metres record time of 4hrs 44min 32sec. This smashed the 5 hours barrier and beat the previous record held by Nottingham University BC by 18min 42secs.

A year later this was beaten by 3min 44sec by a team from Royce's Gym, Wigan who recorded a time of 4hrs 40min 48sec.

Then on Wednesday 14 February 2001, again in aid of Comic Relief and again coached by Jürgen Grobler, a ten-man team from Leander Club competed against the reigning World Record Holders from Royce's Gym (all non-rowing, fitness devotees) at Great Marlow School, (Steven Redgrave's old school), in a head to head contest.

The Leander team, in alphabetical order, were:-

· Ed Coode, member of the 1999 team and World Rowing Champion in coxless fours,

· James Cracknell, member of the 1999 team, World Rowing Champion, Sydney Olympic Gold Medallist, Captain of Leander Club and British Indoor Ergo Rowing Champion,

· Toby Garbett, World Rowing Champion

· Luka Grubor, member of the 1999 team and Sydney Olympic Gold Medallist,

· Richard Hamilton, member of the 1999 team,

· Ben Hunt-Davis, Sydney Olympic Gold Medallist,

· Ian Lawson, National Champion

· Matthew Pinsent, member of the 1999 team, World

Rowing Champion , Barcelona, Atlanta and Sydney Olympic Gold Medallist and British Ergo Record Holder,

· ***Steven Redgrave***, World Rowing Champion, Los Angeles, Seoul, Barcelona, Atlanta and Sydney Olympic Gold Medallist, and

· Steve Williams, member of the 1999 team,

Royce's Gym beat their own World Record by 12min 52sec but Leander went further and knocked 17min 15sec off the record, achieving a new World Record time for 100,000 metres of 4hr 23min 33sec.

See - AWESOME FOURSOME and ERGO ROOM

INTERNATIONAL ENTRIES

All ***entries*** at the Regatta, other than those from the United Kingdom, are referred to as ***overseas entries***.

INVITATION RACES FOR WOMEN

In 1981, as an experiment to assess the feasibility of including races over a shortened course during the normal Regatta programme, the Regatta held two invitation events for women. Four ***coxed fours*** and four ***double sculls*** were invited to race over a course using the Start by the ***Barrier*** as used for the ***Special Race for Schools***. The winners received Regatta medals.

The experiment was repeated in 1982 over an even shorter course starting at Fawley, and an Invitation event for women ***single scullers*** was added - the winner also receiving a Regatta medal. The Stewards considered at that time however that the difficulty of adding the events to an already crowded programme did not justify inclusion of any of the events on a permanent basis.

A single sculls race for women was introduced in 1993 and

this became a permanent feature with the establishment in 1997 of the Princess Royal Challenge Cup.

In 1998 and 1999 invitation races for Women's ***Eights*** took place before the establishment of the Women's Eights event for the ***Henley Prize*** in 2000.

ISIS

Isis is the official name of the Oxford University Boat Club Reserve ***crew*** - and any crew the OUBC President decides to form.

Isis is also the name of the ancient Egyptian fertility goddess and wife and sister of Osiris; Osiris being the name of the Oxford University Women's Boat Club Reserve crew.

Isis is also the alternative name of the ***River Thames*** at Oxford. There are many suggested reasons for naming the river the Isis, but none seem to have any foundation earlier than the 19th century.

One author has suggested that as Isis is an alternative name for the river from its source to the point ***downstream*** of Dorchester where the River Thame flows into the River Thames, that it gives credence for the name ***Tamesis*** - which was the Roman name for the whole river.

A relief carving of Isis can be seen above the centre arch on the ***upstream*** side of ***Henley Bridge*** and on some of the ***Henley Royal Regatta*** winners ***medals***.

See - HENLEY BOAT RACES

ISLANDS

There are five islands on the ***Henley Reach***.

- ***Rod Eyot*** (the phonetic pronunciation is usually 'eye-ot'),
- An island immediately ***downstream*** of Rod Eyot which has no name and which has been almost washed away,

- ***East Eyot***,
- ***Fawley Boathouse*** Island, and
- ***Temple Island***.

Rod Eyot, the first island downstream from ***Marsh Lock***, is the only island with human occupation.
See - RAILWAY

JUDGE
See - STARTING A RACE AT HENLEY, FINISHING A RACE AT HENLEY and UMPIRING A RACE AT HENLEY

JUDGES' BOX
The Judges' Box is on the finish line on the ***Buckinghamshire*** side of the ***Regatta Course***.

Results' / Photographers' Box
Judges' Box

Since 1998, although it was first considered in 1969, it has been double-decked to provide greater visibility for the Judges. The photo-finish video camera was installed in 1983.

The 'electric lamp' fixed to the side of the Judges' Box, which replaced the flag in 1950, is used to indicate to the Timekeeper/Race Recorder in the ***Umpire's launch***, when the ***bow*** of the leading ***boat*** crosses the finish line.

In 1886, when the Finish of the Course was moved from ***Henley Bridge*** to ***Poplar Point***, the Exeter College barge was moored at the Finish post where it served as a Grandstand, Committee Room and Judges' Box.

All Finish Judges at the Royal Regatta are ***Stewards of the Regatta***.

See - FINISHING A RACE AT HENLEY

KENTON THEATRE

This theatre, originally known as New Theatre, is in ***New Street*** approximately 200m from the river.

It was built in 1805 on the site of the old Town Workhouse, the land having been bequeathed to the town by Robert Kenton in 1632. The theatre was not a success and after 1813 the building was used as a non-conformist chapel, a Church of England School, a place of worship while work was being undertaken in St Mary's Church between 1852 and 1854, and, in 1870 was the Church Hall for St Mary's.

After the First World War the building was used as a theatrical store until, in the 1930s it was again used as a theatre.

In 1962 it was closed for repairs and modifications and, in 1965, after local residents appealed for funds to save the building, it was completely restored, and is now recognised as the fourth oldest theatre in England in regular use.

THE KING'S CUP

See - ROYAL HENLEY PEACE REGATTA

THE KINGSWOOD SCULLS

See - ROYAL HENLEY PEACE REGATTA

KNOT

A knot is a measurement of speed as used by aircraft and boats being the equivalent of one nautical mile per hour. A nautical

mile is approximately 2,026.7yds (approximately 1,853.18m) or one minute (one sixtieth of a degree) of the circle of the Earth. To put this in context, a statute mile is 1,760yds (approximately 1,609m) and 1km (1,000m) is approximately 1,094yds.
One knot is approximately 1.15mph or 1.85kph.
See - WEIGHTS AND MEASURES

LABELS

Regatta literature normally differentiates between ***badges***, labels, ***passes*** and ***tickets***.

At Henley, labels are generally designed for attaching to items (not people) eg. labels for cars in the main ***car parks*** or labels for racks used for ***boats*** in the Boat Tent.

LADIES

At Henley, 'Ladies' might refer to the ***Ladies' Challenge Plate*** (an event for men), or to Ladies accompanying Gentlemen - or simply to the Toilets!

Female ***athletes*** in the sport are generally referred to as Women.

THE LADIES' CHALLENGE PLATE

This event for ***eights*** was established in 1845 and the following year was named the Ladies' Challenge Plate because, or so it is believed, the wives of the ***Stewards*** or ladies of Henley presented the trophy to the Regatta. The base was added in 1926.

Until 1966 the 'Ladies', the abbreviated name of this event, was restricted to eights from colleges, schools and certain academic institutions within the United Kingdom although Trinity College Dublin was also permitted to enter.

Since 1966 the qualifications have been changed and the Ladies' is now open to any eight that is below ***Grand*** standard (ie. not a ***heavyweight***, lightweight or ***FISA*** Senior B (under 23) national crew) thus making it second only to the Grand in seniority for eights.

Athletes, other than ***coxswains***, competing in this event are not permitted to compete in any other eight-oared event at the same Regatta.

Because it is usually referred to simply as the 'Ladies' the name has presented problems, particularly as until 1988 the Regatta was a men-only event (apart from ***women*** coxswains since 1974).

Many publications have fallen into the trap of thinking it is an event for women. One national newspaper, in order to be politically correct, even changed references to the 'Ladies' used by its rowing correspondent, to 'Women'.

The present entrance fee for this event is £80 and the Stewards have limited the number of entries to 16.

See - PRINCESS ELIZABETH CHALLENGE CUP and REGATTA TROPHIES

LANDING STAGE

See - BOAT TENT AREA and FIXED STAGE

LEANDER CAR PARK

This car park behind ***Leander Club***, which becomes the ***Competitors' Car Park***, for the five days of the Regatta, is generally referred to, in error, as the Leander Car Park as the Club is the most adjacent property.

The land, originally known as 'The Nook', was purchased by the Regatta in 1938.

LEANDER CLUB

Leander Club, (Note: Not Leander 'Rowing' Club or Boat Club) is based at Henley-on-Thames, and one of the three clubs on the ***Henley Reach***. Leander, with HM The Queen as Patron and HRH Prince Philip and HRH the Prince of Wales as Honorary Life Members, is probably the most prestigious rowing club in the world. Contrary to popular belief, Leander Club has no formal connection with Henley Royal Regatta - other than that most (all except three) of the ***Stewards*** are members of the Club.

The Club was established in Lambeth in London, probably in 1818. It rented a boathouse and rooms in Henley in 1892 and built the Clubhouse on land on the ***Berkshire*** bank next to ***Henley Bridge*** in 1896, the site of the 'Nook Enclosure' when the ***Regatta Course*** had finished at Henley Bridge before 1886.

The Club's boathouse at Putney was retained until 1939 when it was sold to Barclays Bank RC. In 1998, 100 years after building the Clubhouse, work commenced on refurbishing and extending it at a cost in excess of £3 million, over half of which came from the National Lottery.

The Club is believed to have derived its name from a six-oared 'cutter' '*Leander*' kept in a boathouse in London opposite the Houses of Parliament at the beginning of the 19th century. Two other boats used by members at the time were the '*Star*' and the '*Arrow*' hence the inclusion of a star and an arrow on the Club's badge. In 1980 Leander registered the name *Star and Arrow* as an alternative racing name for those ***athletes*** ineligible to race under the Leander title.

The Club's motto is *'Corpus Leandri Spes Mea*' (The body of Leander is my hope, or, My hope rests in the fellowship of Leander). The reason for adopting a hippopotamus (*hippo* - horse, *potamos* - river) as its crest is not known but some believe it to have been because the hippopotamus is recognised as the supreme water mammal - and, cynics would add, the only one with its nose in the air!

The Club did race with blades with scarlet spoons in the early days but since 1898 Leander ***colours*** have been recorded as 'cerise' (light, clear, cherry red) which seems to be neither scarlet or the Leander pink of today - the latter causing the Clubhouse to be nicknamed the 'pink palace'.

Leander athletes compete with pink blades and wear white rowing singlets with the Club's 'pink hippo' motif although most, when not representing the Club, wear the Great Britain international rowing strip as Leander is the main base of the National men's ***heavyweight*** rowing squad.

Up to the end of the 20th century, including the Sydney ***Olympic Games*** in 2000, 34 of the 65 Great Britain ***rowers***, ***scullers*** and ***coxswains*** who have won Olympic gold medals were Leander members. In addition to Olympic gold medals, Leander members have won 33 Olympic silver medals and 4 bronze medals.

The Club Captain is James Cracknell, MBE, who rowed at bow in the Great Britain Olympic Gold medal coxless four in

Sydney in September 2000.

Although Leander had raced at Henley before 1839, having competed against Oxford University in 1831, an event referred to locally at the time as the Henley Regatta, the Club did not compete at the first Henley Regatta in 1839. A Leander ***crew*** is reported to have accompanied the competitors racing for the ***Grand Challenge Cup*** as 'observers' and Mr JD Bishop of Leander was the ***Umpire*** - on horseback. Leander won the Grand Challenge Cup in 1840 since when the Club has won the trophy a further 26 times (apart from the six occasions when it was won by ***composite*** crews comprising one or more Leander members).

The Leander membership rules have changed over the years. From the end of the 19th century, membership of Leander was mainly from Oxford and Cambridge universities. Then from the late 1950s non-Oxbridge international oarsmen were admitted and then those who have distinguished themselves within the sport.

In 1997, before the Club applied for Lottery money to modernise the 100-year old Clubhouse and boathouse and to provide a more efficient training base for the National men's heavyweight squad, the members agreed to allow women to become members. This was fortunate and timely as it was unlikely Lottery money would have been made available had the membership remained restricted to men.

Leander has six categories of membership - Ordinary, Life, Honorary, Cadet, Associate and Temporary.

The qualification for Ordinary membership, the largest category, is good fellowship, proficiency in oarsmanship at a very high level eg. international selection, Henley winner, and/or a dedicated service to the sport.

Ordinary, Life and Honorary members are entitled to wear

all the Club's colours (pink tie, pink socks and pink cap) and Club buttons without restriction. Cadet members are entitled to wear the full Club colours and buttons only when representing the Club at a Regatta.

Associate membership, the second largest category, has no rowing prerequisite. Associate and Temporary members are not entitled to wear the Club's colours or buttons although Associate members are allowed to wear other colours as detailed by the Committee - at the present time this is restricted to the blue 'hippo' tie.

During the Royal Regatta the Leander ***dress*** regulations are similar to those of the ***Stewards' Enclosure***. Gentlemen are required to wear lounge suits, jackets or ***blazers*** with flannels (trousers -usually white) and a tie or cravat. Ladies are expected to wear dresses or formal outfits with hats, and, as with the Stewards' Enclosure, the hemline must be below the knee. Divided skirts, culottes or trousers of any kind are forbidden. The Club reserves the right to refuse entry to anyone dressed in a manner which is inappropriate for the occasion.

Outside the Regatta period the dining and accommodation facilities of the Club are available to non-members for conferences, luncheons, dinner parties and weddings.
See - AWESOME FOURSOME and INDOOR ROWING

THE LEANDER CUP

See - ROYAL HENLEY PEACE REGATTA

LEANDER WAY

This is the private road, owned by the Regatta, which leads from the A4130 road to ***Leander Club*** and ***Lion Meadow*** - with access to the public ***footpath*** that crosses Lion Meadow.
See - REGATTA HEADQUARTERS

LEFT LUGGAGE TENT

Situated outside the main entrance to the ***Stewards' Enclosure***, this facility is for Members of the Stewards' Enclosure and their Guests who are not permitted to take parcels and other property into the Enclosure.

LETHEBY AND CHRISTOPHER

Letheby & Christopher, of Northolt, Middlesex, a company established in 1900 and since 1992 part of the Compass Group, is the catering ***contractor*** responsible for managing the restaurants and bars in the ***Stewards' Enclosure***.

The other companies providing specialist catering management and corporate hospitality services in the UK as part of the Compass group include ***Payne & Gunter***, National Leisure Catering and Leith's.

LIFEGUARD SERVICES

Colwick Park LifeGuards of Nottingham provide the water rescue services on the river at the Regatta.

LIGHTWEIGHT

See - HEAVYWEIGHT

LINE MEN

Until the middle 1970s the Regatta employed men at the start of the ***Regatta Course*** to throw lines to the ***bow athlete***, when there was a cross wind, to prevent the ***boat*** being blown off course once it was straight. One lineman would be stationed in a ***punt*** (known as a line punt) which was fixed in the centre of the Course between the two competitors. The other would be either in the line punt attached to the outside of the

Buckinghamshire side of the Course or standing on the ***Berkshire*** bank, depending on the direction of the wind.

The line would be pulled away by the lineman when the ***Umpire*** shouted 'Are You Ready' immediately before shouting 'Go' (the old starting instructions).
See - STARTING A RACE AT HENLEY

LION MEADOW

Lion Meadow, leased by the Regatta from 1926 and purchased in 1939, is one of the three main official Regatta ***car parks***. Available only to members of the ***Stewards' Enclosure***, it is situated immediately behind the Boat Tent between the road and ***Remenham Lane*** with the main access via ***Leander Way*** or Remenham Lane.

Car park ***labels*** are sold to reserve a parking place for all five days of the Regatta; those who had a reserved space the previous year being allocated the same space provided they apply before the end of March.

The road across Lion Meadow from the Stewards' Enclosure to Remenham Lane was constructed in 1948. It was covered with an awning for visitors to the ***Olympic Games*** Regatta and, in subsequent years, for ***Members of the Stewards' Enclosure*** and their guests, to walk to the ***Luncheon Tent*** in ***Selwyn's Meadow;*** the meadow having been purchased the same year. In 1967 the awning was moved from the road to Selwyn's Meadow to cover the entrance to the Luncheon Tent. In 1985 the Luncheon Tent was moved to the enlarged Stewards' Enclosure.

It is believed Lion Meadow was so named because the Red Lion Hotel used it for grazing horses when the latter was a coaching inn.

A public footpath crosses Lion Meadow from Leander

Way to a point on the Remenham Lane by the storage sheds. See - CAR PARKS and LITTLE LION

LIST OF ENTRIES AND COLOURS OF THE CREWS

The Regatta publishes this within days of the closing date for ***entries***.

Competitor clubs are listed in alphabetical order (under each event) together with their ***identification number***, except for the ***Silver Goblets***, ***Double Sculls***, ***Diamonds*** and ***Princess Royal*** events where the individual competitors are listed in alphabetical order in addition to their clubs and identification numbers. The List also shows the number of competitors entered in each event and the maximum number permitted by the ***Stewards*** thereby indicating how many will have to be eliminated by means of the ***Qualifying Races*** before the ***Draw***.

The Regatta makes available a copy of the List to each club that has entered the Regatta and also to each individual competitor entered in the Silver Goblets, Double Sculls, Diamonds and Princess Royal events.

Details of the ***Colours*** of the ***Crews*** are later added to the reverse of the sheet. The full 'List of Entries and Colours of the Crews' can be purchased by the public from ***Regatta Headquarters***, from the Boat Tent Official in the ***Boat Tent Area*** or from ***Higgs & Co***.

LITTLE LION

This is the informal name for the piece of land separated from ***Lion Meadow*** by the road from the ***Stewards' Enclosure*** to ***Remenham Lane***. The ***Mobile Bank*** is situated on the edge of Little Lion facing the road.

Part of Little Lion is used as a car park for the ***Stewards of the Regatta***.

LITTLE WHITE HART HOTEL

The Little White Hart, occasionally referred to as the 'White Hart' which was its name in the 18th century, is one of two ***Brakspear's*** public houses that face the river (the other is the ***Angel on the Bridge***).

The Little White Hart, which may have been built in the late 17th century, was rebuilt circa 1900. It is situated on ***Riverside*** next to the Brakspear's Conference Centre (the old ***Henley Rowing Club*** boathouse) and is uniquely positioned with an uninterrupted view down the centre of the ***Regatta Course***. In the early days of the Regatta, when the Course finished approximately 20 yards ***downstream*** of ***Henley Bridge***, stands were erected along Riverside in front of the Little White Hart.

The Little White Hart is also the base for those involved with the annual ***Swan*** Upping ceremony.

LOCAL AMATEUR SCULLING RACE

This event was established at the Regatta in 1846 the prize being a model silver wherry

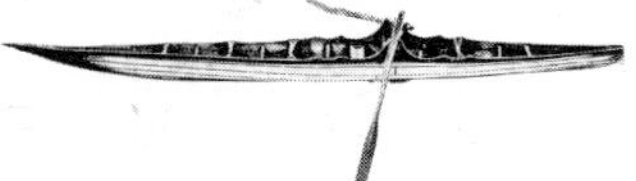

hence the event also being called the 'Silver Wherry'.
(Note: A wherry was an open decked ***sculling boat*** with a high pointed ***bow*** and stern used in the 17th century as a ferry particularly in London)

Initially entries were restricted to ***scullers*** who lived in Henley and this was extended 1848 to include any that lived within 12 miles of the town.

The event was withdrawn in 1858 through lack of interest.

LOCKS AND WEIRS

The ***River Thames*** flows 220miles (354km), from its source 15miles ***upstream*** of Cricklade, to the sea - and falls 234ft (72m). To control the fall/flow of water there are 44 locks and 133 weirs between Cricklade and Teddington, each lock having one or more adjacent weirs. The ***Environment Agency*** estimates that without locks and weirs the depth of water in the summer would be only 2ft!

The early locks were known as flash (or flush) locks and worked in conjunction with a paddle and rimer weir. This

Paddle & Rimer Weir at Northmoor

consisted of a line of posts (rimers) across the river. Flat boards on the end of a posts (paddles), were then lowered into the river between the rimers and the flow of water forced the paddles against the rimers thereby making a barrier to hold back the water. The usual way for a boat to move ***downstream*** or upstream was for sufficient paddles and rimers to be removed to create a gap. The boat was then either swept through the gap on the flow of water if it was travelling downstream, or pulled through it against the flow of water if it was travelling upstream. Either way was not easy and could result in the amount of water in the higher reach being substantially reduced and flooding in the lower reach, thus the name 'flash' or 'flush' lock.

The last flash lock to be replaced, the one at Eaton Hastings, was known to be in regular use in 1935 two years before it was removed in 1937, with boats queuing up to go through in convoy to avoid the reach losing too much water.

Leonardo da Vinci is credited with having designed the first lock with gates although the design and method of construction has naturally changed considerably since the 16th century.

The first 'pound lock' built in the United Kingdom and probably the first in Europe, was that on the River Thames at Swift Ditch, Abingdon in 1624. Although now disused it has survived and is currently being restored.

Many of the original pound locks near to Henley were designed in the late 18th century by the Reverend Humphrey Gainsborough, minister at the Congregational Chapel in Henley and brother of Thomas Gainsborough the painter. These include ***Marsh***, Shiplake and Sonning locks upstream of Henley, and ***Hambleden***, Temple, Marlow and Boulters locks downstream.

When a boat enters a pound lock the gates will close behind it. The water level in the lock chamber will then be allowed either to fall (by opening the sluices under the tail/downstream gates) if the boat is travelling downstream, or rise (by opening the sluices under the head/upstream gates) if the boat is travelling upstream. The effect will be to lower or raise the level of the water so that when the gates ahead of the boat are opened the boat is on the same level as the water ahead of it.

The 44 locks are managed by the ***Environment Agency*** and are manned throughout the year, from 9am to 7pm in the summer and 9.15am to 4pm in the winter. Special arrangement are made at Marsh and Hambleden Locks during Regatta week

Some locks provide a range of services for boat owners such as the supply of water, including drinking water, charging points for electric boats, sewage pumpout facilities, refuse disposal and toilets.

Locks also display the red and yellow ***stream*** caution boards to warn river users of adverse river conditions.

LONDON CATERING SERVICES

LCS London Catering Services, of Keswick Road London, is the catering ***contractor*** responsible for The Regatta Brasserie', restaurant and bar, in the ***Regatta Enclosure***.

LOST PROPERTY

The Lost Property Tent in the ***Stewards' Enclosure*** is situated by the Main Entrance to the Enclosure.

Regatta Staff are instructed to remove to the Lost Property Office any items left on chairs and seats, other than the reserved seats in the ***Grandstand***.

The Tent also has an access point from outside the Enclosure, which is available for a limited period for the use of ***Members*** and Guests recovering items after the Enclosure has closed.

All items of Lost Property remaining at the end of the Regatta are held in the ***Secretary***'s Office at ***Regatta Headquarters***, until the end of September.

LUNCHEON AND TEA TICKETS KIOSK

This is situated in the ***Stewards' Enclosure*** between the ***Coffee & Liqueur Bar*** and the ***Bandstand***.

LUNCHEON TENT

The Luncheon Tent is situated at the ***downstream*** end of the ***Stewards' Enclosure*** between the ***Seafood Restaurant*** and the ***Regatta Enclosure***.

Between 1948 and 1985 the Luncheon Tent was in ***Selwyn's Meadow*** and a road was built across ***Lion Meadow*** to ***Remenham Lane*** in 1948 for visitors to the Olympic Games Regatta and subsequently for ***Members of the Stewards' Enclosure*** and their Guests to access it.

Luncheon and Tea tickets can be purchased in advance or from the ***Luncheon and Tea Tickets Kiosk*** on the day, subject to availability.

Admission times for the three-course luncheon are 11.45am until 1pm for the first sitting and from 2.15pm until 3.00pm for the second sitting.

Tea is served between 4pm and 6pm.

MARSH LOCK

Marsh Lock, so named because the land immediately ***upstream*** of the lock is liable to flooding, marks the upstream end of the ***Henley Reach***.

In the fifteenth century when Marsh was a 'flash ***lock***' there were five mills on the site.

The original pound lock, like Hambleden Lock and many

others on the Thames, was designed in the late 18th century by the Reverend Humphrey Gainsborough, minister at the Congregational Chapel in Henley and brother of Thomas Gainsborough the painter. The lock, built in January 1773 and rebuilt in 1788 and 1886, is situated on an island linked by two horseshoe bridges designed to carry the towpath round

the mill, which is situated on the west, Oxfordshire, side of the river.

The lock chamber is 41.19m (135ft 2in) long, 6.42m (21ft 1in) wide, 2.18m (7ft 2in) deep when full of water and has a 'dropfall' (the distance between the level of the water upstream of the lock and the level on the Henley Reach ***down-stream*** of the lock) of 1.33m (4ft 4in).

Marsh Lock is 75.55km (46.95miles) upstream of the Teddington Boundary Obelisk, beyond which the river is the responsibility of the Port of London Authority, and 142km (88.23miles) downstream of Cricklade Bridge, the generally

accepted limit of navigation on the river. It is 1.52km (.95mile) upstream of ***Henley Bridge*** and 5.21km (3.24miles) upstream of ***Hambleden Lock*** at the other end of the Henley Reach.

Marsh Lock has three weirs, including one of the few remaining paddle and rimer (sometimes spelt 'rhymer' or 'rymer') weirs.

It also has a Thames Salmon Trust 'salmon ladder' which is sponsored by the Arbib Foundation. This was installed on 17 May 1996.

The lock is manned between 9am and 7pm although during Regatta week this is changed to accommodate the increase in the number of boats on the river. It has no facilities for boat users and no public toilets - yet.

See - ENVIRONMENT AGENCY - THAMES REGION

MARSH MEADOWS

This is the stretch of land on the Oxfordshire side of the river, ***upstream*** of ***Henley Bridge***, between ***Mill Meadows*** and ***Marsh Lock***.

The strip of embankment along Marsh Meadows, together with the embankment by Mill Meadows, provides the only local authority authorised over-night moorings on the ***Henley Reach***

MEDALS

Each winning ***athlete*** at the Royal Regatta receives a medal which he keeps - except the winners of the ***Goblets*** and the ***Diamonds*** each of whom receive a cup, and the winner of the ***Princess Royal*** who receives a brooch.

On one side of every medal, surrounded by a laurel wreath, is the inscription 'HENLEY REGATTA. ESTABLISHED 1839' (Note: Henley Regatta not Henley Royal Regatta)

Below this inscription the medals for the ***Ladies'***, ***Henley Prize***, ***Stewards'***, ***Prince Philip***, ***Queen Mother***, ***Britannia***, ***Men's*** and ***Women's Quads***, ***Fawley*** and ***Double Sculls*** also have the name of the event. These ten have the heads of ***Isis*** and ***Tamesis*** in relief on the other side of the medal surrounded with the words *ISIS ET TAMESIS*

The other six, the ***Grand***, ***Thames***, ***Temple***, ***Princess Elizabeth***, ***Visitors'*** and ***Wyfold***, have an image in relief of the respective trophy on the other side surrounded by the name of the trophy. The medals presented to the winners of the Goblets between 1967 and 1996, the period when the goblets were not presented, were similarly designed. The Grand and Thames have the additional words *PRIZE MEDAL* round the bottom of the medal.

Every medal is engraved with the date on the edge.

See - REGATTA TROPHIES

MEDIA

The media, principally press reporters, have their own room at the Regatta accessible from the ***Boat Tent Area***.

In 1955 the Regatta established a Press Committee to co-ordinate relations with the press but this is now managed by the Regatta's Press Officer.

In order to protect the privacy of ***Members*** and their guests, television cameras and journalists (unless they are Members in their own right) are not allowed in the ***Stewards' Enclosure***.

Newspaper coverage of the Regatta is varied. *The Times*,

Daily Telegraph, *Independent* and *Guardian* and their Sunday equivalent newspapers report rowing events in some detail although even their coverage is far from as comprehensive as it was forty years ago. The tabloid press usually comment on the amount of ***Pimm's***, strawberries and champagne consumed, or seek out the more sensational stories and pictures - and their reporters always seem to be present when attractive ladies in short dresses are turned away from the entrance of the Stewards' Enclosure.
See - FOOD AND DRINK

MEMBERS' STAND

See - GRANDSTAND

MEMBERSHIP OF THE STEWARDS' ENCLOSURE

Members of the ***Stewards' Enclosure*** are occasionally referred to, in error, as being a 'Member of the Regatta'. Sometimes members are even mistakenly referred to as ***Stewards***.

Membership is by application to the Stewards of the Regatta and necessitates being nominated and seconded by members. Members of the Stewards' Enclosure have no say in the running of the Regatta although there have been many ***Membership Surveys*** during the 20th century, carried out specifically so that the Stewards could be made aware of the views and opinions of members. The last two surveys were in 1988 and 1999.

Membership in 1919, when the Stewards' Enclosure was established, was restricted to 300. It had risen to 700 by 1939 and by the 2000 Regatta was 6,474 of which 6,094 were full members. The other 380 were Overseas Members who had elected to pay a nominal annual subscription to retain their membership whilst overseas. Overseas members do not receive any badges although should the member return and wish to attend the Regatta he can upgrade his membership at any time and receive his full badge entitlement by paying the full membership subscription.

Membership of the Stewards' Enclosure has been restricted for many years in order to avoid overcrowding in the Enclosure. By 2001 there were over 1,300 on the waiting list for membership, approximately 50% having a rowing background. Applications from those who have competed at the Regatta (approximately half of those on the waiting list) can take several years before membership is approved. The waiting list is reviewed in March each year in the light of those who have died or who have had their membership withdrawn because they have committed a misdemeanour such as failing to pay a bar bill or their annual subscription. Few members resign their membership. With only approximately 120 membership vacancies becoming available each year, those on the waiting list who have not competed at the Regatta can expect to wait up to 12 years before their application is given consideration by the Stewards.

8.5% of members of the Enclosure are ***women*** who have been eligible for membership since December 1946. 1946 was also the first year that a full list of Members was printed and distributed.

Members of the Stewards' Enclosure, most of whom have rowed at the Regatta, are issued with an enamelled Personal Membership ***Badge*** each year. The colour of the badge changes each year and the design changes approximately every ten years. These badges are also popular collectors' items and collections have been sold at auction over the years. Past enamelled badges can be purchased from the ***Regatta Shop*** and blue enamelled badge key rings, without a date, are also a popular sale item.

Since 1983, when the popularity of the Regatta was increasing rapidly and ticket touts started to appear, members' enamelled badges have been engraved on the reverse with a number, which identifies the member to whom it has been issued. Similarly the 'free allocation' guests' badges issued to members have the same number printed on them as that on the member's badge thereby easily identifying the member to whom they have been issued. (Note: This number changes each year and is not the personal number of the member on Regatta files)

The numbers on any other guests' badges bought by members, bearing in mind that only members are permitted to buy badges for the Stewards' Enclosure, are noted by the Regatta. The reason for this is that Members are responsible for the conduct of their guests and they are advised annually that if they allow their guests to flout the established codes of behaviour in the Enclosure they 'place their continued membership at risk'.

Members are allocated a total of eight Guests' Badges, two for Wednesday, Thursday and Friday and one for Saturday and Sunday. The colours of the Guests badges, like the colours of the badges for the ***Regatta Enclosure*** and the covers of the ***Regatta Programmes***, are changed daily and are issued in pink, green, grey, yellow and blue.

Those wearing Members' or Guests' Badges are also entitled to enter the ***Regatta Enclosure*** and the ***Boat Tent Area***.

The 1999 Membership Survey revealed that over 30% of members were aged over 60 and less than 8% were under the age of 30.

MEMBERSHIP SURVEYS

Over the years the ***Stewards'*** have sought the views of Members of the ***Stewards' Enclosure*** on a range of matters.

The last two surveys took place in July 1988 and October 1999 and produced a 63% response in 1988 and 45% in 1999 - the higher figure in 1988 being attributed to the survey taking place immediately after the Regatta unlike the 1999 survey.

The most significant findings from the 1999 survey, valid in view of the high level of response, included:-

· 97.5% agreeing with the banning of mobile phones in the Stewards' Enclosure (not covered in the 1988 survey), and

· 75% wanting the dress code in the Stewards' Enclosure to be retained.

It was also possible to estimate from the responses that the attendance figures in the Stewards' Enclosure in 1999 were 14,000 on Wednesday, 16,000 on Thursday, 20,000 on Friday, 16,500 on Saturday and 12,500 on Sunday.

The 1999 survey also revealed that 53% of the membership was over the age of 50 compared with 39% in 1988, and that less than 8% were under the age of 30 compared with 20% in 1988.

A significant number agreed that children under the age of 10 should continue to be excluded from the Stewards' Enclosure, and a small percentage wanted the return of closed circuit television particularly so that races on the early part of the ***Regatta Course*** can be seen in the Enclosure. This was a justifiable response as a recent review has shown that in 82% of races the competitor that is ahead at the ¼ mile ***signal*** stays ahead to win the race. The percentage increases at the ***Barrier*** where 86% of those ahead go on to win.

THE MEN'S QUADRUPLE SCULLS

The decision to establish the Men's ***Quadruple Sculls*** event was taken at a meeting of the ***Stewards*** in December 2000.

The event is open to any quad below ***Queen Mother*** standard (ie. not a ***heavyweight***, lightweight or ***FISA*** Senior B (under 23) national crew).

Athletes competing in this event are not permitted to compete in any other quadruple sculling event at the same Regatta.

The present entrance fee for this event is £50 and the Stewards have limited the number of entries to 16.

At present there is no trophy for the Men's Quadruple Sculls.

See - REGATTA TROPHIES

THE MILE & ONE EIGHTH RESTAURANT

The Mile & One Eighth Restaurant, established in 1994, is situated at the ***upstream*** end of the ***Luncheon Tent*** in the ***Stewards' Enclosure***. Seating is at tables for 12, and reservations can be made in advance for this all-day restaurant facility which includes morning coffee and Danish pastries, a three-course waitress-served luncheon and strawberry cream tea. The restaurant opens at 10.30am each day (11am on Sunday) and drinks can be purchased throughout the day.

MILL MEADOWS

The stretch of land on the Oxfordshire side of the river ***upstream*** of ***Henley Bridge***, between Boathouse Reach (the line of house by ***Hobbs & Sons***) and ***Marsh Meadows***. Mill Meadows has public bowling and putting facilities and children's play grounds.

The strip of embankment along Mill Meadows, together with the embankment by Marsh Meadows provides the only local authority-authorised over-night mooring on the ***Henley Reach***.

MINIMUM WEIGHT

This rule, introduced in 1869, refers to the minimum weight that must be carried by a ***coxed crew***. If the weight of the ***coxswain*** is below this figure, ***dead-weight*** must be carried to bring the weight up to the minimum specified for the ***event*** entered.

The other minimum weight rule introduced in 1869, which specified a minimum weight for a coxswain below which he was not allowed to compete, was abolished by the ***Stewards*** in December 2000.

See - DEAD-WEIGHT and STEWARDS' CHALLENGE CUP

MOBILE BANK

See - BANKING FACILITIES

MOBILE PHONES

Since 1996 mobile phones have not been allowed in the ***Stewards' Enclosure***.

MOORINGS DURING THE REGATTA

During the Regatta the General Directions of the

Environment Agency are that:-

· no boat may secure to any of the piles of the ***Regatta Course***,

· no boat may be moored unattended alongside the ***booms***,

· manually propelled boats may be moored to the ***towpath*** alongside the Regatta Course one abreast only and provided no obstruction is caused to competitors proceeding to the Start,

· manually propelled boats may be moored to the booms outside the Regatta Course (except in the practice area and in the area between the mooring prohibition notices at ***Fawley***), provided no obstruction is caused,

· open power driven boats ie. those without awnings or cabins, may moor one abreast only to the Regatta Course booms on the ***Buckinghamshire*** side, ***downstream*** of the Course Pile - which is a pile marked by the Environment Agency with a notice to this effect, again provided no obstruction is caused to the ***navigation*** channel. (Note: All other power driven boats may not moor to the Regatta Course booms), and

· no boat shall moor to banks or booms in the area between the mooring prohibition notices at Fawley or to the Course booms from the Barrier to Temple Island.

On ***Fawley Meadows***, moorings on the ***upstream*** meadow (the meadow next to ***Phyllis Court Club***) together with moorings on the stretch of bank downstream from the ***Fawley Meadows Hospitality Village***, can be reserved by contacting the Secretary's Office in advance of the Regatta. No mooring is permitted on the land in front of the Hospitality Village.

Mooring on Regatta land downstream of ***Fawley Court*** is allowed on a day to day basis.

NATIONAL RIVERS AUTHORITY

The NRA took over responsibility for the full length of the

River Thames, from Cricklade to Teddington, from the ***Thames Water Authority***, in 1989 and subsequently passed it onto the ***Environment Agency*** in 1996.

NAVIGATION

The general rules of navigation are that when two boats approach each other they should pass to the right (port side to port side) 'when it is safe and practical' so to do.

In awkward conditions, such as when approaching bridges, boats going ***upstream*** should give way to boats travelling ***downstream***. Any boat overtaking another has a duty to keep clear while manoeuvring.

Powered boats should always slow down when approaching unpowered boats and should always give way to sailing boats. Powered boats and sailing boats must give way to rowing ***boats***.

The cruising speed of a powered boat should be about the same as walking pace. River craft using the ***Henley Reach*** outside the period when the ***Regatta Course*** is under construction or being dismantled are required to keep to normal navigation rules. On the Henley Reach this means craft keeping to the ***Berkshire*** side when proceeding downstream, using the second arch from that bank when going under ***Henley Bridge***; and keeping to the ***Buckinghamshire/***
Oxfordshire side when going upstream using the second arch of the Bridge counting from the Town side.

Regattas and ***head of the river races*** are allowed to establish special navigation rules.

The ***Environment Agency*** Rules of Navigation on the ***Henley Reach*** are changed downstream from ***Henley Bridge*** to accommodate the building of the Regatta Course and again for the five days of racing. At a predetermined date, depending on the state of the Course, ***pleasure boats*** travelling upstream and downstream, and ***crews*** and ***scullers*** travelling downstream towards the start of the Course, are required to keep off the Course, leaving that for crews and scullers travelling upstream.

During the Regatta the Environment Agency directions for non-competitors and non-official boats are that for 30 minutes preceding, and during, periods of racing:-

· manually propelled boats may navigate outside the Course and Practice Area and may, if necessary, cross the Course through the openings in the booms provided a race is not in progress,

· power driven boats may be navigated outside the Course and Practice Area on the Buckinghamshire side but must not stop or turn round or otherwise interfere with the Regatta or the navigation of other boats,

Results' / Photographers' Box

· sailing boats may navigate only under oars or mechanical power and shall not have a sail hoisted,

· boats in the navigation channel, ie. the area between the booms on the Buckinghamshire side of the Course and the Buckinghamshire bank, are required to keep to the right hand side of the channel and obey the normal navigation rules of passing approaching boats on the port (left) side, and

· all boats will give way to racing boats travelling to the start.

Competitors are not allowed to practice on the Course during the hours of racing and those travelling downstream to the Start are not allowed to turn into the Practice/Warm Up Area until 400m downstream of ***Temple Island***.

Competitors must proceed to the Start down the navigation channel on Wednesday Thursday and Friday morning. Congestion in the navigation channel however reaches a peak towards the end of the Regatta. As this coincides with fewer races, competitors going to the Start are allowed, from Friday afternoon, to proceed down the Course to the gap in the booms by the ***Regatta Enclosure***, and to then continue down the Berkshire side of the river.

NEW COURSE

This was the Course used at the Regatta from 1886 to 1922.
See - REGATTA COURSE

NEW STREET

The street that joins ***Riverside*** by ***Hooper's*** opposite to the ***Boat Tent Area***.

NOT ROWED OUT

This is the verdict given when one or more of the competitors fails to continue racing before reaching the finish line eg. in the event of a competitor being unable to continue racing after hitting the booms or as a result of equipment failure.
(Note: A ***crew*** that finishes a race without its ***cox*** is deemed not to have completed the Course)

NUMBERS ON BOATS

See - IDENTIFICATION NUMBER

OAR

The sport differentiates between oars, as used in ***rowing***, and

sculls as used when ***sculling***. Both are usually referred to as '***blades***' but never as 'paddles'.

Both oars and sculls have a 'spoon' - the flattened end of the oar/scull that goes into the water. This is usually painted with the colours of the club.

OARSOME FOURSOME

The popular name, and official Australian registered trademark, of the Australian 1992 and 1996 ***Olympic*** Gold Medal ***Coxless Four*** of Nick Green, Mike McKay, Andrew Cooper and James Tomkins(1992) and Drew Ginn replacing Andrew Cooper (1996).

In 1998 the ***crew*** (Green, McKay, Ginn and Tomkins) were beaten in the semi final of the ***Stewards' Challenge Cup*** by the ***Awesome Foursome*** (Cracknell, ***Redgrave***, Foster and Pinsent) who went on to win the Stewards' for the second year.

The 'Oarsome Foursome' did not defend their title in the Sydney Games in 2000. A faster Australian four, known as the 'Gruesome Fewsome', was selected and came third behind the Great Britain and Italian fours.

OFFICIAL BOATS

In addition to the umpire launches the Regatta operates a number of official boats. These include the privately owned slipper launch *L'Amazon*, the workboat ***Black Piglet*** owned by the Regatta, *Impey*, hired for use by the contractors dealing with the Regatta commentary, and the Goose Patrol boat used to keep ***Canada geese*** off of the ***Regatta Course***.
See - FLAGS

OLD COURSE

This was the Course used at the Regatta from 1839 to 1885.
See - REGATTA COURSE

OLYMPIC GAMES

Before the first Olympic Games in 1896, Baron Pierre de Coubertin (himself an oarsman) attended Henley Royal Regatta and subsequently used the Regatta's management structure as a role model for the International Olympic Committee - the governing body of the Olympic Games.

Rowing (including ***sculling***) has therefore been represented at every Olympic Games except the unofficial Athens Games of 1906; although there are no results from the first Olympic Regatta planned for Easter in 1896 as this was abandoned because of bad weather and insufficient international participation.

Up to the end of the 20th century, including the Sydney Games in 2000, Great Britain ***crews*** and ***scullers*** won a total of 21 Olympic titles/championships. Individually 65 Great Britain rowers, scullers and ***coxswains*** have won a total of 74 gold medals. The most notable year was 1908 at the Olympic Regatta held at Henley when, relying on veteran oarsmen from ***Leander*** for the second eight, Great Britain won all four gold medals, the ***eights***, ***coxless fours***, ***coxless pairs*** and ***single sculls*** - in 1908 there were only four events and only nine countries participated. This remains Britain's best ever Olympic rowing gold medal tally.

The best known rowing Olympic Gold Medallists are ***Steven Redgrave***, who has won five Gold Medals (1984, 1988, 1992, 1996 and 2000), Jack Beresford Junior, who won three (the single sculls in Paris in 1924, the coxless fours in Los Angeles in 1932 and the ***double sculls*** in Berlin in 1936 - JB also won silver in the single sculls in Antwerp in 1920 and the eight in Amsterdam in 1928), and Matthew Pinsent, who has also won three, (the coxless pairs in Barcelona in 1992 and Atlanta in 1996 and the coxless fours in Sydney in

2000).

The Olympic Games have been held twice in Great Britain; in 1908, when the Games planned for Rome were cancelled and Italy withdrew following the 1906 eruption of Mount Vesuvius, and 1948. On both occasions, in the absence of a suitable still water course, the Olympic Regatta took place at Henley - the only town to host the Olympic Regatta twice.

In 1908 the Royal Regatta barred foreign entries because of the close proximity of the Olympic Games. The Olympic Course, an extension of the ***Regatta Course***, was 1½ miles long (2,414.02m) and, as with the Regatta Course, competitors raced ***upstream***. The Start was well ***downstream*** of ***Temple Island*** and the Finish upstream of the present finish line at Poplar Point.

Since 1912 all racing in the Olympic Games has been over a still water, 2,000m (1mile 427yds) course - the standard distance for multi-lane international events; except in 1948 at Henley. On this occasion the Regatta Course was shortened by 183m (200yds) to 1,929m, to compensate for the ***stream***, and the booms were removed to enable three abreast racing (racing had been two abreast in 1908). It would have been extremely difficult to have built a 'straight' 2,000m course for three abreast racing on the ***Henley Reach***. In 1948 there were seven events and 27 countries participated. Great Britain won gold medals in the coxless pairs and the double sculls.

Henley was also the venue for the Olympic Canoe Regatta in 1948, which took place two days after the finish of the rowing Regatta.

Interestingly two of the three members of the ***FISA*** Fairness Committee at the Sydney Games were Henley ***Stewards*** as was the FISA doctor.

In the Sydney games of 2000, Great Britain won two gold medals, the eights and the coxless fours. This was the first time since the Stockholm Games of 1912, when a Leander crew had represented Great Britain, that Great Britain had won the eights event, the Blue Riband event. The eights silver medal in 2000 went to Australia reversing the outcome of the final of the ***Grand Challenge Cup*** less than three months earlier. On that occasion the Australian crew, entered as Australian Institute of Sport, beat the Great Britain eight, rowing as Leander Club and Queen's Tower Boat Club (but with R Thatcher in the ***crew*** in place of F Scarlett), by 1½ lengths. See - AWESOME FOURSOME and INTERNATIONAL OLYMPIC COMMITTEE

OPEN STAND
See - FAWLEY STAND

OUTRIGGER
The bracket (referred to as a rigger) fixed to the side of a racing ***boat*** to hold the ***oar/scull*** (which fits into the rowlock which is a form of gate, which swivels on a pin at the furthest point from the side of the boat).

The first timer outriggers were used at Henley was in the ***Diamonds*** in 1845.

OVERSEAS COMPETITOR BADGES
These enamelled metal badges, valid for the five days of the regatta are sold to competitors from overseas allowing them access to the ***Boat Tent Area*** and all ***Enclosures***.

OVERSEAS ENTRIES
Entries at the Regatta, other than those from the United

Kingdom, are referred to as Overseas Entries and the country of domicile is shown against the name of the club on the ***List of Entries*** and in the ***Regatta Programme***.

The first overseas entry was from the USA in 1872 (two entries being received from the Atlanta Rowing Club) and the first ***Regatta trophy*** to go overseas was in 1878 when a coxless four from Colombia College, Canada won the ***Visitors' Challenge Cup***.

Ever since entries have been received from overseas, the Regatta has held written agreements from each National Association and Federation to ensure that Henley conditions of entry are accepted and that clubs and ***athletes*** are appropriately qualified for the event for which they are entered. In 1896 and again in 1905 the ***ARA*** wanted the Regatta to ban overseas entries because many countries didn't have the same definition of an ***amateur*** as the ARA - but the ***Stewards*** disagreed. Indeed it was as a result of some overseas entries in the 1920s and 1930s and the liberal definition of an amateur used by some other countries, that contributed to the Stewards redefining the status of an amateur in 1938.

In 1954, Russia entered the ***Grand*** and ***Stewards' Challenge Cups***, the ***Silver Goblets and Nickalls' Challenge Cup***, the ***Double Sculls Challenge Cup*** and the ***Diamond Challenge Sculls***, (winning the Grand, Stewards' and Goblets). This was the first time a complete national team had competed for trophies at Henley although, to comply with Henley rules, the team entered under club names.

Most entries from overseas are of a high standard although the increase in recent years coupled with the improvement in the quality and number of home entries has necessitated some overseas competitors having to Qualify.

The sesquicentennial (150th) anniversary of the Regatta in

1989 attracted a record overseas entry of 126 - which has not been surpassed.

OXFORD COLLEGE SERVANTS

The Oxford College Servants, also known as Oxford College Scouts, provided the security attendants in the ***Stewards' Enclosure*** for many years. In 1982, the increasing demands on their time and the need of the Regatta for greater numbers of attendants to deal with a rapidly increasing membership contributed to the decision of the Regatta to use private security organisations.

OXFORDSHIRE

The land on the ***Mill Meadows***, ***St Mary's Church***, ***Phyllis Court Club*** side of the river from ***Marsh Lock*** to the county boundary, which is opposite ***Remenham Club***, is situated in the county of Oxfordshire.

The county ***downstream*** of Oxfordshire is ***Buckinghamshire***.

For parliamentary purposes the Oxfordshire side of the ***Henley Reach*** is part of the Henley-on-Thames constituency.

OXON

Oxon is the abbreviation for ***Oxfordshire***.

OYSTER BAR

See - CHAMPAGNE & PIMM'S BAR

PADDLE

When a ***boat*** is being ***rowed*** or ***sculled*** other than when it is racing or practising racing, the action is often referred to as 'paddling'.

Paddle is also the name of a short oar as used when propelling a ***punt*** or dragon boat but it is incorrect to refer to an '***oar***' as a paddle.

Obviously 'paddle' is also the description given to dabbling one's feet, or wading, in shallow water - something not encouraged at Henley or in the river generally.
See - WEIL'S DISEASE

A PAIR

This, and the description 'pair-oar', describes two ***athletes*** '***rowing***' a ***boat***. The boat is also called a 'pair' or a 'pair-oar'.

A pair can also be referred to as a ***coxless*** pair or a ***coxed*** pair.
(Note: Two athletes '***sculling***' a boat is referred to as a '***double***')

At Henley the only event for pairs is for coxless pairs for the ***Silver Goblets and Nickalls' Challenge Cup***.

The ***fastest recorded time*** at the Regatta taken by a coxless pair over the ***Regatta Course***, (1mile 550yds), (***SG Redgrave*** & MC Pinsent, Leander Club in 1995) is 6min 56sec - a speed of 9.86knots or 11.36mph (18.28kph).

PARK FARM MEADOWS

This is the 18½ acres of land on the ***Buckinghamshire*** side of the river between ***Fawley Court*** and ***Temple Island***, purchased by the Regatta in 1955.

In 1966 scenes for the film 'Half a Sixpence' were filmed on the edge of the woodland (also known as the '***Bushes***') at the ***upstream*** end of Park Farm Meadows.

PASSES

Regatta literature normally differentiates between ***badges***,

labels, passes and ***tickets***.

At Henley, passes are generally personalised with the names of the recipient/wearer eg. ***press*** passes and staff passes - the latter also includes a photograph for added security.

PATRON

Her Majesty The Queen is Patron of the Regatta.

The first Patron was Thomas Stonor, the 3rd Lord Camoys, who was Patron from 1844. Then in 1851 the ***Stewards*** decided to seek Royal Patronage to help the finances of the Regatta. Lord Camoys wrote to HRH Prince Albert (before he became Prince Consort) who consented to become the first Royal Patron of the Regatta, following which it received its Royal prefix. Lord Camoys then became Vice Patron and, in 1864, became the Regatta's first ***President***.

After the death of the Prince Consort in 1861, HM Queen Victoria consented to the title being retained and, on the accession of each monarch since the death of Queen Victoria, the Regatta has applied for and received notification that Royal Patronage will continue.
See - ROYALTY

PAYNE AND GUNTER

Between 1976 and 1996, Paynes originally of Shepherd's Bush and then Chiswick, who subsequently became Payne & Gunter, organised the Regatta's Official Hospitality facility on ***Fawley Meadows***. In 1996 the company merged with ***Letheby & Christopher***, the catering ***contractors*** in the ***Stewards' Enclosure*** and became part of the Compass Group.
See - FAWLEY MEADOWS HOSPITALITY VILLAGE

PE

The abbreviated name of the ***Princess Elizabeth Challenge Cup***.

PEACE REGATTAS

Special Regattas were organised after each of the World Wars See - ROYAL HENLEY PEACE REGATTA (the 1919 Regatta) and ROYAL HENLEY REGATTA (the 1945 Regatta)

PEDESTRIAN WALKWAYS

These are interlocking platforms for use in inclement weather so that people do not have to walk in mud.

Following the very wet Regatta of 1988, emergency Pedestrian Walkways have been hired by the Regatta each year and kept in store on site in case of need. They were first laid in the ***Stewards' Enclosure*** in 1991.
See - REGATTA WEATHER

PHILLIPS TRADITIONAL RIVERCRAFT AND MARITIME EPHEMERA AUCTION

Since 1986 Phillips Auctioneers have held an Auction in the Regatta Boat Tent in the ***Boat Tent Area*** on the Saturday after the Regatta. Items for sale include a wide range of memorabilia including Henley winners medals, collections of the enamelled ***badges*** issued to ***Members*** of the ***Stewards' Enclosure***, paintings, boating artifacts, models, flags and a selection of boats in and out of the water.

PHOTO-FINISH

See - FINISHING A RACE AT HENLEY

PHOTOGRAPHERS

Accredited photographers can use the ***Photographers' Box*** by the finish of the ***Regatta Course*** and the ***Photographers' Platform*** next to the ***Progress Board***. The Regatta also appoints an 'Official' photographer who takes photographs of every race, competitors in training and the Prize ceremony.

George Bushell & Son, established in Henley in 1919, were official Regatta photographers for many years. In 1988, when the business finished, George Bushell, grandson of the founder, generously gave the company's negatives and plates to the Regatta. The Regatta now has photographs of many races since 1887, all races from 1946 to 1983 and most of the races since 1983.

The present photograph contract is held by Wokingham Photographic, based in the same shop in Hart St Henley used by Bushell's.

PHOTOGRAPHERS' BOX

This is the two tiered structure on the ***Buckinghamshire*** side of the ***Regatta Course*** 20m ***upstream*** of the ***Judges' Box***. It is reached by a boat from the ***Press Box catwalk*** on the opposite side of the Course and is for accredited photographers only.

The Photographers' Box is also known as the ***Results' Box*** as the outcome of each race is shown on boards on the front of the structure. An ***Environment Agency*** Official is based on the Photographers' Box to help guide boats through the narrow part of the ***navigation channel***.

See pictures on page 146 and 173

PHOTOGRAPHERS' PLATFORM

This is situated on the ***Buckinghamshire*** side of the ***Regatta Course*** outside the ***booms*** on the ***upstream*** side of the ***Progress Board***.

Access is by boat for accredited photographers only.

PHYLLIS COURT CLUB

Phyllis Court Club is situated on the ***Oxfordshire*** bank, the opposite side of the river from the Regatta ***Enclosures*** - and occupies approximately 250m of riverbank at the finish of the ***Regatta Course***.

The site of Phyllis Court may have been a river crossing point for Romans and Saxons and there have been reports of the remains of a bridge having been found in the river at this point.

In 1347 the Manor of Fillets as it was known and which was part of Windsor Great Forest, was given by King Edward III to John de Molyns, Treasurer of the Kings Chamber and Keeper of the Royal Hawks and Falcons. A manor house was built on the site and surrounded by a moat with a drawbridge - the remains of the moat were cleared in 1906 to make the waterway to the river.

In 1622 Phyllis Court was sold to Judge, Sir James Whitelock (sometimes spelt Whitelocke and sometimes Whitlock) who owned ***Fawley Court***. His son, Judge and Parliamentarian, Sir Bulstrode Whitelock inherited the property and, because of his support for Parliament, the house, like Fawley Court, was attacked at the beginning of the Civil War and occupied by Royalist troops under Prince Rupert. When the property was recovered by Parliamentary forces, Sir Bulstrode was appointed Governor of the garrison by Oliver Cromwell and moved into the building, Fawley Court having been severely damaged by Royalist forces and made uninhabitable. In 1643 bricks from the partially demolished fortified manor house of Phyllis Court were used to build the wall along the river - which ends at the Henley landmark of the '***Hole in the Wall***'.

Parliamentary forces captured Greenland, the last Royalist stronghold in the area, in 1644, and Sir Bulstrode was made Governor of Henley by Oliver Cromwell in 1646. He then finished the demolition of Phyllis Court and rebuilt the house in 1648.

Following the restoration of the monarchy and in order to avoid having to sell Phyllis Court to pay the heavy fines imposed on him for supporting Cromwell, Sir Bulstrode gave Phyllis Court to William his eldest surviving son by his second marriage.

The house then changed hands a number of times. It was demolished in 1785, rebuilt, demolished again and then rebuilt between 1837 and 1838, immediately before the establishment of the Regatta; and it was partially rebuilt and refurbished in 1976 following a serious fire. The Grandstand was built in 1912 for the visit to the Regatta of King George V and Queen Mary. It was improved in 1913 and renovated in 1993 and is now a permanent structure able to offer dining and entertaining facilities throughout the year.

Over the years Phyllis Court has received many Royal visits. Queen Anne, the Consort of James I, stayed in 1604 and, in December 1688, when the property was owned by William and Mary Whitelock, William of Orange, who also stayed at

Fawley Court, stayed at Phyllis Court on his way to London with 15,000 troops for the 'Glorious Revolution'.

The Phyllis Court 'Club' was founded as a proprietary club by Roy Finlay on 2 June 1906; he and his father having taken a lease over the property, which was then owned by WD Mackenzie of Fawley Court.

The grounds of Phyllis Court were used for entertaining by the Regatta for many years in the 19th century. In 1908 over 100 foreign competitors were entertained when the ***Olympic Games*** Regatta was held at Henley.

Phyllis Court remained open during the First World War although the grounds were requisitioned by the Royal Flying Corps.

In 1924 the Prince of Wales, later and briefly Edward VIII, became patron.

On 1 January 1937 the club changed from being a proprietary club to a members' club.

During the Second World War the Club was requisitioned by the Government as a WAAF Officers Mess for the Central Photographic Unit based at Medmenham. It later became the base for a secret organisation making models to help with the planning of missions such as the Dambusters raid and the Allied landings in France. During the latter years of the war it became a rest home for American aircrews.

In 1945 the Regatta considered purchasing the Club but Club members voted against a sale at a Special General Meeting of the Club held on 29 May 1946.

In addition to providing a wide range of facilities for its members, Phyllis Court, which has eleven en-suite bedrooms, also offers bed and breakfast accommodation as well as facilities for private conferences and meetings.

See - PROTESTS

PILES

Approximately 250 piles are used in the construction of the ***Regatta Course***, where, with the 220 ***booms*** that are floated between most of them, they help prevent ***pleasure boats*** interfering with the races.

A further 300 or more piles are used as supports for the various boxes and stages on the river.

PIMM'S

Pimm's is the name of the drink associated with summer social events and in particular with the Regatta. The Classic Pimm's drink consists of a measure of Pimm's Original No 1 Cup (gin based) and three measures of lemonade and served with ice and slices of lemon, cucumber, apple and oranges and a sprig of mint.

The number of Pimm's drunk each year at the Regatta, approximately 30,000 pints, together with the amount of champagne and the volume of strawberries and cream consumed are often used by the tabloid press as a guide to the success or otherwise of the Regatta.

See - CHAMPAGNE & PIMM'S BAR and FOOD AND DRINK

PINEAPPLE CUP

This is the description of the silver gilt cup presented instead of a medal to the winner of the ***Diamond Challenge Sculls***. It is so named because the surface design has the appearance of the outside of a pineapple.

PINK COTTAGE

Situated on the ***Buckinghamshire*** bank approximately 250m ***upstream*** of ***Hambleden Lock***, Pink Cottage is the name given by local oarsmen to ***Ferry Cottage*** (the previous building on the site having been painted pink many years ago). The cottage marks the starting line for the four local ***Head of the River Races***.

PINK PALACE

A popular name for the ***Leander*** Clubhouse linking the Club's colour with its pre-eminence on the river.

THE PIPE

A natural gas pipe crosses the ***Regatta Course***, buried in the bed of the river in 1983, between ***Temple Island*** and the ¼ mile ***Signal Box***.

PLEASURE BOATS

The term 'pleasure boats' is used to describe those boats that are not racing ***boats*** or ***official boats***. It includes boats pro-

Pleasure boats at the Fawley Narrows

pelled by petrol or diesel engines or electric motors, such as large passenger boats, cabin cruisers, launches and 'tin fish' (small metal boats with outboard engines). It also includes non-racing hand propelled boats such as ***skiffs***, dinghies, ***punts*** and ***canoes*** that are propelled by ***oars*** or paddles - or poles in the case of punts.

Old photographs of the Regatta confirm the stories that it was possible to walk from one side of the river to the other via pleasure boats at the beginning of the 20th century. However, the number of hand propelled pleasure boats has diminished considerably since then. In the 20 years from 1980 the number of boats available for hire fell 65% and in the 10 years from 1990 the number of privately owned boats fell 28%. Such is the concern of the ***Environment Agency***, particularly as a survey has revealed that one of the reasons for the decline is the high cost of boating, that it is actively taking steps to help increase the number of all pleasure boats using the river, including racing boats.

Although pleasure boats have always been popular at Henley there has been a continual problem keeping them off the ***Regatta Course***. In the early days a cannon/maroon was fired to let boaters know that a race was in progress. In 1889 steam and electric launches patrolled the Course and in 1891 electric bells were fixed to ***piles*** along the Course to warn boats to keep clear when a race was in progress. In 1892 a man was stationed at the ¼ mile ***signal*** specifically to keep pleasure boats off the Course.

In 1899, after a number of accidents, including some caused by boats tied to piles but swinging onto the Course in front of racing boats, the entire ***Buckinghamshire*** side of the Course was ***boomed*** - the bays on the ***Berkshire*** side having been boomed since 1884.

In recent years, organising pleasure boats in the ***navigation*** channel has also been difficult. In 1956 and again in 1988 the river authorities instigated a system requiring river traffic, other than competitors and official boats, to move up or down the river in convoy at specific times during the day. In 1988 there was even talk of closing the Regatta part of the ***Henley Reach*** to pleasure boats during the Regatta period.

During the Regatta the Environment Agency issue navigation and mooring instructions specifying what pleasure boats can and can't do at the Regatta.

The maximum speed for power driven pleasure boats on the ***River Thames***, ***upstream*** of Teddington, is 8km per hour (5mph) 'over the bed of the river'. The Environment Agency has set up 'transit marks' at various points consisting of two pairs of black and white poles with a red triangle topmark, which are set so that a boat moving at 8 kph will take 1 minute to travel from one pair to the next. Despite this, any boat when dealing with an emergency is exempted from the speed limit.

All non-manual powered craft are required to have the name of the boat, as shown on the launch certificate, clearly marked on either side of the bow and on the stern. They are also expected to carry a life-jacket or buoyancy aid for every person on board.

Pleasure boats used on the freshwater Thames are not permitted to have lavatories on board that can be discharged into the river.

Electric boats, which cause less pollution than petrol and diesel powered boats, are encouraged by the Environment Agency who have installed nine electric power points over the length of the Thames, upstream of Teddington, for charging boat batteries.

Most narrow boats are used on narrow waterways and canals hence their name. They were designed originally for transporting goods but are now used mainly for holidays although a large number are used as homes throughout the year.

Salter Bros. of Oxford provide daily passenger boat services on the Thames during the summer linking up the many river-side towns - a service Salter's has provided since 1888. See - MOORINGS DURING THE REGATTA, SPEED LIMIT ON THE RIVER and SALTER'S STEAMERS

POLICE

The Thames Valley Police appear in force at the Regatta, over 200 officers being in attendance including mounted police, dog handlers, marine unit patrols and members of the Tactical Support Group. The police estimate that on the Saturday of the Regatta crowds of over 200,000 can be expected.

From the middle 1970s the police presence on the ***River Thames***, ***upstream*** of Teddington, was by way of the police boats *Sit Pax*, *Ubivis* and *In Valle Thamesis* (approximate English translation being 'Let there be peace wherever in the Thames Valley' - *Ubivis* being a boat that was kept on a trailer so that it could be put into the water 'wherever' it was needed.) (Note: The motto of the Thames Valley Police is *Sit Pax In Valle Tamesis*)

In the 1990s, boats that remained permanently in the water proved to be impractical. By 1998, following financial cutbacks, the police presence on the river was by way of a number of small boats which, like *Ubivis,* can be transported easily and quickly to the river by road.

POPLAR POINT

This is the name of the bend in the river, at the finish of the ***Regatta Course***. This was approximately 300m from the end of the Course before 1886 when the Finish was at ***Henley Bridge***. It was so named because poplar trees have always grown at this point.

Two trees have been planted at Poplar Point in recent years. One is in memory of Kenneth Payne, ***Steward*** of the Regatta and Member of the ***Committee of Management*** 1938 - 1988; the other in memory of Peter Coni, OBE, QC, Steward from 1975 and ***Chairman*** 1977 - 1993.

PRACTICE AREA

This is the 600m stretch of river, also known as the Warm Up Area, that is reserved for competitors immediately ***downstream*** of the start of the ***Regatta Course***.
See - BUOYS and ERGO ROOM

PRESENTATION CUP FOR FOUR OARS WITHOUT COXSWAINS

This trophy was introduced in 1869 following the incident in 1868 in the ***Stewards' Challenge Cup*** which was then an event for coxed fours, when WB Woodgate rowing in the Brasenose College, Oxford coxed four, arranged for the ***cox***, FE Weatherly, to jump overboard at the start of the race. Woodgate had built a contraption enabling him to ***steer*** the ***boat*** from the no 3 position and Brasenose won the race easily - but were then disqualified.

The Presentation Cup for Four Oars without Coxswains was included in the programme for 1869 with the same entry qualifications as the Stewards'. It was not repeated until 1872 and then there were only two entries, one of which withdrew before the race. In 1873 the Presentation Cup was discontinued and the Stewards' Challenge Cup was made coxless. In 1874 the ***Visitors'*** and ***Wyfold Challenge Cups*** followed suit.

PRESENTATION OF PRIZES

This takes place on the Sunday of the Regatta from the centre of the ***Fawley*** Stand in the ***Stewards' Enclosure***, usually at 6pm after the last final has been decided.
See - PRIZES and REGATTA TROPHIES

PRESIDENT

There have been only four Presidents since the Regatta was

established in 1839. From 1864 to 1881 the President was Thomas Stonor, the 3rd Lord Camoys and from 1881 to 1897 it was Francis Stonor, the 4th Lord Camoys. Sir Harcourt Gold OBE was President for one year in 1952.

John L Garton, CBE was appointed President in 1977, after retiring as Chairman (1965 - 1977)

PRESS

See - MEDIA

PRESS BOX

The Press Box, equipped with telephone points for rowing journalists, is situated at the finish of the ***Regatta Course*** and offers a unique head-on view of races.

Access, for accredited journalists only (not ***photographers*** who have their own box and platform), is via the ***catwalk*** by the ***Stewards' Enclosure towpath*** gate at the ***downstream*** end of the ***Boat Tent Area***.

PRESS TENT

The Press Tent is situated next to the ***First Aid Tent*** in the ***Boat Tent Area*** and has direct access to the ***Bridge Bar***.

THE PRINCE PHILIP CHALLENGE CUP

Instituted in 1963 for ***coxed fours***, the trophy was presented by Prince Philip. The ***Book of Honour***, where the names of winners are recorded, was added in 1964.

The event, usually referred to simply as the 'Prince Philip', is the senior coxed fours event at the Regatta - the unrestricted entry qualifications being the same as for the ***Grand***, the ***Stewards'***, the ***Henley Prize*** and the ***Women's Quadruple Sculls***, being for any club ***crew*** of international standard - except that no one, except ***coxswains***, is permitted to compete in the Prince Philip and any other four-oared event at the same Regatta.

The entrance fee for this event is £50 and the ***Stewards*** have limited the number of entries to 16.

See - REGATTA TROPHIES

THE PRINCESS ELIZABETH CHALLENGE CUP

The event, often referred to as the 'Princess Elizabeth' or simply as the 'PE', was established on an experimental basis for public school ***eights*** in 1946 when HRH Princess Elizabeth visited the Regatta. The silver cup and cover trophy, designed by Flaxman and made in London in 1802 by WM Hall, was presented to the Regatta in 1957 by Captain and Mrs Eric Noble of Harpsden Court and the base was added the same year - the trophy used to that date was then sold.

The races in 1946 were over a shortened course but, since 1947, ***crews*** have raced over the full ***Regatta Course*** and in 1948 the Princess Elizabeth was given permanent status.

Originally, crews were allowed to enter the ***Ladies'*** and the Princess Elizabeth at the same Regatta although if a ***crew*** reached the final of the Ladies' it had to withdraw from the Princess Elizabeth. Since 1950 entries have been for 'either' the Ladies or the Princess Elizabeth.

The entry requirements now refer to secondary schools and, since 1964, entries from overseas schools have been permitted. In 1997 the age limit was restricted to exclude any competitor who will have reached the age of nineteen by the end of the Regatta.

Only one crew per school can enter the Princess Elizabeth and ***athletes***, other than ***coxswains***, competing in this event are not permitted to compete in any other eight-oared event at the same Regatta.

The entrance fee for this event is £80 and the ***Stewards*** have limited the number of entries to 32.

See - REGATTA TROPHIES

THE PRINCESS ROYAL CHALLENGE CUP

The Princess Royal Challenge Cup was established in 1997 as the prize for women's single sculls, following the introduction of a ***single sculling*** race for ***women*** in 1993.

The silver cup and cover trophy is the work of Joseph Jackson of Dublin and is hallmarked 1800.

Each winner receives a set of miniature crossed sculls to keep.

In 1993, 1994 and 1995 the Women's Single Sculls event as it was then known, was part of the ***FISA*** World Cup.

Entry was unrestricted until 1999 since when, in order to

maintain a high quality and to reduce the number of entries, which required the majority to '***qualify***', those entering are required to be of not less than ***ARA Senior*** 1 status, or the international equivalent status, in sculling.

The entrance fee for this event is £30 and the ***Stewards*** have limited the number of entries to 16.

See - REGATTA TROPHIES

PRIZE TENT

This is situated in the ***Stewards' Enclosure*** next to the ***Regatta Shop*** behind the ***Grandstand***. All the ***Regatta trophies*** are on display in the Prize Tent during the five days of the Regatta together with other trophies and paintings and occasional displays mounted by organisations connected with Rowing or the Thames.

PRIZES

The Regatta refers to the ***Regatta trophies*** and the ***medals*** presented to the winning finalists as 'prizes'

PROGRESS BOARD

The progress of each race is shown on a frame situated on a box on the ***Buckinghamshire*** side of the Course - facing the

Grandstand in the ***Stewards' Enclosure***.

On the first three days of the Regatta, when more than one race is on the Course at the same time, the Progress Board, first used 1920, is able to show the position of each competitor and the ***Barrier*** and ***Fawley*** times.

Sadly the individual clocks, added in 1960 to show the time that had elapsed since the start of each race, have not been used since 1970.

Picture courtesy of Henley Stewards

Some years ago the Regatta adapted the frame and boards so that spectators on the Phyllis Court side of the river could read the names but this was not continued.

PROJECT OARSOME

The business plan of the ***ARA***, part of its Forward Planning, is to attract, support and retain young people in ***rowing***, from the age of 11. This involves introducing rowing to schools and communities with no rowing history by way of linking 104 mainly state schools to 52 adjacent established rowing clubs. The aim is to increase the school-age rowing population by 33% to around 6,000 competitive ***athletes***.

Project Oarsome, established in 2000 is financed by Sport England through the Sport England Lottery Fund, the Henley ***Stewards' Charitable Trust*** and the rowing clubs involved in the Scheme.

On the ***Henley Reach***, ***Henley Rowing Club*** and ***Upper Thames Rowing Club*** are project leaders.

PROTESTS

The Regatta occasionally experiences marches and protests from groups wishing to use the occasion to gain publicity for their cause. The first recorded occasion was in 1919 when militant suffragettes made protests at the Regatta. In 1960 a person or group wrote the words 'Ashes to Ashes Dust to

Dust' in large letters on the ***Phyllis Court*** river wall. The purpose wasn't clear but the words were, the letters remaining clearly visible for nearly ten years afterwards (**See background to 1967 picture on page 198 opposite**). Recent marches have included the Right to Work, Anti-Apartheid and Bash the Rich protest groups.

PUBLIC ENCLOSURE

After the 1966 Regatta, the contract that the Funfair had with the Regatta to use ***Blandy Meadow***, ***downstream*** of the ***General Enclosure***, was not renewed. As a result a 'Public Enclosure' was established in 1967 in its place. In 1971 the Public Enclosure was merged with the General Enclosure and became the ***Regatta Enclosure***.
See - FAIRGROUND

PUBLIC SCHOOLS CHALLENGE CUP

The Public Schools Challenge Cup was established at the Regatta in 1879 for ***coxed fours*** from public schools rowing on fixed ***seats*** in clinker ***boats***. This event was withdrawn in 1885 following which Marlow Regatta bought the trophy for £45. Apart from the one occasion in 1919 when the trophy was brought back from Marlow to be presented for fixed seat clinker fours at the ***Royal Henley Peace Regatta***, it has been presented at Marlow Regatta.

PUBLIC SLIPWAYS AND LAUNCHING SITES

With the co-operation of the ***Environment Agency***, many towns on the river maintain slipways so that members of the public can launch boats usually brought to the river on a trailer.

Henley has only one public slipway, which is situated at

the downstream end of ***Riverside*** next to ***Hoopers*** at the bottom of ***New Street***.

PUNT

This was the most popular pleasure boat at the Regatta during the first 100 years of the Regatta's history.

A punt is a flat-bottomed, square ended boat, the bottom sloping up at each end. It can be between 20ft (6.1m) and 27ft (8.2m) long and up to 3ft (1m) wide and is propelled either by using a pole, which is pushed against the bed of the river, or by a ***paddle*** - or even with a small outboard engine clipped to the side. A punt propelled by a team of 'paddlers' would be referred to as a 'dongola'.

Holidays on the river using a punt or a ***skiff*** were very popular in the late 19th and early 20th centuries. The boat was converted into a form of tent by stretching a cover, usually green canvas, over a number of hoops along the length of the boat.

Punts are also used for racing. This involves two classes of boat, the 'Two Foot' class being a punt approximately 25ft (7.62m) long and 2ft (61cm) wide, which can be poled by one or two ***athletes***, and a 'Best' class which is the same length but 15in (46cm) wide and which is poled by one athlete. 'Best' class racing, using the narrower punt, requires a high degree of balance and co-ordination for the athlete to remain upright.

The punting championships (of the World) established in 1896, are held in August annually on the Thames at Maidenhead and organised by the Thames Punting Club.

A QUADRUPLE SCULL

This describes four ***athletes*** 'sculling ' a ***boat*** and is also called a quad. The boat is also called a 'quadruple scull' or a 'quad'.

(Note: Four athletes '***rowing***' a boat is referred to as a '***four***')

Quadruple sculls are normally ***coxless*** (***coxswains*** are only added to very junior ***crews***). Quads at Henley are coxless.

At Henley, Quadruple Sculls compete for the ***Queen Mother*** and ***Fawley Challenge Cups***, the ***Women's Quadruple Sculls*** and the ***Men's Quadruple Sculls***.

The ***fastest recorded time*** at the Regatta taken by a men's quadruple scull over the ***Regatta Course***, (1mile 550yds), (Società Canottieri Eridanea & SC Firenze, Italy for the Queen Mother Challenge Cup in 1989) is 6min 15sec - a speed of 10.94knots or 12.6mph (20.28kph).

QUALIFYING RACES

Qualifying Races, known as 'Eliminating Races' from when they were introduced in 1928 until 1964, take place on the Friday afternoon and evening before the ***Draw*** (which takes place on the Saturday before the Regatta).

When the number of competitors for an event exceeds the maximum laid down in the ***Qualifying Rules***, the ***Committee of Management*** decides, based on recent form, who should be required to justify their inclusion in the Draw.

From 1928 the races, which have also been referred to as the 'getting-on' races, were side by side races but since 1975 they have operated in the same way as ***head of the river races*** whereby each competitor is required to race over the ***Regatta Course*** and is timed. The fastest, together with those who have not been required to 'qualify', are included in the Draw. Any subsequent withdrawals before the Draw are replaced with the fastest of the non-qualifiers. Those who fail to qualify and do not reach the Draw are deemed not to have competed in the Regatta and the names of the athletes are not included in any of the Regatta Records.

In 1998, 324 competitors raced for 96 places in the Regatta. The outcome was that as a result of withdrawals and Qualifying races 311 competitors were put into the Draw from a record 552 entries.

The poor quality of many of those involved in the Qualifying Races in 1998 prompted the ***Stewards*** to review the entry requirements in some of the small ***boats*** events in order to keep the number of those required to qualify to a minimum.

Since 1956 the results of the Eliminating/Qualifying Races have been shown in the ***Regatta Programme*** although since 1975 when the system changed (see above) no times have been shown. Those who qualify are shown in alphabetical order and those who fail are shown in finishing order.

An ***athlete*** who fails to qualify for an event is prohibited from competing for that event by substituting in another crew. See - QUALIFYING RULES and under name of individual ***Regatta trophy*** for details of the limit on the number of entries for each event.

QUALIFYING RULES

There have always been specific rules setting out the qualifying requirements for competitors entering each event.

In December 2000 the ***Stewards*** announced the outcome of a very comprehensive review of the Qualifying Rules. As a result, from 2001, the various events at the Regatta have been grouped under different levels of competence.

The premier events for ***eights***, ***coxless fours***, ***coxed fours*** and ***quadruple sculls*** are, as they were before 2000, respectively, the ***Grand***, ***Stewards'***, ***Prince Philip*** and ***Queen Mother*** Challenge Cups.

The second level is the ***Ladies Challenge Plate*** for eights, the ***Visitors' Challenge Cup*** for coxless fours (there is no comparable level for coxed fours) and the ***Men's Quadruple Sculls***.

The third level is the ***Thames Challenge Cup*** for eights, the ***Wyfold Challenge Cup*** for coxless fours and the ***Britannia*** for coxed fours. (there is no comparable level for quadruple sculls).

The ***Temple Challenge Cup*** for eights is the only event on level four leaving the ***Princess Elizabeth Challenge Cup*** for eights and the ***Fawley Challenge Cup*** for quadruple sculls on level five.

With regard to the three events for women, the ***Henley Prize*** for eights is comparable to the Grand, the ***Women's Quadruple Sculls*** to the Queen Mother and the ***Princess Royal*** to the Diamonds.
See - QUALIFYING RACES and under name of individual ***Regatta Trophy*** for more details.

THE QUEEN MOTHER CHALLENGE CUP

The trophy was so named because the decision to introduce this event in 1981 was taken at a meeting of the ***Stewards*** in 1980, the year Her Majesty Queen Elizabeth the Queen Mother celebrated her 80th birthday.

The event, usually referred to simply as the 'Queen Mother' is the senior ***quadruple sculls*** event at the Regatta - the unrestricted entry qualifications being the same as for the ***Grand***, the ***Stewards'***, the ***Henley Prize*** and the ***Women's Quadruple Sculls***, being for any club ***crew*** of international standard.

The entrance fee for this event is £50 and the Stewards have limited the number of entries to 16.
See - REGATTA TROPHIES

RACE CONTROL

The ***Committee of Management*** sets out the timetable for racing and a small group of ***Stewards*** and officials, known as Race Control, deal with any changes that might be necessary during the day eg. incorporating re-rows into the timetable following ***dead heats***, changing the times of races because of accidents involving competitors.

The main base for Race Control is at the top, ***upstream*** end, of the ***Floating Stand***. Since 1998, Race Control officials have been able to see and listen to proceedings at the start by means of a CCTV camera mounted on a pile near to the ***start platforms***.

RACE RECORDER

See - RACE REPORTS

RACE REPORTER

See - COMMENTARY AT HENLEY

RACE REPORTS

A Timekeeper, assisted by a Race Recorder, follows each race standing in the stern of the Umpire's launch and prepares 'an accurate and unbiased account of the race' on a Race Report sheet - in triplicate.

The position of the race, ie. which competitor is leading and by how much, at each of the ***signals*** and at ***Fawley*** and the Finish, is recorded on the sheet together with the ***Barrier***, Fawley and Finish times

.... 19........ (Day / Date)	RACE NUMBER.................... HOUR....................
EVENT....................................	UMPIRE....................................
Weather....................................	
BERKS (No. 1)	BUCKS (No. 2) ....

	WIND		RATES OF STROKE		LEADER		TIMES TAKEN
	Direction	Force	Berks (No. 1)	Bucks (No. 2)	Station	Distance	
Start	○						
First Minute			¼............. ½............. Full.............	¼............. ½............. Full.............			
¼ Mile	○						
BARRIER							Mins Secs
½ Mile	○						
FAWLEY							Mins Secs
¾ Mile	○						
1 Mile	○						
1⅛ Miles							
FINISH							Mins Secs
JUDGE'S VERDICT	WINNER				Station	Distance	

NOTES:—

....

....

....

....

.... Timekeeper's Signature

The direction and force of the wind at the Start and at the ¼ mile signal, the ½ mile point and the ¾ mile and mile signals are also shown. The yellow pennants on the piles next to the ***signal boxes*** are used to identify the wind direction and to help estimate force eg. nil, light, moderate, strong and very strong.

The ***rate of stroke*** of each of the competitors after ¼, ½ and a full minute of the race are recorded together with the rate of stroke at the ¼ mile signal, the Barrier, the ½ mile point, Fawley, the ¾ mile, mile and $1^1/_8$miles signals and at the Finish.

Throughout the race, details are advised by the Timekeeper/Race Recorder to the member of the ***commentary*** team who also stands at the back of the Umpire's launch and relays them by radio to the commentary point on the top deck of the ***Floating Stand***.

Finally, immediately after the race, after the verdict of the Judges at the Finish has been recorded and a brief report on the race has been added, the Report is signed by the Timekeeper and distributed by ***runners***.

The Race Report is taken to the Committee Room in the ***Secretary's Tent***. A copy is taken to the Results Records team who record the result and times on the ***Results Boards*** in the ***Stewards' Enclosure***. They also advise the ***Henley Standard*** official who is responsible for updating the ***Regatta's Web Site***. The second copy is taken to the ***Boat Tent Area*** where an Official records the result and times on the notice board after which it is taken to the ***Press Tent***.

Various other officials pass the information to the ***Regatta Enclosure***, the Start Officials, the ***Fawley Meadows Hospitality Village*** and ***Temple Island***.

The information in the race reports is subsequently used when compiling the ***Regatta Records*** Books.

From the early days of the Regatta races were timed by an official at the Finish who observed the Start through a telescope. It was the opinion of Mr JF Cooper, ***Secretary of the Regatta*** 1883-1919, that this system was not perfect and that, quote, 'no reliance whatsoever must be placed on the old times as recorded at any rate before the 1880s' unquote. One presumes he meant over the 'Old' ***Regatta Course***, which finished near to ***Henley Bridge***, and before 1886 when the 'New' Course was established.

From 1906 ***Stewards*** have been responsible for timing the races. Race recording duties were undertaken by volunteers until the 1951 Regatta when Stewards were made responsible for these duties as well.

RADIO AND TELEVISION

The BBC first broadcast live radio programmes from the Regatta in 1946 - the commentator being John Snagge who also commentated on the ***University Boat Race***.

Closed circuit television, using a camera at the ***Barrier*** and another at the ***General Enclosure***, was first used at the Regatta in 1963. This was supplemented between 1964 and 1968 when the coverage was linked to the BBC live television broadcast, the BBC using initially four cameras by the ***Regatta Course***, one on an ***umpire's launch*** and one in the area of the Boat Tent.

ITV was awarded a contract for live television coverage in 1971 and 1972.

In 1983 and 1984 Henley again experimented with closed circuit television for the benefit of those in the ***Enclosures*** and the ***Fawley Meadows Hospitality Village***, but it was not a success and was discontinued.

Rowing does not lend itself well to television. This is because it is difficult to show the distance one competitor is ahead of another during a race unless the camera can accompany the race along the side of the Course - which is difficult at Henley. In addition, over long courses such as Henley, a competitor that goes ahead after a couple of minutes racing usually stays ahead, which does not make exciting television.

This was borne out in the 1999 ***Membership Survey*** which highlighted a desire by a small percentage of members of the ***Stewards' Enclosure***, for the return of closed circuit television particularly so that races on the early part of the Regatta Course can be seen in the Enclosure. This was a justifiable response as a recent review has shown that in 82% of races the competitor that is ahead at the ¼ mile ***signal*** stays ahead to win the race. The percentage increases at the ***Barrier*** where 86% of those ahead go on to win.

Notwithstanding this, television camera teams are at Henley each year although in recent years coverage of the Regatta has been restricted to occasional programmes on one or more evenings. These usually consist of live interviews from the river-bank which are intermixed with recordings made earlier, the interest being generally in the personalities and events around the Enclosures rather than the racing.

To maintain the private garden party atmosphere, television cameras are not allowed into the Stewards' Enclosure.

A commercial Radio Station, broadcasting on 107FM was based in the ***Competitors' Car Park*** in 1996.

RAILWAY

Special trains run between London and Henley on the five days of the Regatta in addition to the normal service.

The Regatta owed much of its popularity with the public in Victorian England to the Great Western Railway, which reached Twyford in 1839 the year of the first Regatta. A branch line from Twyford to Henley was opened in 1857.

There were two failed attempts to build a railway across and along the Henley Reach.

In January 1894 speculative plans were published to build a railway from London to Cheltenham and Mid Wales which would involve a line connecting up Marlow, Medmenham, Remenham, Henley, Harpsden, Shiplake, Caversham and Reading; but nothing came of this.

Then, in 1897, the Great Western Railway Company announced plans for a new line to be built between Marlow and Henley thereby providing a route for trains between High Wycombe and Paddington via Marlow and Henley. This would have involved a line from south of Mill Lane, crossing the river using one of the ***eyots***, through ***Thamesfield***, which was to have been a new station, over the London to Oxford road (now the A4130 road) and along an embankment by the side of ***Lion Meadow***.

In the light of the fierce opposition GWR offered a compromise which would have involved a station on the allotments land next to where the ***Henley Cricket Club*** field is now and a tunnel through the hill to Marlow. Eventually the Henley Town Council agreed to the tunnel scheme provided the station was built on the Henley side of the river.

Notwithstanding this the whole idea was still not acceptable to the ***Thames Conservancy***, landowners, oarsmen and many members of Parliament such that in March 1898, GWR withdrew the Bill, much to the regret of the Henley Council.

The ***Chairman*** of the ***Committee of Management*** of the Regatta wrote subsequently to the newspapers thanking those who had assisted in opposing the scheme.

RATE OF STROKE

The Rate of Stroke relates to the number of ***strokes*** taken by a competitor in one minute, generally referred to in the sport as the 'rating'. At Henley, rating is also referred to by the official commentators as the 'rate of striking'.

Rating has been described in rowing books as the 'beat'

but this is not in common use other than in the world of ***drag-on boat*** racing.
See - RACE REPORTS

RECORDING THE RACES
See - RACE REPORTS

RED LION HOTEL
The Red Lion Hotel, a former coaching inn, can be dated back to 1533. It is situated on the corner of Hart Street and ***Riverside***, by ***Henley Bridge*** on the opposite side of the river from ***Leander Club***.

Well known visitors to the Red Lion, which is reputed to be haunted, include Charles I in 1632, the Duke of Marlborough who used it as a stopping point between London and Blenheim, the poet William Shenstone who, it is claimed, wrote a poem on one of the window panes, Dr Samuel Johnson and James Boswell in 1776, and George III in 1788 and the Prince Regent (who became George IV). The Oxford and Cambridge ***crews*** stayed at the Red Lion when they came to Henley in 1829 for the first ***University Boat Race*** and, more recently, Grace Kelly, later to be HSH Princess Grace of Monaco, stayed at the Red Lion in 1947 when her brother JB(Jack) Kelly Jnr won the ***Diamond Challenge Sculls***.

The paved area on Riverside, in front of the Red Lion, is

known as the Red Lion Lawn, and was lawn until the 1980s.

This area, referred to at the time as 'Lion Lawn' marked the Finish of the 'Old' ***Regatta Course*** from 1840, after the finish line used at the first Regatta had been moved about 30yds ***downstream*** of the bridge for safety reasons, to 1885 when it was moved to ***Poplar Point***.

See - CHANTRY HOUSE and ROYALTY

Sir Steven Geoffrey REDGRAVE, CBE

The first Olympian to win Gold Medals at five successive Olympic Games in an endurance sport.

Born 23 March 1962.

Height 1.93m (6ft 4in); Weight 105kg (16½st)

Started rowing at Marlow RC while at Great Marlow School.

First competed at ***Henley Royal Regatta*** in 1980.

Elected a member of ***Leander Club*** 1987 and subsequently made an Honorary Member.
Elected a ***Steward of Henley Royal Regatta*** in 1996 and to the ***Committee of Management*** in December 1998
Made Member of the British Empire (MBE) for Services to Rowing in 1987 and Commander of the British Empire (CBE) in New Year's Honours List 1997.
Announced his retirement from international rowing on 31 October 2000 at the age of 38.
Received a Knighthood for services to rowing in 2001 New Year's Honours List.

OLYMPIC GAMES (5 Golds, 1 Bronze)

1984: Los Angeles - Gold - Coxed Four with MP Cross, RGM Budgett, AJ Holmes and AC Ellison cox.
1988: Seoul - Gold - Coxless Pair with AJ Holmes.
- Bronze - Coxed Pair with AJ Holmes and PJ Sweeney cox.
1992: Barcelona - Gold - Coxless Pair with MC Pinsent.
1996: Atlanta - Gold - Coxless Pair with MC Pinsent.
2000: Sydney - Gold - Coxless Four with JE Cracknell, TJC Foster and MC Pinsent.

HENLEY ROYAL REGATTA ENTRIES (19 wins)

Competed every year from 1980 to 2000 with the exception of Olympic Years 1992 and 1996.

Grand Challenge Cup (*eights*)

Has never competed in this event.

Stewards' Challenge Cup (*coxless four*)

1993 - won - Leander Club and University of London crew with RJ Obholzer, RH Manners & BF Hunt-Davis.
1997 - won - Leander Club and Oxford University crew with JE Cracknell, TJC Foster and MC Pinsent - this was the 2000 GB Olympic Gold Medal winning crew.

1998 - won - Leander Club crew with JE Cracknell, TJC Foster and MC Pinsent - this was the 2000 GB Olympic Gold Medal winning crew.

1999 - won - Leander Club and Queen's Tower Boat Club crew with JE Cracknell, ER Coode and MC Pinsent.

2000 - won - Leander Club crew with JE Cracknell, TJC Foster and MC Pinsent - this was the 2000 GB Olympic Gold Medal winning crew.

Prince Philip Challenge Cup (***coxed four***)

1984 - won - Marlow Rowing Club and University of London Tyrian Club with MP Cross, RGM Budgett, AJ Holmes and AC Ellison cox - this was the 1984 GB Olympic Gold Medal winning crew.

1995 - won - Leander Club with JG Michels, LST Reed, MC Pinsent and N Chugani cox.

Queen Mother Challenge Cup (***quadruple scull***)

1981 - lost in final - Maidenhead Rowing Club and Marlow Rowing Club crew with M Carmichael, DA Clift and ER Sims.

1982 - won - Marlow Rowing Club and Thames Tradesmen's Rowing Club crew with ER Sims, MP Cross and DA Clift.

Silver Goblets & Nickalls' Challenge Cup (***coxless pair***)

1986 - won - Leander Club and Marlow Rowing Club with AJ Holmes - this was the 1988 GB Olympic Gold Medal winning coxless pair.

1987 - won - Leander Club and Marlow Rowing Club with AJ Holmes - this was the 1988 GB Olympic Gold Medal winning coxless pair.

1988 - withdrew after first heat - Leander Club with AJ Holmes who injured a rib in training - this was the 1988 GB Olympic Gold Medal winning coxless pair.

1989 - won - Leander Club with SN Berrisford.
1990 - withdrew before semi-final - Leander Club with SN Berrisford who had a back injury.
1991 - won - Leander Club with MC Pinsent - this was the 1992 and 1996 GB Olympic Gold Medal winning coxless pair.
1993 - won - Leander Club with MC Pinsent - this was the 1992 and 1996 GB Olympic Gold Medal winning coxless pair.
1994 - won - Leander Club with MC Pinsent - this was the 1992 and 1996 GB Olympic Gold Medal winning coxless pair.
1995 - won - Leander Club with MC Pinsent - this was the 1992 and 1996 GB Olympic Gold Medal winning coxless pair.

Double Sculls Challenge Cup

1980 - lost in semi-final - Hollingworth Lake Rowing Club and Marlow Rowing Club with DA Clift.
1981 - won - Maidenhead Rowing Club and Marlow Rowing Club with ER Sims.
1982 - won - Marlow Rowing Club with DA Clift.

Diamond Challenge Sculls (***single scull***)

1983 - won - Marlow Rowing Club.
1985 - won - Marlow Rowing Club.
1986 - lost in final - Marlow Rowing Club.

See - AWESOME FOURSOME, INDOOR ROWING and ROWING HALL OF FAME

REFEREES

Umpires, not 'referees', control ***rowing*** and ***sculling*** events although in the USA umpires are often referred to as referees.

REGATTA AFFILIATION

Since 1958 every regatta that wishes to use the ***ARA*** Rules of Racing, ARA licensed umpires, etc is required to be affiliated to the ARA. ***Henley Royal Regatta***, which has its own ***Constitution and Rules***, is not subject to the ARA Rules of Racing, but has been voluntarily affiliated to the ARA since 1975.

REGATTA COURSE

(See plan on page 16)

One of the reasons Henley was chosen for the first ***University Boat Race*** was because, in 1829, it had the longest stretch of open, relatively straight, water on the ***River Thames***.

So when the people of Henley established the Regatta in 1839, the Course used was from a point 'opposite a ditch in front of the Temple' of ***Temple Island***, ***upstream*** to ***Henley Bridge***, the competitors having to pass under the bridge.

After the first year for safety reasons the finish line was moved about 30yds ***downstream*** of the bridge opposite the steps to the ***Red Lion*** Lawn - where it remained until the 'New Course', with the finish at ***Poplar Point***, was established in 1886. The 'Old Course', used from 1839, was wide enough for more than two competitors to compete in the same race but it was not straight - the bend at Poplar Point favouring the competitor on the ***Berk***s ***station***.

There were many complaints about the Course not being fair because of the bend at Poplar Point and there was even reference in 1851 to problems caused by the remains of a small island, at the head of Temple Island, which acted as a breakwater deflecting the ***stream***. In 1871, to prevent competitors cutting the corner at Poplar Point and then keeping to the ***Berkshire*** bank to avoid the stream, posts with flags on were put in line from the Point to the second arch of Henley

Bridge. Unfortunately one competitor hit the first post and, although the system was tried again in 1872, it was not a success and was abandoned. In 1879, to avoid competitors using the bays on the Berkshire side of the river towards the end of the Course, a rope was strung between posts from a point by Bushy gate (this is the name of a gate on the towpath just upstream from where Remenham Club now stands) and Poplar Point but it was not a success and was not tried again.

An idea was put forward in 1884 to cut off the bend at Poplar Point but this was rejected.

Piles had been used more successfully to mark the Course nearer to the Start and in 1884 and in 1885 piles were used to mark all the bays on the Berkshire side of the river to prevent competitors taking advantage of the slack water. In 1886 both sides of the Course were piled.

The 'New Course' from 1886, was the same length as the Old Course but, at 150ft, was narrower. The width was reduced further still in 1887 to 135ft and in 1888 to 120ft.

The New Course started on the ***Buckinghamshire*** side of the river, near to the downstream end of Temple Island, and finished at Poplar Point where the present Course finishes. Nevertheless it was still not straight having a bend at Remenham Rectory (next to the ***Barrier***) and another just downstream of ***Fawley Court***, although this time the competitors on the ***Bucks*** station had a slight advantage.

In 1897 the width was reduced to 110ft and in 1899, due to the continual accidents between racing ***boats*** and ***pleasure boats*** which had featured regularly since the 1850s, and following the problems in 1897 and 1898 when the Course had to be adjusted to accommodate a fallen tree, ***booms*** were used between the piles along most of the Buckinghamshire side of the Course from the Barrier to the Finish, and partly on the

Berkshire side - with sliding booms to allow pleasure boats to cross. This was a big success and in 1900 booms were used to mark the Course along the length of Temple Island and in 1902 more booms were added to the Berkshire side.

This not only solved much of the pleasure boat problem, it made the Course much fairer. Then, in 1897, problems associated with the '***bushes*** wind' were first recorded. This relates to the possible benefit afforded to competitors on the Bucks station as a result of the protection from the wind given by the trees and bushes on the Buckinghamshire side of the river downstream from Fawley.

But the Course still wasn't straight, having the two slight bends, one by the ***Barrier*** and one by ***Fawley Boathouse***.

Before the 1923 Regatta, ½acre of Berkshire bank and some of Temple Island were removed with the agreement of Lord Hambleden and Mr WD Mackenzie respectively. This enabled the 'Experimental' Course to be used in 1923. It started halfway up the Berkshire side of Temple Island, using the 'barge channel' as it had been referred to, and finished a little upstream of Poplar Point. It was 80ft wide and 110yds shorter than the previous courses - but it was straight.

The present 'Straight Course' has been used since 1924. It starts at the downstream end of Temple Island on the Berkshire side and finishes at Poplar Point.

The possibility of widening the Course to enable three or four boat racing has been considered from time to time and rejected by the ***Stewards***. In 1970 the Regatta gave serious consideration to a four lane racing course and looked at three options. They were all dropped, two because the owners of the land that would have needed to have been purchased refused to sell, and the third because it would have required the removal of Poplar Point and much of the ***Stewards' Enclosure***.

In 1961 marker ***buoys*** were used in the gaps in the booms and in 1962 buoys, 50ft apart (reduced to 40ft in 1963), were used to mark the sides of the Course from the Start to the ¼ mile signal. In 1970, because of the high replacement cost of the 60ft booms, the Course was buoyed from the Start to Fawley. Since 1981 and the continued improvement in the finances of the Regatta, the Course has again been boomed from the top of Temple Island.

The present Course is just wide enough for three crews to 'row' side by side with their blade tips almost touching, as instanced at the sesquicentennial (150th) celebrations on 14th

June 1989 when the first race for the Town Cup was re-enacted. Nevertheless it has not been wide enough for three competitors to 'race' together side by side since before 1886, although the Henley Rules still take the precaution of stipulating that ' no more than two boats shall contend in any one heat.'

The traditional length of the Course has always been 1mile 550yds (2,112m or 1mile, 2furlongs and 5chains!) although before 1967 the actual distance between the Start and Finish posts was 1mile 570yds. Between 1891 and 1966, boats were started with their 'sterns' at the starting post (referred to in the sport as a 'sterns-on' start). Therefore the ***bow*** of an ***eight*** (an eight being traditionally 60ft or 20yds long) would travel 1mile 550yds to the Finish. The bows of small boats travelled further. To ensure boats started level, each was measured before they raced and ***umpires*** were issued with details of the lengths of boats in each race. They then instructed the men in the ***stake boats*** (predecessors of the ***start floats*** and the ***start platforms***) to pull the longer of the two boats back by an appropriate amount.

This anomaly over the distance the boats travelled was removed in 1967 when the fixed stake boats were changed to moving 'start floats'. The bows of all boats could then be aligned on the same point (bows-on start), 1mile 550yds from the Finish - effectively giving the smaller boats a slightly shorter distance to travel than hitherto.

The position of the ***Fawley Box***, which used to be exactly halfway between the Start and Finish 'posts', remained unchanged so is now 60ft nearer to the new start line than the finish line.

In 2000 the start floats were replaced with floating start platforms although the aligning principle remained unchanged.

The strength of the stream and the direction of the wind can give one competitor a slight advantage over the other but generally the effects are minimal. The Stewards are ever anxious to ensure the Course is 'fair' and publish figures each year in the ***Regatta Programme*** showing the number of races that have taken place since the Second World War and the percentage of wins on each station excluding ***dead heats*** and races ***not rowed out***. Of the 10,133 races up to and including the 2000 Regatta, 51.48% were wins on the ***Berks*** station and 48.52% on ***Bucks***. The wins at the 1995 and 1997 Regattas were divided evenly between the stations.

Times are recorded at the Barrier (2,089ft from the start), Fawley (3,435ft from the start) and the Finish. The Fawley time is then shown in large numbers on the upstream side of the Fawley Box for the benefit of spectators in the Enclosures.

There are five ***Signal Boxes*** along the Course each with a wooden frame 13ft (4m) high. By positioning the boards in the frame the signal shows the position of the race at that point. In addition there is a box at Fawley, a ***Progress Board***, which has a ***Photographers' Platform*** on the upstream side, opposite the ***Grandstand*** in the Stewards' Enclosure, and a ***Judges' Box*** on the finish line. All these structures, with the exception of the ¾ mile signal are on the Buckinghamshire side of the Course so that spectators in the ***Grandstand*** in the Stewards' Enclosure can see them clearly. The ¾ mile signal is the exception because if it were positioned on the Buckinghamshire side it would block the view of the time boards on the Fawley Box.

Upstream of the Finish are the ***Stewards' Box*** and the ***Press Box*** on the Berkshire side and the ***Photographers' Box/Result's Box*** on the Buckinghamshire side - which is Oxfordshire at this point.

From the Wednesday before the Regatta until the end of the Regatta ***crews*** and ***scullers*** training on the Course are requested not to obstruct others. Those coming up the Course have absolute right of way at all times over those ahead of them.

Between 1920 and 1989 the Course was built by a small group of men employed by ***Hobbs and Sons***. Since 1990, the team has worked for ***Freeboom***, the company established by the supervisor, John Fenn.

Work on the Course commences in April when sighting posts are put in at the Start and Finish for the Berkshire line of booms. Until recently their positions in the river were located by tape measure coupled with aligning them, with the aid of a telescope, with the third drainpipe on the wall of the building next to the ***Little White Hart Hotel*** on ***Riverside***. The present system of ensuring two straight lines of piles and booms covering the 1mile 550yds of the Course, which is now a universally recognised feature of the Regatta, is a closely guarded trade secret!

Removing the piles, booms and buoys and all the associated timber involved in constructing the Regatta Course as well as the various boxes and walkways, and storing them under ***Regatta Headquarters***, takes a little over a month.

REGATTA ENCLOSURE

The Regatta Enclosure is situated on the Berkshire bank ***downstream*** from the ***Stewards' Enclosure***. It was established in 1971 by merging the ***General*** and ***Public Enclosures***.

Members of the public may purchase ***badges*** at the gate subject to availability - in the interest of safety and to avoid overcrowding, the number of badges available daily is limited to 2,000. A Regatta Enclosure badge will entitle the wearer to enter the ***Boat Tent Area***. The colours of the Regatta Enclosure badges, like the colours of the Guests badges for the Stewards' Enclosure and the covers of the ***Regatta Programmes***, are changed daily and are issued in pink, green, grey, yellow and blue.

Competitors, 'non rowing' journalists and children under the age of 14 are allowed in free of charge, and there is a facility for 'baby changing'.

The Regatta Enclosure is very informal and there are no dress regulations but picnics, dogs, televisions, tape recorders and portable radios are not permitted. There are restaurant facilities in the Enclosure and a licensed bar provided by

London Catering Services who manage the Regatta Brasserie where a table can be reserved for lunch or for the whole day. There is also a Grandstand although seats cannot be reserved.

REGATTA HEADQUARTERS

Regatta Headquarters is the building on the ***Berkshire*** side of the river next to ***Henley Bridge*** opposite the ***Angel on the Bridge*** public house

Before the Second World War the Regatta operated from a number of premises including 24 Market Place in Henley.

In 1940, when 24 Market Place was commandeered for war use, the office moved to Wargrave and then to the Conservative Club at 74 St James's Street, London. In October 1945 the ***Regatta*** acquired the lease of Baltic Cottage in Henley on the corner of ***Thames Side*** and Friday Street and moved back to Henley. The lease on Baltic Cottage expired in December 1964 but the Regatta was permitted to remain there until March 1966 when it moved to the Henley Squash and Badminton Club for a few months before taking up residence in the ***Stewards' Enclosure*** earlier than normal for the 1966 Regatta. The Office returned briefly to Friday Street before moving to rooms at the back of ***Leander Club*** in September 1966 for seven months. The Office then moved into Bridge House immediately opposite the entrance to

Leander Way, on 4 April 1967 having purchased it in 1962. This then became the Official Regatta Headquarters and was renamed Regatta House.

Financial problems subsequently necessitated the need to sell Regatta House and to move again. Between 1975 and 1985 the Regatta again used two rooms in Leander Club, expanding into temporary cabins in the Regatta's car park behind Leander during the weeks leading up to the Regatta.

With the improvement in the Regatta's finances in the early 1980s, the Regatta purchased the derelict ***Carpenters Arms*** public house on the southeast corner of Henley Bridge in 1983. The Carpenters Arms was subsequently demolished and the present Headquarters built using that site, together with the site of the adjacent boathouse (which had been leased by the Regatta from 1864 until it had been purchased in 1904). The new building was designed by the Terry Farrell Partnership and built by JM Jones Limited, at a cost in the region of £1.2m.

The new building was opened on 16 April 1986 by Her Majesty The Queen, Patron of the Regatta, accompanied by His Royal Highness Prince Philip, Duke of Edinburgh.

Regatta Headquarters' unique design has won many awards including the Financial Times Architecture at Work Award in 1987, the Royal Institute of British Architects Architecture Award in 1988 and a Wokingham District Council Design Award in 1994.

Regatta Headquarters, as with the Angel on the Bridge on the opposite side of the river, has within its basement, 5m ***upstream*** of Henley Bridge, one of the stone arches of the original bridge believed to date from 1170.

Regatta Headquarters has three levels. There is a store and wet dock on the ground floor, with four overhead electric gantries for lifting heavy equipment from the barges. The middle floor has a large Committee room overlooking the river, a shop and a storage area as well as offices for the ***Chairman***, ***Secretary*** and the five permanent staff. The ***Badge Office*** is situated in the front of the building to the left of the entrance, with the office on the right-hand side being used for most of the year by ***Sodexho Prestige***, the company that manages the official ***Fawley Meadows Hospitality Village*** and the facilities offered during the Regatta on ***Temple Island***. The office used by Sodexho Prestige becomes the ***Crews***' Enquiry Office from the beginning of June and is occupied by the team dealing with Entries. The upper floor contains the ***Regatta Secretary's*** accommodation.

Regatta Headquarters is closed on weekends and Bank Holidays, and from the Thursday before, until the Wednesday after, the Regatta.

Apart from these dates:-

· the ***Secretary's Office*** and the shop for the sale of ***Regatta Merchandise*** in Regatta Headquarters are open to the public from 9.30am to 1pm and 2pm to 5pm, Monday to Friday, and

· the Badge Office in Regatta Headquarters is open to the public from 1 May until the Thursday before the Regatta from 10am to 1pm and 2pm to 4pm Monday to Friday.

See - ROYALTY

REGATTA LOTTERY

Between 1976 and 1985 a Lottery was organised each year by the ***Stewards***, the proceeds of which were devoted to Regatta funds

REGATTA MAGAZINE

There are three magazines that have this title:-

· The Royal Regatta produced its own magazine to mark the

sesquicentennial (150th) anniversary of the Regatta in 1989, and it was known as the Regatta's Magazine,

· The official magazine published by the ***Amateur Rowing Association*** which is distributed to all registered members of the ***ARA***, is titled ***Regatta Magazine***, and

· The Henley Regatta Magazine, which is an independent magazine, published annually by Watts Media Limited of Watlington who publish County Magazine, and has no connection with the Regatta other than the name.

REGATTA MEMENTOES

See - REGATTA MERCHANDISE

REGATTA MERCHANDISE

In 1976, as a means of increasing income, a Regatta shop was established and in 1987 the trading arm of the regatta, ***Henley Royal Regatta Limited***, was formed. Since then the sale of Regatta related merchandise has grown and can be bought throughout the year.

The three shops on the Regatta site are located:-

· within the ***Stewards' Enclosure*** behind the ***Grandstand***, which is open during the five days of the Regatta,

· by the main entrance to the ***Boat Tent Area***, this shop with public access, is open from the Friday, ***Qualifying Races*** day, to the Sunday, Finals Day, of the Regatta, and

· in the ***Fawley Meadows Hospitality Village*** which is open during the five days of the Regatta.

Outside the Regatta period, merchandise can be purchased from ***Regatta Headquarters*** during normal office hours (9.30am to 1pm and 2pm to 5pm, Monday to Friday) or by mail-order. The ***Regatta's web site***, www.hrr.co.uk, also has shop pages where items can be purchased on-line.

Members of the Stewards' Enclosure are regularly advised of additions to the range of goods on sale and those wishing to add their names to the non-Members mailing list for merchandise can do so by contacting Regatta Headquarters.

REGATTA PROGRAMME

A Programme is produced each day by the Regatta and has been printed by local printers ***Higgs & Co*** since 1886.

The Programme includes a list of the races for the day, details of the competitors in each race and the ***Draw*** for each event. Since 1886 it has also shown the weights of the ***athletes*** and ***coxswains*** in st (stones) and lb (pounds) and, since 1947, the average weights, excluding coxswains, of ***eights***, ***fours*** and, since 1981, ***quads***.

The Programme also shows statistical and historical information about the Regatta and the ***Regatta Trophies***, and, after the first day, gives the results of all races on previous days. It also provides details of the Programme of Music to be played throughout the day by the band in the ***Stewards' Enclosure***.

Questions are sometimes asked as to why the competitor on the No 2 station is listed first in the Programme. This is because, traditionally, the first name drawn for each race has the ***Berks*** (***Berkshire***) No 1 ***station*** which is on the left of the ***Regatta Course*** from the race ***umpire's*** perspective. However a spectator in the ***Enclosures*** looking down at the race as set out in the Programme and then across and down the river at the race, expects to see the competitor, furthest away from him in the Programme, to be furthest away from him on the Course (on the Bucks No 2 station), with the competitor closest to him (on the Berks No 1 station), to be listed closest to him in the Programme.

The colours of the covers of the Regatta Programmes, like the colours of the Guests badges for the Stewards' Enclosure and the badges for the ***Regatta Enclosure***, are changed daily and are issued in pink, green, grey, yellow and blue.

Programmes are on sale each day from kiosks on the Regatta site and from tents inside the Stewards' and Regatta Enclosures.
See - WEIGHING-IN and WEIGHTS AND MEASURES

REGATTA RECORDS

The Official Records Books of the Regatta have been published since 1903 giving details of all Regattas since 1839. These include individual races, the names of competitors, the ***weather*** conditions, a summary of each Regatta and the changes that have taken place during the year. Since 1841 the weights of competitors have been shown and, since 1947, the average weights (excluding the ***coxswains***) of ***eights***, ***fours*** and, since 1981, ***quads***. ***Fawley*** times have been shown since 1903 and ***Barrier*** times since 1929 although Barrier times may have been taken before 1928 and not entered in the records.

Records Books covering recent years, together with a limited number of volumes relating to earlier Regattas can be purchased from the ***Regatta Shop***. (See full list of titles of Regatta Records Books at the end of this book)

'Regatta Records' can also refer to the ***fastest recorded times*** that competitors have travelled over the Regatta Course, the penultimate entry in the ***Regatta Programme***.

REGATTA SECRETARY

See - SECRETARY OF THE REGATTA

REGATTA SERVICE

Since the 1930s a special service for those attending the Regatta has taken place in ***St Mary's Church***.

Until 1974 the Regatta Service took place at 10am on the Sunday before the Regatta but changed to the Sunday of finals day in 1974. The service is usually conducted by the Rector of St Mary's and the ***Committee of Management*** invite the 'preacher' but do not influence his subject, resulting in the parable of the unjust steward often being selected as the theme!

REGATTA SHOP

See - REGATTA MERCHANDISE

REGATTA SOUVENIRS

See - REGATTA MERCHANDISE

REGATTA TROPHIES

The Regatta offers 19 events which are competed for annually, 16 of which have trophies - The Grand Challenge Cup, The Ladies' Challenge Plate, The Thames Challenge Cup, The Temple Challenge Cup and The Princess Elizabeth Challenge Cup for eights. The Stewards' Challenge Cup, The Visitors' Challenge Cup and The Wyfold Challenge Cup for coxless fours. The Prince Philip Challenge Cup and The Britannia Challenge Cup for coxed fours. The Queen Mother Challenge Cup and The Fawley Challenge Cup for quadruple sculls. The Silver Goblets and Nickalls' Challenge Cup for coxless pairs. The Double Sculls Challenge Cup and, for single sculls, The Diamond Challenge Sculls. The event for the Men's Quadruple Sculls (new in 2001) does not have a trophy

There are three events for women, the Henley Prize for eights, the Women's Quadruple Sculls (new in 2001) and The Princess Royal Challenge Cup for single sculls - the Princess Royal being the only one that has a trophy.

See under names of individual trophies/events for more details

(Note: The names of the Henley Royal Regatta trophies and events are interrelated, the abbreviated name of a trophy often being used to describe an event eg. it is acceptable to say that the Grand [the Grand Challenge Cup] is the senior event at the Regatta, and an entry in the Diamonds [the Diamond Challenge Sculls] means an entry in the men's single sculling event)

Each winning athlete receives a medal except for the winners of the Goblets and the Diamonds who each receive cups and the winner of the Princess Royal who receives a miniature, crossed ***sculls***, brooch.

From the beginning, the Regatta trophies, as at most Regattas, were taken away by the winners who retained them for a year. While waiting to be presented with their trophy at the ***Prize*** Giving Ceremony, winning ***athletes*** would sign a guarantee that they would ensure the trophy was properly engraved and returned before the next Regatta.

The ***Stewards*** decided in 1975, after difficulties had been experienced returning trophies from overseas, that no trophy would leave the UK. This rule was extended a few years later and now all trophies presented to the winning finalists are recovered after the Ceremony and kept by the Regatta. Each winner receives a photograph of the trophy and special arrangements are made if a trophy is requested for a particular function eg. an annual dinner or crew reunion.

The full names of the winners are engraved on the trophies and written/printed into the ***Books of Honour*** that accompany the Grand and Prince Philip Challenge Cups.

When not in the ***Prize Tent*** in the ***Stewards' Enclosure*** the Grand (the original Cup) and a changing display of others, including a Diamonds 'pineapple' Cup and the case containing the Diamond Challenge Sculls are on display in ***Regatta***

Headquarters. The trophies not on display are kept in secure storage

The Royal Regatta refers to its trophies, and the ***medals*** and cups presented to winners, as prizes.
See - CHALLENGE CUPS

REGATTA WEATHER

The Regatta is often remembered for its extremes of weather.

Heavy rain with thunder and lightning was recorded at the first Regatta in 1839 and has featured at Henley on numerous occasions ever since. Indeed many Regattas before the First World War were held in torrential rain.

In recent times the wet Regattas of 1963 and 1988 when the ***enclosures*** became mud baths, and the strong ***stream*** of 1968 (the strongest since 1883 when records were started) which swept away many of the fixed landing stages, are well documented. The water level in 1968, when 3½ inches of rain fell in 12 hours, was also higher than at any other Regatta since records began.

Following the very wet Regatta of 1988, emergency ***Pedestrian Walkways*** have been hired by the Regatta each year and kept in store on site in case of need. They were first laid in the ***Stewards' Enclosure*** in 1991.

The ***Qualifying Races*** of 1994 saw one of the more dramatic changes in the weather in living memory on the Henley Reach. On that Friday the hot sunny afternoon gave way at around 7.30pm to a very violent thunderstorm, the heavy rain and low cloud reducing visibility to almost zero for some fifteen minutes. There were around 70 competitors on the water at the time and many had to take refuge on the fields around ***Temple Island*** to avoid sinking. No one was injured but racing had to be adjourned until the next morning.

There have also been some very hot and humid Regattas. In 1976, with the temperature in excess of 90ºF (32.2ºC) and with high humidity, gentlemen in the Stewards' Enclosure were allowed to remove their jackets - the one and only occasion this has been permitted.

Generally speaking, and apart from the extremes referred to above, the weather, particularly rain, whilst naturally causing concern to spectators, has a minimal effect on the racing.

The Regatta does not take out wet weather insurance cover.

See - FLOODING

REGATTA WEB SITE

In 1999 the Regatta established its own Web site, www.hrr.co.uk. This site contains general information about the Regatta and, as soon as they are available, details of the ***Entries*** and the ***Draw***. The racing results and the daily timetable are published each day as soon as they are available.

REMENHAM

Remenham embraces most of the land on the ***Berkshire*** side of the river from ***Hambleden Lock*** and Aston Ferry, to the

Church of St Nicholas

fields along the Wargrave Road as far as ***Marsh Lock*** and, going back from the river to the houses at the top of ***White Hill***.

The actual village of Remenham is small, the centre being the Church of St Nicholas situated at the fork in ***Remenham Lane*** near to the ***Barrier***.

REMENHAM CLUB

Remenham Club is situated on the ***Berkshire*** bank just ***downstream*** of the 1mile ***signal*** on the ***Regatta Course***. The Club, (Remenham Club Limited), was formed in 1909 by Members of the Metropolitan and up-river clubs, London, Thames, Twickenham, Molesey, Kingston, Staines and Vesta, as a meeting place at Henley for past and present rowing men, their families and personal friends.

The Clubhouse was built in 1911. Members of the Club must have competed for their Founding Club at Henley Royal Regatta or in other regattas to indicate to the Committee a proficiency in oarsmanship.

REMENHAM COURT

This is the white Georgian house, also known as 'Remenham Lodge' and 'The White House', which lies back from the river on the side of the hill opposite the mile signal. The estate includes the meadow between the house and the river next to the ***Regatta Enclosure***.

In 1957 the ***Stewards*** considered purchasing the property for ***Regatta Headquarter***s and would have used the meadow in the front and ***Green's Field***, which was also part of the estate, for car parking. In the event the Stewards did not proceed partly because of the price and partly because Green's Field had grazing rights, which might have prevented it being used as a car park - although a year later they bought Green's Field and bought out the grazing rights.

The late Richard Burnell, in his book *Henley Royal Regatta, A celebration of 150 years*, published in 1989 when corporate hospitality was at its peak and when the meadow was being used privately for this purpose, expressed strong views on this decision. Burnell, a 1948 Olympic Gold medallist and a ***Steward of the Regatta*** from 1966, wrote that in his opinion the ***Committee of Management***, of whom his father the late Lieut.-Colonel CD Burnell, DSO, OBE, was a member at the time, 'made a blunder of some magnitude' in not proceeding with the purchase. He considered, admittedly with hindsight, that it would have been 'the best bargain Henley ever bought'.

THE REMENHAM CUP
See - ROYAL HENLEY PEACE REGATTA

REMENHAM FARM

Remenham Farm, which is owned by the Copas Partnership, covers most of the land on the Berkshire side of the river, from a point opposite the ***Fawley Boathouse*** inlet, ***down-stream*** past ***Hambleden Lock*** to the Flower Pot landing stage. The landing stage is the site of the Aston Ferry, which operated until the 1950s

The Regatta declined to bid for the purchase of Remenham Farm when it was up for sale in 1957 and did not bid when it was sold to the Copas family in 1976.

During the Regatta the land downstream of the ***Barrier*** is used for the ***Temple Island Enclosure***. The land ***upstream***, between the Barrier and a point opposite the ***Fawley Box***, is

used for private car parking and as a public amenity area.
See - COPAS LAND

REMENHAM LANE

Remenham Lane runs from the A4130 road at the bottom of

White Hill by the Little Angel Inn, to Remenham Church.

During the Regatta the Lane is restricted to one way traffic giving access to the Official Regatta ***car parks*** and to parking on land owned by ***Remenham Farm***. There is public footpath access to the ***towpath*** at the ***Barrier*** for pedestrians via the road to the left of the Church and, during the Regatta, for cars with access to Remenham Farm and to the private enclosure by the start of the ***Regatta Course*** (***Temple Island Enclosure***).

RESCUE LAUNCHES

The Colwick Park Lifeguard Club of Nottingham provides the four rescue launches used during the five days of the Regatta and at the ***Qualifying Races***.

REST TENT

See - CREWS' LOUNGE

RESULTS BOARDS

Full results of all races are exhibited throughout each day on the two Results Boards in the ***Stewards' Enclosure*** (situated between the ***Secretary's Tent*** and the ***Grandstand*** and between the ***Grandstand*** and the ***Fawley Stand***). Results are also recorded on a board by the Boat Tent Official's Tent in the ***Boat Tent Area*** and on the side of the Stand in the ***Regatta Enclosure***. There are also Results Boards in the ***Fawley Meadows Hospitality Village***, on ***Temple Island*** and on the Tent of the ***Start Judge/Aligner*** at the start of the ***Regatta Course***.

RESULTS' BOX

See - PHOTOGRAPHERS' BOX

RIGGER

The bracket (referred to originally as an outrigger) fixed to the side of a racing ***boat*** to hold the ***oar/scull*** (which fits into the rowlock which is a form of gate, which swivels on a pin at the furthest point from the side of the boat).

RIPARIAN OWNER

A Riparian owner is one who owns the river-bank. Such ownership normally carries with it ownership of the river bed to the centre line of the river.

THE RIVER AND ROWING MUSEUM

The Museum, consisting of three main galleries dedicated to the history of the ***River Thames***, to Rowing and to the Town of ***Henley***, is situated on the Henley town side of the river on ***Mill Meadows***. The site is ½ mile ***upstream*** from ***Henley Bridge*** and on the opposite side of the river to ***Henley Rowing Club***.

The ***Stewards of the Regatta*** were advised in November 1948 of a plan to establish a Rowing Museum and Library in Henley. They were unable to support this but did offer non-financial help if it were to be a museum of a general nature of which rowing formed a part; but nothing came of the plan.

Then, nearly forty years later, Christopher Dodd, rowing journalist, author and Editor of ***Regatta Magazine***, and David Lunn-Rockliffe retired Chief Executive of the ***Amateur Rowing Association*** instigated their idea of a rowing museum in January 1988. A meeting subsequently took place under the Chairmanship of Peter Coni, OBE,QC, ***Chairman*** of the Regatta's ***Committee of Management*** and member of the Executive Committee of the ARA, to explore the idea of a National Rowing Museum.

The original 'Steering' Committee included Diana Cook, antiquarian bookseller, Roger Davis, Chairman of the Rowing Foundation (a Charity set up by the ARA to help junior rowing), John Howard, Henley Councillor and ***Steward*** of the Regatta, Dr Richard Marks, Director of the Brighton Pavilion, Dr Noel Snell, former Mayor of Henley, Richard Way, Boat Builder and Restorer, Charlie Wiggin, Accountant and Ivan Pratt, Chief Executive of the ARA.

The scope of the Museum was subsequently expanded to include the ***River Thames*** and Henley. Mill Meadows was selected in 1989 as the most suitable site and the Town Council agreed a lease requiring a token annual rental of a single rose; but sadly Peter Coni and Roger Davis had died before the lease was signed in 1994.

The 'Steering' Committee was subsequently replaced with a Board of Trustees and the finished building was opened to the public by local resident Phillip Schofield on Saturday 29 August 1998.

Her Majesty The Queen opened the museum officially on

6 November 1998, nearly eleven years after the idea had first been put forward.

The Museum, situated on the Henley Flood plain and designed by David Chipperfield architects to resemble a boat-house, is built on piles to prevent any problems in the event of the river flooding. The cost, which at the outset was expected to be less than £4m, had risen to around £20m by the time the building was finished. With two Lottery applications declined, a range of individuals and organisations provided the financing, the largest contributor being the Arbib Foundation. The Museum was fortunate that Martyn Arbib, Founder and Chairman of the Henley based company Perpetual plc, was Deputy Chairman of the Steering Committee and subsequently the Board of Trustees.

The Museum has received many awards, including the RIBA award for Architecture, the National Heritage's 'Museum of the Year' in November 1999 and 'Building of the Year' in June 2000 by the Royal Fine Arts Commission Trust.

The Thames Gallery provides a comprehensive guide to the river including information on its ecology, economy, geology, history, navigation and wildlife.

The Rowing Gallery traces the quest for speed by manually propelled craft from the age of the Athenian Trireme (Greek warship propelled by three decks of rowers) to the latest Olympic achievements. Among artifacts in the Rowing Gallery is the ***boat*** used by Oxford to win the first ***University Boat Race*** at Henley in 1829; and the boat used by ***Steven Redgrave*** and Matthew Pinsent to win the ***Olympic Coxless Pairs*** title, Great Britain's only gold medal in any sport in the Atlanta Games in 1996.

Henley Royal Regatta was the first corporate member of the Museum's ***Rowing Hall of Fame***.

The Henley Gallery tells the story of the town from its earliest times to the present day, with particular emphasis on the Regatta for which the town is famous.

The Museum and its Riverside Café are open daily from 10am throughout the year except Christmas Eve, Christmas Day, New Year's Eve and New Year's Day.

Conferences, weddings and social functions for up to 100 people can be held in the Thames room and the whole museum is available for evening functions, private viewings and receptions.

RIVER THAMES

The river was named ***Tamesis*** in Roman times and Temese by the Anglo-Saxons.

The river flows 220miles (354km), from its source 15miles ***upstream*** of Cricklade Bridge, to the sea - and falls 234ft (71m).

This statue of 'Thames' (Old Father Thames) is at St John's

Lock, the first Thames lock, 10miles ***downstream*** from Cricklade.

Although the river flows from Gloucestershire in the west to London in the east, it meanders to such a great extent that from ***Marsh Lock*** to ***Henley Bridge*** the river has turned through 135° and is flowing from South East to North West.

In 1770, rather than make the whole river more navigable, the Thames Navigation Commissioners considered constructing a canal from Sonning to Isleworth effectively bypassing Henley. Members of the clergy on the investigating committee objected to this but were then criticised for their lack of knowledge of river matters. So they nominated the Reverend Humphrey Gainsborough, minister at the Congregational Chapel in Henley and brother of Thomas Gainsborough the painter to represent their interests. Humphrey Gainsborough subsequently designed and superintended the construction of all the locks in the vicinity of Henley including Sonning, Shiplake, Marsh, Hambleden, Temple, Marlow and Boulters. The idea of a canal was not raised again.

The river '***stream***' flows from Marsh Lock through Henley Bridge, down the ***Regatta Course*** and past ***Temple Island*** to ***Hambleden Lock***. Thus the competitors at the Royal Regatta, and at all other rowing events held on the ***Henley Reach***, except for the ***Henley Boat Races*** and the Boxing Day Eights races at ***Henley Rowing Club,*** race upstream. They also race 'uphill' as the river is approximately 5cm (2 inches) higher at the finish of the Regatta Course than it is at the start of the Course at the bottom of Temple Island!

The 150 miles (241km) of non-tidal, freshwater between the source of the river and the Teddington Boundary Obelisk, beyond which the river is the responsibility of the Port of London Authority, provides much of the domestic water used in the Thames Valley and $^{2}/_{3}$ of London's drinking water.

The river at Henley is not tidal.

See - ENVIRONMENT AGENCY - THAMES REGION

RIVER THAMES SOCIETY

The River Thames Society was established in 1962 as a Registered Charity for the protection and promotion of the river.

The aims of the Society are:-

· To protect the natural beauty of the river, adjacent lands and buildings of historical and architectural interest and to promote nature conservation,

· To support and contribute to the efforts of other organisations with similar interests in the river, and

· To preserve and extend amenities and to encourage the use of the river for all purposes.

The RTS is divided into 6 branches enabling it to monitor all activity on the water and along the banks. This includes checking planning applications from the source to the sea through its River Warden Scheme. Each branch organises meetings and other social activities during the year and the Society publishes its own quarterly Journal *'Thames Guardian'*. The ***Henley Reach*** is in the 'Middle Thames' branch of the RTS.

Over the years the RTS has been responsible for establishing the concept of the Thames Barrier, the nine River Users Groups and, in 1978, the Thames Heritage Trust.

RIVER USERS GROUPS

The ***River Thames Society***, with the co-operation of the Thames Water Authority (now the ***Environment Agency***) established nine RUGs. These comprise of representatives of organisations that have an interest in ensuring the river and the banks of the river are not spoilt in any way.

The nine RUGs cover the river from Cricklade to Tower Bridge.

The ***Henley Reach*** is watched over by RUG Area 6, which

is responsible for the stretch from ***Marsh Lock*** to Boulters Lock (Maidenhead).

RIVERSIDE

This stretch of river-bank, road and properties, also known as 'Waterside', is on the town (Oxfordshire) side of the river between ***Henley Bridge*** and the bottom of ***New Street***/Wharf Lane - opposite the Regatta ***Boat Tent Area***.

Until 1886 when the ***Regatta Course*** finished at the bridge, large stands for spectators were built along this road. After the Finish moved to ***Poplar Point***, the corner where Riverside joins New Street continued to be a convenient location for local people to watch the Regatta.

Brakspear's Henley Brewery own much of Riverside and in 2000 put forward plans to build a pedestrian walkway along the edge of the river from the ***Angel on the Bridge*** public house, under Henley Bridge to New Street.

ROD EYOT

This is the first ***island downstream*** of ***Marsh Lock*** (the phonetic pronunciation is usually 'eye-ot' although occasionally 'eight' or 'ait').

Rod Eyot, situated in the middle of the river, is the only

island of the five on the ***Henley Reach*** that is inhabited.

There is another island immediately downstream of Rod Eyot (see picture below) but this has no name and, in recent

years, has been almost washed away as a result of strong streams and high water levels in the winter.
See - EYOT

ROW OVER

In the event of a competitor being unable to race, the opponent of that competitor is required to row over the ***Regatta Course*** at the appointed time. If there is only one entry in an event or if all except one withdraw or are unable to compete, the remaining competitor must row over the Course to be entitled to receive the trophy.

ROWERS

Athletes who row rather than ***scull***.

ROWING

Rowing is Britain's oldest team sport.
Rowers propel a ***boat*** with one ***oar*** each. ***Scullers*** have a ***scull*** in each hand. Rowing is occasionally referred to as sweep-oared rowing.

There are three types of boat used by rowers - a ***pair***, a ***four*** and an ***eight***.

'Rowing' is also the name given to one of the actions of a ***crew*** in moving the boat, 'rowing' being faster than '***paddling***'.
(Note: The oars used in rowing should be referred to as oars or blades but not as sculls)
See - ATHLETES

ROWING CLUBS ON THE HENLEY REACH
There are three rowing clubs on the ***Henley Reach*** - ***Henley Rowing Club***, ***Leander Club*** and ***Upper Thames Rowing Club***.

Phyllis Court Club is not a rowing club but has a rowing section for its members, with a boating area at the ***downstream*** end of the Club land.

ROWING HALL OF FAME
This relates to a list of persons and institutions considered by a group organised by the ***River and Rowing Museum at Henley***, as great performers, great coaches or great 'shapers' of rowing.

Launched in 1997, the first performers to be recognised were ***Steven Redgrave*** and Matthew Pinsent and the first institution was ***Henley Royal Regatta***.

ROWLOCK RALLY
Established in 1969 by Henley Round Table, the Rowlock Rally is a race by some 50 boats, mainly ***skiffs***, from Oxford to Henley, usually in April to raise funds for Round Table charities.

ROYAL HENLEY PEACE REGATTA
No official Regattas were held in the five years between 1915

and 1919 inclusive.

On Saturday 5 July 1919 the ***Stewards*** organised a Peace Regatta known as the Royal Henley Peace Regatta, to distinguish it from the usual Regatta. It was held over four days and 10 specially commissioned trophies were offered.

- The King's Cup for ***eights*** for ***crews*** consisting of Allied forces,
- The Fawley Cup with an entry requirement similar to the ***Thames Cup***,
- The Elsenham Cup which was similar to the ***Ladies' Challenge Plate***,
- The Leander Cup for Allied Forces ***fours***,
- The Wargrave Manor Cup which was similar to the ***Wyfold Challenge Cup***,
- The ***Public Schools Cup*** which was for fixed ***seat*** clinker fours, the trophy being brought back from Marlow Regatta for the occasion,
- The Hambleden Pairs,
- The Kingswood Sculls,
- The Remenham Cup for clinker eights, and
- The Temple Cup for clinker fours (these last two being held over a shortened course of 1 mile.)

There was also a race for Oxford and Cambridge trial eights. (Note: 'Clinker' refers to a method of constructing a boat by overlapping planks ie. where one of the long sides of each of the planks running the full length of the hull overlaps the long side of the plank next to it) There are few clinker boats used today for rowing. Skiffs are usually clinker built.

ROYAL HENLEY REGATTA

No official Regattas were held in the six years between 1940 and 1945 inclusive.

On Saturday 7 July 1945, two months after the cessation of hostilities in Europe, the ***Stewards*** organised a special peace Regatta known as the Royal Henley Regatta - to distinguish it from the usual Regatta. There was insufficient time to organise a regatta on the scale of the 1919 Peace Regatta so competitors raced three abreast over a shortened 1 mile course and three trophies were offered:-

- The Danesfield Cup for open ***eights*** - won by Imperial College BC,
- The Hedsor Cup for School eights which was won by Radley, and
- The Barrier Cup for ***scullers*** which was won by WEC Horwood of Quintin BC.

ROYALTY

HM The Queen is Patron of the Regatta. Although Her Majesty officially opened the new ***Regatta Headquarters*** in 1986, she has not visited the Regatta since 1946 when she did so as HRH Princess Elizabeth.

In 1851 HRH Prince Albert (before he became Prince Consort) consented to become the first Royal Patron of the Regatta following which it received its Royal prefix. After his death, HM Queen Victoria consented to the title being retained and on the accession of each Monarch since the death of Queen Victoria the Regatta has applied for and received notification that Royal Patronage will continue.

Prince Albert did not visit the Regatta and it was not until 1887, Queen Victoria's Golden Jubilee Year, that the Regatta received its first Royal visit, which was also the largest Royal visit in the Regatta's history. On that occasion, Friday 1 July 1887, the King of Denmark, the King of Hellenes, the Prince and Princess of Wales, Prince Albert Victor, Prince George, the Princesses Louise, Victoria and Maud of Wales, the Hereditary Princess of Saxe-Meiningen, the Duke of Sparta and Prince George of Greece visited the Regatta.

The first and only visit to the Regatta by a reigning British Sovereign was in 1912 when King George V with Queen Mary and Princess Mary arrived in Henley on the Royal Train and were then rowed to the Regatta in the Royal Barge. They had tea at ***Greenlands*** and followed the final of the ***Grand Challenge Cup*** before Queen Mary presented the Prizes.

The Duke and Duchess of Connaught attended the 1919 Peace Regatta and the Duchess presented the Prizes.

In 1921 the Prince of Wales who later became King Edward VIII visited and presented the Prizes. Prince Henry Duke of Gloucester attended in 1923 and Prince George, Duke of Kent visited in 1928 and presented the Prizes. Their Royal Highnesses the Duke and Duchess of York, who later became Their Majesties King George VI and Queen Elizabeth, attended in 1931 and the Duchess of York presented the Prizes.

Then at the centenary Regatta in 1939 the Duke of Kent visited and presented the Prizes.

Their Royal Highnesses Princess Elizabeth, who became HM Queen Elizabeth, and Princess Margaret visited in 1946 and Princess Elizabeth presented the Prizes. Princess Elizabeth also graciously agreed to the new trophy for the race for schools being named the ***Princess Elizabeth Challenge Cup***.

The next visit was in 1964 when HM Queen Elizabeth the Queen Mother, accompanied by HRH the Princess Margaret Countess of Snowdon and the Earl of Snowdon, visited to mark the 125th anniversary of the Regatta. Her Majesty also presented commemorative medals to members of the Harvard

crew who were celebrating the 50th anniversary of their winning the Grand Challenge Cup in 1914.

HRH Prince Philip, Duke of Edinburgh, visited in 1968, HRH the Princess Alexandra, The Hon Mrs Angus Ogilvy, visited in 1976 and presented the Prizes, and HRH the Princess Anne visited in 1977.

There have been many royal visits by members of the Royal Family since 1977. Those that have presented the Prizes are:-

- HRH Prince Michael of Kent 1980, 1984 and 1989.
- HRH Prince Andrew 1985,
- HRH Princess Anne, The Princess Royal, who presented the Prizes in 1988 and 1999, and
- HRH Prince Philip, Duke of Edinburgh 1998.

The visit by HSH Princess Grace of Monaco who presented the prizes in 1981 was significant because her father JB Kelly Snr, who won the single sculls title at the ***Olympic Games*** of 1920, had not been allowed to compete at the Regatta in 1920. Her brother JB (Jack) Kelly Jnr had won the ***Diamond Challenge Sculls*** in 1947 and 1949.

On 16 April 1986 Her Majesty The Queen, Patron of the Regatta, accompanied by His Royal Highness Prince Philip, Duke of Edinburgh opened the new ***Regatta Headquarters***.
See - AMATEUR STATUS

RUDDER

A flat piece of wood, plastic or metal that protrudes into the water at, or near to, the stern of a ***boat*** to enable the boat to be steered. The rudder on a racing boat is normally at the bottom of a short pin which extends through the boat. Lines are attached to the top of the pin which then pass along the top of the stern deck and then along the sides of the boat to the ***cox*** or the ***athlete*** responsible for ***steering***.

Generally all racing boats, except single and ***double sculling*** boats, use rudders.

RUGs

See - RIVER USERS GROUPS

RULES OF RACING AT HENLEY

Henley has its own Constitution and Rules and, unlike other regattas in the country, but like the ***University Boat Race***, is not run under ***ARA*** Rules. Nevertheless Henley Rules are similar to those of the ARA and ***FISA***.

RUNNERS

At the Regatta 'runners' is the traditional name given to the group of temporary junior assistants attached to the ***Secretary***'s Office to cover the period leading up to the Regatta and to assist afterwards with the clearing up.

In the sport 'runners' can also refer to the rails or grooves for ***seats*** in ***boats***.

SAFETY

All officials of the sport of rowing are aware that the welfare and safety of competitors and spectators is paramount. In addition, all ***ARA*** and ***FISA*** licensed ***umpires*** are trained to deal with emergencies particularly those occurring during a race.

It is a condition of competing at the Regatta that all athletes are able to swim a minimum of 100yds in light clothing and shoes. Coxswains are required to wear life-jackets or buoyancy aids at all times when on the water.

The Regatta provides medical and first aid services

throughout the hours of racing. In addition, umpires and ***umpire launch*** drivers work closely with the ***rescue launches***, the First Aid service and the Regatta Doctor in the event of an incident during a race, the most likely being an ***athlete*** falling into the water.
See - BOATS

ST JOHN AMBULANCE
Members of St John Ambulance are stationed at a number of places around the Regatta site. During the Regatta they expect to deal with around 600 people. Their main base is in the ***First Aid Tent*** in the ***Boat Tent Area*** but they also have first-aid stations on ***Fawley Meadows***, in ***Phyllis Court*** and at ***Remenham Farm*** on land opposite ***Temple Island***.

ST MARY'S CHURCH
St Mary's Church is the parish church of Henley with origins dating back to 1204. It has three significant links with the Regatta.

· The traditional ***Regatta Service*** is held at 10am on the Sunday, finals day, of the Regatta,

· Its 96ft tower, (118ft to the top of the turrets) built circa 1540 of flint and stone with a peal of eight bells, is often used by photographers to obtain the ideal view of the length of the ***Regatta Course*** (see cover picture), and

· The tower is also used by ***coxswains*** as a target when ***steering*** up the ***Henley Reach*** towards the town.

The flag pole was replaced in June 2000 with a shorter pole which is also a cellular radio antenna for one2one mobile phone users.

The grave of James Nash, the first ***Secretary*** of the Regatta is in the churchyard 80ft to the north of the church tower.

See - AMATEUR ROWING ASSOCIATION

SALTER'S STEAMERS

The Oxford based company Salter Bros., established in 1858, owns a fleet of 'steamers', large passenger boats so named because when they were first introduced they were steam powered.

Salter's provided a twice-daily passenger service on the ***River Thames*** between Oxford and Kingston until 1973.

The company still provides a passenger service on the river between May and September. In addition to carrying passengers between Oxford and Abingdon, Marlow and Windsor and Windsor and Staines, it operates a daily service with trips from Reading to Henley and back and another service on Tuesdays, Wednesdays and Thursdays from Marlow to Henley and back.

The stopping point at Henley is ***Mill Meadows***, but for many years it was Singers Wharf by ***Singers Park***, immediately upstream of the ***Angel on the Bridge***. Later it was the pier at ***Hobbs & Sons***, now adapted for the *New Orleans*.

SCULL

The word 'scull' is used in the sport in three ways.

- An ***athlete*** can 'scull' ie. ***sculling*** a ***boat***,
- A sculling boat can be called a 'scull' although the full description 'sculling boat' is more often used, and
- A 'scull' is one of a pair of sculls as used by a sculler to

propel the boat.
(Note: A common mistake is to spell 'scull' with a 'k' - 'skull')
See - OAR

SCULLERS
Athletes who ***scull*** rather than ***row***

SCULLING
Scullers propel a ***boat*** with a ***scull*** in each hand. ***Rowers*** have one ***oar***.

There are three types of boat used by scullers at Henley. A ***single sculling*** boat for one person (usually referred to as a sculling boat rather than a 'sculler'), a ***double*** scull and a ***quadruple*** scull (a quad).
(Note: The sculls [the ***blades*** not the boats] used in sculling should be referred to as sculls or, as two are needed by each ***athlete***, a pair of sculls. It is also acceptable to refer to them as blades but not as ***oars***)
See - ATHLETES

SEA CADETS
See - TS GUARDIAN

SEAFOOD RESTAURANT
The Seafood Restaurant, established in 1985, is situated between the ***Fawley Bar*** and the main ***Luncheon Tent*** in the Stewards' Enclosure. The restaurant offers a wide range of seafood and shellfish together with a selection of wines and champagnes.

The restaurant opens at 11.45am each day and advance reservations are not available.

SEAT

Seats in racing ***boats***, also referred to as 'sliding' seats, are normally on four or eight wheels, depending on whether the seat moves along grooves or rails/runners - referred to as the '***slide***'.

Sliding seats were first seen at Henley in 1872 but there had been reports of scullers in 1871 sliding on broader than normal, fixed 'thwarts' (seats) with the aid of grease. Even after 1872 competitors continued to race with fixed seats using grease such that in 1882 a rule was introduced requiring fixed seats to be no more than 6in wide/long.

See - CREWS

SECRETARY OF THE REGATTA

The Secretary is the senior salaried executive of the Regatta. He is supported by a small permanent staff who are based in the ***Regatta Headquarters*** - apart from the eleven days of the Regatta when they operate from the ***Secretary's Tent*** in the ***Stewards' Enclosure***.

There have been only eight secretaries in the 162 years of the Regatta, since it was established in 1839:-

- the joint Secretaries Messrs J Nash the instigator of the Regatta, and C Towsey from 1839 to 1853,
- C Towsey 1853 - 1883
- JF Cooper 1883 - 1919
- WH Barff, DSO 1919 - 1938
- LD Williams 1938 - 1958
- AL Alexander, CBE 1958 - 1971
- PA Hannen 1971 - 1975, and
- the present Secretary, Richard S Goddard, who was appointed on 13 October 1975.

SECRETARY'S OFFICE

See - REGATTA HEADQUARTERS

SECRETARY'S TENT

On the Thursday before the Regatta the ***Chairman*** of the ***Committee of Management*** and the ***Secretary of the Regatta*** and their staff move, with their desks and equipment, from their base in ***Regatta Headquarters*** to temporary premises in the ***Stewards' Enclosure*** and remain there for the duration of the Regatta. The temporary office is known generally as the Secretary's Tent.

Whilst in the Secretary's Tent in the Stewards' Enclosure, the Secretary's Office is open on the Friday and Saturday before the Regatta and throughout Regatta week, re-opening in Regatta Headquarters a few days after the Regatta.

SEEDING

Although seeding of competitors was considered by the ***Stewards*** in 1950 the Regatta has only allowed seeding in the ***Diamonds*** and the Women's Single Sculls (now the ***Princess Royal***) in 1993, 1994 and 1995 when these events were part of the ***FISA*** World Cup

See - SELECTION

SELECTION

Before the ***Draw*** the ***Stewards*** often 'select' certain competitors who they would prefer not to meet in the first round of their event - usually because they are of a high standard or from the same part of the world.

In the late 1930s the Stewards considered that a school ***crew*** racing in the ***Ladies'*** and having to race over the ***Regatta Course*** twice in one day would be at a disadvantage if the second race was against a college crew. So a form of selection was used to ensure school crews did not meet college crews in the first two rounds which were rowed on the opening day of the Regatta.

It must be emphasised that the Henley 'selection' process, introduced in 1969, is not the same as seeding and it is not acceptable for it to be referred to as such.

A degree of seeding based on ***FISA*** ranking did take place in the ***Diamonds*** and the Women's single sculls, now the ***Princess Royal***, events in 1993, 1994 and 1995 when both counted as a round of the FISA World Cup.
See - DRAW

SELWYN'S MEADOW

Selwyn's Meadow, also known as Selwyn's Field, is the 3½ acres of land on the south side of ***Barn Cottage*** next to ***Butler's Field***.

From approximately 1869 this land had been the cricket field of ***Henley Cricket Club*** and, from around 1928, the home of Henley Tennis Club.

The Regatta purchased the land from the Selwyn family in 1948 and Barn Cottage in 1983. Selwyn's Meadow was used by the Regatta initially as a site for the ***Luncheon Tent*** for the 1948 ***Olympic Games*** and then for the Luncheon Tent for members of the ***Stewards' Enclosure***.

Following the move of the Luncheon Tent to the enlarged Stewards' Enclosure the land became part of the Butler's Field car park.

SENIOR

The ***Amateur Rowing Association*** operates a system whereby events are classified Senior, Junior or Veteran. Any ***athlete*** can compete in the senior class irrespective of sex, weight or age although there are separate women and lightweight classes at senior level.

There are six status levels in the Senior classification. The highest level is 'Elite' followed by Senior 1, Senior 2, Senior 3, Senior 4 and finally, 'Novice' level.

Athletes (excluding ***coxswains***) are awarded points for wins in certain events up to a maximum of 12 points. The lowest status level at which a crew can compete is determined by the total of the points held by the athletes in the ***crew***. Points won by athletes in '***rowing***' events are not included when determining the number of points held by ***sculling*** crews, and vice versa. The lowest status level at which a ***single sculler*** can compete is determined by his personal total of points won in sculling events.

Henley uses the ARA status system to determine the minimum qualification status for entries in the ***Silver Goblets and Nickalls' Challenge Cup***, the ***Double Sculls Challenge Cup***, the ***Diamond Challenge Sculls*** and the ***Princess Royal Challenge Cup***.

THE SEVEN-OAR CREW

In 1842 the Cambridge Subscription Rooms ***crew*** which had won the ***Grand Challenge Cup*** in 1841 and were therefore due to meet the winner of the heats in the 1842 final were accused by others of planning to strengthen their crew with ***athletes*** from their University Boat Club crew should the Boat Club crew be eliminated in the heats. An appeal was made to the ***Stewards*** but they pointed out that there was no rule against an athlete competing twice in the same event. This was considered unfair by the challengers, and Oxford University Boat Club, who were drawn against Cambridge University Boat Club, withdrew.

After the Regatta the Stewards introduced rules preventing athletes from rowing in two ***crews*** for the same event and also preventing athletes being substituted by anyone once they had raced.

In 1843, the Oxford University Boat Club crew, competing for the Grand Challenge Cup, won its first race ***easily*** but before the final against Cambridge Subscription Rooms, the ***stroke***, FN Menzies, fell ill and was unable to row. Cambridge were asked to allow a substitute to be introduced but they had no wish to apply to the Stewards for leniency in view of their involvement in events in 1842 which had prompted the new rule. So Oxford went to the Start with the ***bow seat*** empty. R Lowndes had moved from bow to 7 and GR Hughes from 7 to stroke. Cambridge objected to racing seven men but Lord Camoys, the acting Steward of the Regatta, said there was no rule against it. So the crews raced - and the seven men of Oxford won, the official result being 'nearly a length'.

See - CHALLENGE CUPS

SIGNAL BOXES

There are five Signal boxes (occasionally referred to as telegraph signals) along the ***Regatta Course***. Each signal box has a wooden frame which shows the position of the race at that point. These boxes are approximately 5ft square and consist of a platform some 3ft above the surface of the river and a frame 13ft (4m) high. When a race passes a signal box the ***station*** number of the leading competitor is raised to the top of the frame using a pulley and sash cord system. The other number is then raised to a level appropriate to the position of that competitor in relation to the leader eg. if the distance is one length then the number is raised until

the top is level with the bottom of the number of the leader.

The Signal boxes are located at the ¼ mile, ***Barrier***, ¾ mile, 1mile, and $1^1/_8$miles positions and are all on the ***Buckinghamshire*** side of the Course except for the ¾ mile signal. The reason is that they are designed to be seen by spectators in the ***Grandstand*** in the ***Stewards' Enclosure***, possibly with the aid of binoculars, and when they were first used most would have been hidden from view by trees ***down-stream*** of the ***Enclosures*** had they been on the ***Berkshire*** side. The ¾ mile signal is the exception because if it were on the Buckinghamshire side it would block the view from the Grandstand of the time boards on the ***Fawley Box***.
(Note: The 1mile, and $1^1/_8$miles signals are also referred to as the 'milepost' and the 'mile and an eighth')
See - RACE REPORTS

THE SILVER GOBLETS and NICKALLS' CHALLENGE CUP

The Silver Goblets and Nickalls' Challenge Cup is competed for by for ***coxless pairs***. The event was established in 1845 when Silver Wherries (models of 17th century ferryboats see - LOCAL AMATEUR SCULLING RACE for picture) were presented to the winners. (Note: A wherry was an open decked ***sculling boat*** with a high pointed bow and stern used in the 17th century as a ferry particularly in London)

Since 1850, after many requests, Silver Goblets have been given to the winners to keep in place of the wherries. Since then the event has been referred to simply as 'The Goblets'.

In 1895 the Silver Peg Cup was donated by Tom Nickalls to commemorate the achievements of his sons, Guy and Vivian having won the Silver Goblets together and with others in each of the previous five years. In fact during the 13 years between 1885 and 1897, the brothers won the ***Grand*** three times, once rowing together in the same ***Leander*** crew, the ***Ladies***' once, the ***Stewards'*** four times, twice rowing together in the same London RC ***crew*** and once together in the Magdalen College, Oxford crew, the Goblets eight times, three times rowing together in the same pair, and the ***Diamonds*** six times.

The presentation of the personal goblets was stopped after 1967 for cost reasons and winners were given medals instead. In 1997 the Regatta recommenced the practice and, in addition, at a special ceremony, presented goblets to the 1968 - 1996 winners.

The entry qualifications are unrestricted other than that, at the date of entry, the pair shall be at least ***ARA Senior*** 1 status, or equivalent international status, in rowing.

Notable recent winners include ***Steven Redgrave*** who has won this event seven times - four times with Matthew Pinsent, twice with Andy Holmes and once with Simon Berrisford.

The entrance fee for this event is £40 and the Stewards have limited the number of entries to 16.

See - REGATTA TROPHIES

SINGER'S PARK

This is the small garden area on ***Thames Side*** in front of the Old Rectory and next to the ***Angel on the Bridge***. The area is believed to have been maintained by the Rector of Henley in 1853 and subsequently renamed after Councillor Singer when the Town Council took over responsibility for its maintenance.

Singer's Park has a landing stage for boats - known as Singer's Wharf. This was used for many years as the stopping point for ***Salter's Steamers***.

SINGLE SCULL

This describes one ***athlete*** ***'sculling'*** a ***boat'***. The boat is also called a single scull or a sculling boat.

(Note: It is incorrect to refer to one athlete in a boat as 'rowing' the boat)

At Henley athletes in single sculls compete for the ***Diamond Challenge Sculls*** and ***Princess Royal Challenge Cup***.

The ***fastest recorded time*** at the Regatta taken for the Diamond Challenge Sculls over the ***Regatta Course***, (1mile 550yds), (V Chalupa, Dukla Praha, Czechoslovakia in 1989) is 7min 23sec - a speed of 9.26knots or 10.67mph (17.16kph).

The ***fastest recorded time*** at the Regatta taken for the Princess Royal Challenge Cup over the Regatta Course, (1mile 550yds), (MH Brandin, Kungälvs Roddklubb, Sweden in 1995) is 8min 6sec - a speed of 8.44knots or 9.72mph (15.64kph).

See - OAR

SKIFF

A skiff is a wide, open decked boat that can be ***rowed*** or ***sculled***, being designed for single, ***double*** or treble ***sculling*** or ***pair oared*** rowing with a ***cox***.

Holidays on the river using a skiff or ***punt*** were very popular in the late 19th and early 20th centuries - as instanced in the Jerome K Jerome novel 'Three Men In A Boat' written in 1889. The boat was converted into a form of tent by stretch-

ing a cover, usually green canvas, over a number of hoops along the length of the boat.

Skiffs usually have fixed ***seats*** (ie. not sliding seats) and are approximately twice as wide as the rowing/racing ***boats*** described elsewhere in this book and as such they do not normally require ***outriggers***.

Skiffs are normally ***pleasure boats*** but there is a Skiff Racing Association founded in 1901 which has six affiliated clubs, all except one, the Granta Skiff Club of Cambridge, being based on the Thames. Between them they organise over 20 events between May and October each year.

SKIRT POLICE

A BBC television programme in November 1999 referred to the security staff at the entrance to the ***Stewards' Enclosure***, who refuse entry to anyone incorrectly dressed, particularly ladies with a dress hemline that is not below the knee, as the Henley 'Skirt Police'. This name was probably made up for the programme as there is no record of it being used at Henley.

SODEXHO PRESTIGE

Sodexho Prestige of Kenley, Surrey, is responsible for managing the Regatta's Official Hospitality Village on ***Fawley Meadows***.

Town & County, part of the Gardner Merchant Leisure, Sodexho Alliance Group, was awarded the Fawley Meadows contract in 1997. On 21 February 2000 Gardner Merchant Leisure changed its name to Sodexho since when Town & County, being one of the four companies in the group responsible for the major events part of the business, has managed the Fawley Meadows Hospitality Village under the name of ***Sodexho Prestige***.

The other companies now providing specialist catering management and corporate hospitality services in the UK under the Sodexho Prestige name are Ring and Brymer, Brookes and Gilmore & Pether.

See - FAWLEY MEADOWS HOSPITALITY VILLAGE

SPARE MEN'S PAIRS RACE

This is an informal event that takes place on the Tuesday before the Regatta.

It is believed to have started in the 1930s but being an unofficial event there is little written history. Organised by Jesus College Boat Club, Cambridge, entry is offered to the spare men who are not entered for the Regatta but who accompany a ***crew*** from overseas so as to be available in the event of a substitute being needed.

Usually up to eight pairs race on the ***Regatta Course*** from a free start at the ***Barrier*** - free start meaning that the ***boats*** are lined up from the bank without the use of ***stake boats***. Each race is umpired from a bicycle on the ***towpath*** and members of Jesus College BC organise the Start and Finish.

The invitation by way of a notice (black writing on red paper, black and red being the JCBC colours) is sent to overseas entries. Details of the event are subsequently posted on a notice board in the ***Boat Tent Area***.

The original trophy is believed to have been mislaid in the 1970s and Jesus College provided a new one in 1976 to commemorate the quincentenary (500 years anniversary) of the college. After it has been presented to the winners at an informal ceremony in the Boat Tent Area, the trophy remains on display with the ***Regatta trophies*** in the display cabinets in ***Regatta Headquarters***.

SPECIAL RACE FOR SCHOOLS

This event was introduced in 1974 for those students who were unable to attend the Regatta until the weekend due to examination requirements. The Special Race took place over a shortened course from a point just ***upstream*** of the ***Barrier***.

The trophy for this event was presented to the Regatta in 1985 by his family in memory of Nicholas Young who rowed for Westminster School and St. Catherine's College, Oxford.

After 1989, when the school examination timetable was changed, there was no further need for the Special Race. So in 1990 an event for school and college eights with no age restriction, unlike the Princes Elizabeth, was established and this became the ***Temple Challenge Cup*** in 1992. The Nicholas Young trophy was not used for the Temple but became the ***Fawley Challenge Cup***.

SPEED LIMIT ON THE RIVER

The maximum speed for most power driven boats on the Thames ***upstream*** of Teddington, is 8kph (4.32***knots*** or approximately 5mph) 'over the bed of the river' so that the speed of the ***stream*** is taken into consideration. The ***Environment Agency*** has set up 'transit marks' at various points consisting of two pairs of black and white poles with a red triangle topmark, which are set exactly so that when navigating at 8kph it will take 1 minute to travel from one pair to the other.

Rescue boats used by rowing clubs, regattas and ***head of the river races***, and other boats when dealing with an emergency, are exempt from the basic speed limit, as are licensed rowing coaching launches when being used for coaching and registered ***umpire launches*** when being used for umpiring.

In 1989 R-C Hansa Dortmund, Germany won the ***Grand***

Challenge Cup in a record time of 5minutes 58seconds thereby covering the ***Regatta Course*** at a speed of 11.47knots or 13.2mph/21.24kph.
See - PLEASURE BOATS

STAKE BOATS
Henley first used stake boats (flat-bottomed ***punts***) in 1862 - stake boats being boats secured to stakes (***piles***) to enable officials to hold the sterns of the ***boats*** before the start of a race. Before 1862 competitors would hold a 'bung' attached by a rope to a pile - similar to the way bumping races are started at Oxford.

From 1891 the racing boats were measured and the stern of the longest boat in a race was pulled back by the Stake Boat Official. In later years the Henley stake boats were fixed in wooden pens which had markings along the sides to assist with this task of ensuring the ***bows*** of both boats were level.

In 1967 Henley changed to ***start floats***, which could be moved approximately 30ft towards or away from the new, common to all events, starting line; and in 2000 changed to ***start platforms***.
See - REGATTA COURSE and STARTING A RACE AT HENLEY

START
Because the ***Regatta Course*** is raced against the ***stream*** (ie. ***upstream***), competitors at Henley are referred to as going 'down' to the Start (rather than 'up').

START FLOATS
The Regatta changed from ***stake boats*** to start floats in 1967 and used them until 1999. As the name suggests, a start float

consisted of a platform on floats although the principle of the Stake Boat Official lying down and holding the stern of a ***boat*** before the start of a race still applied.

Start floats were introduced to enable all races to be started on a common starting line. Each start float was connected by a chain to ***piles*** on the river bed and was moved backwards and forwards by winding the chain over a wheel. In later years the mechanical system for moving the start floats presented problems, so in 2000 the Regatta introduced ***start platforms***.

See - REGATTA COURSE re details of the 1967 change in the starting procedure.

START JUDGE

All Start Judges at the Royal Regatta are ***Stewards of the Regatta*** and most are licensed ***ARA*** umpires.

The Start Judge and his assistant, based in a tent by the starting line, ***align*** the ***bows*** of the ***boats*** in each race. They have radio communication with the two officials on the ***start platforms***. They also have a bell, introduced in 1969, which is used to stop a race in the event of a false start.

The Start Judge also has a set of tools for emergency boat repairs.

See - STARTING A RACE AT HENLEY

START PLATFORMS

The Regatta changed from ***start floats*** to start platforms (start pontoons) in 2000. These platforms are based on the starting system used in the 1997 World Championships in Aiguebelette, France.

They operate under the same principle as the start floats, which had been used for 32 years, except that instead of having to rely on being moved by a handle and chain attached to ***piles***, each floating platform 'finger' slides backwards and forwards under a base platform fixed to piles. The principle

of the official lying down and holding the stern of a ***boat*** before the start of a race still applies.
See - REGATTA COURSE and STARTING A RACE AT HENLEY

START PONTOONS
See - START FLOATS and START PLATFORMS

STARTING A RACE AT HENLEY
A Competitor is required to be in position at the Start with the stern of the ***boat*** held by the official on the ***start platform*** ready for the boat to be ***aligned*** by the ***Start Judge***, two minutes before the advertised time of the race. A clock is positioned ***downstream*** of the Start for this purpose. Unlike most regattas, competitors at Henley are not called to the Start and are expected to be there on time. Competitors who are late may be disqualified or warned by the ***Umpire***, such warning being treated as if the competitor had made a 'false start' (see below).

Generally, races at Henley are not started before the time specified in the ***Regatta Programme***. This principle is strictly observed from Friday afternoon when the ***navigation*** rules are changed and competitors are allowed to proceed to the Start down the ***Regatta Course*** from the Finish to the downstream end of the Enclosures where they can go through the gap in the Berkshire line of ***booms***.

Competitors are also required to start the race with the full complement of ***athletes*** in the boat in accordance with the rules for the event eg. ***coxed*** boats must start (and finish) the race with the ***cox*** on board.

The Start Judge will align the boats by instructing the officials on the start platforms by radio to push out or pull back the boats until the bows are level with the starting line.

Meanwhile the ***Umpire's launch*** will have arrived at the Start, with the Umpire, the driver, the Timekeeper, the Race Recorder, the Race Reporter, who is a member of the ***Commentary*** team, and up to eight passengers.

The Start Judge will indicate to the Umpire that the competitors are being aligned by switching an indicator light situated on the Berkshire bank, known as the Aligner's 'traffic lights', to red. When the Start Judge considers the competitors are level he will switch the light to green.

Then, approximately one minute before the time the race is due to start, the Umpire will stand up in the launch. He will then name the two competitors, starting with the competitor on the ***Berks station***, and explain the start procedure - and in particular the words he will use to start the race. In some instances, where an overseas competitor is involved, an interpreter will have accompanied the Umpire to ensure his instructions are understood.

The Umpire will then tell the competitors to get ready.

When the Umpire is satisfied that the competitors are ready to race, he will, without the use of a megaphone, give the warning command 'Attention' and will raise a red flag above his head. After a pause he will say 'Go' and simulta-

neously bring the flag down to one side.

Until the Umpire says the word 'Attention' the starting procedure can be held up by either of the competitors. This is usually done by the cox, or the member of the ***crew*** responsible for the ***steering*** in a ***coxless*** boat, raising a hand. ***Scullers***, who cannot do this easily, usually shout to the Umpire if they are not ready.

Once the Umpire has said the word 'Attention' only he can hold up the start of the race irrespective of any protestations by any of the competitors. The time span between 'Attention' and 'Go' is not defined and can vary - this is done to avoid competitors anticipating the word 'Go'. An excessive pause can result in the Umpire recommencing the procedure.

Since 1960 a microphone has been positioned on a pile (post) by the Umpire's launch to enable the start to be broadcast to those in the Enclosures over the public address system. The Start Judge also records the starting instructions given by umpires so that the procedures used can be checked later for consistency. If the ***bow*** of a boat crosses the starting line after the word 'Attention' but before the word 'Go' it has made a false start. This is brought to the attention of the competitors by the Start Judge ringing a bell and by the Umpire waving his red flag and instructing the competitors to stop. (Note: At Henley, unlike any other Regatta held under ***ARA*** or ***FISA*** Rules, the Umpire does not use a bell) The Start Judge will then raise a card to indicate to the Umpire the station number of the competitor that made the false start.

When the competitors are back on the Start the Umpire will, if appropriate, name and warn the competitor that made the false start. The Umpire will disqualify a competitor who refuses to start again, or who makes two false starts.
See - FINISHING A RACE AT HENLEY, RECORDING A RACE AT HENLEY, STEWARDS' CHALLENGE CUP and UMPIRING A RACE AT HENLEY.

STATIONS

This is the name of the part/side of the ***Regatta Course*** on which each competitor has been drawn in a race. They are referred to in the ***Regatta Programme*** as No 2 ***Bucks*** and No 1 ***Berks***. (See - REGATTA PROGRAMME for explanation as to why the No 2 station is listed first in the Programme)

Bucks is the abbreviation for ***Buckinghamshire***, the county on the side of the river, from ***Hambleden Lock upstream*** to the county boundary, which is opposite ***Remenham Club***. The county ***upstream*** of Buckinghamshire is ***Oxfordshire*** (viz. ***Henley-on-Thames*** is in Oxfordshire) although the No 2 station continues to be called the Bucks station for the rest of the Course.

Berks is the abbreviation for ***Berkshire***, the name of the county on the ***Enclosures*** side of the river, from Hambleden Lock upstream to ***Marsh Lock***.
See - DRAW

STEERING

Boats are normally steered by a ***rudder***, which is turned by the ***cox*** by lines attached to a bar on the top of the ***rudder*** pin. In a ***coxless*** boat, lines from the rudder run along the side of the boat to the top of the shoe of the athlete responsible for steering who, by swivelling his foot, is able to turn the rudder and steer the boat. As with a cox, the athlete that steers the boat is usually in charge and gives the instructions to the others.

In a ***coxless four***, a ***quad*** and a ***pair***, the steering is usually undertaken by the bow athlete who, being positioned at the front of the boat, can turn his head to see ahead more easily than the others. The need to be able to see ahead is less important in a ***crew*** racing on a straight course such that the steering in such circumstances is often undertaken by the most experienced athlete irrespective of his position in the boat.

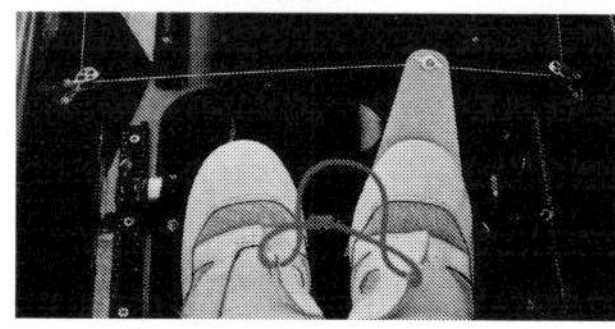

The athlete responsible for the steering in a coxless four is shown in the ***Regatta Programme***.

Single and ***double sculling boats*** do not use rudders and are steered by the athlete(s) exerting greater or lesser pressure on one of their sculls.

STEERING MARKS

Steering Marks, first used at Henley in 1963, are a form of gun sight constructed at the start of the ***Regatta Course*** behind the ***start platforms*** as a steering aid for ***coxless boats***.

Also referred to as the 'Ys and Balls', the Steering Marks each consists of two posts. One is a short post with a large 'V' on top, fixed to the back of the start platform. The second is a pile with a large red florescent 'ball' on top, driven into the river bed approximately 30m downstream of the 'V'.

By aligning the boat so that the athlete(s) can see the ball in the bottom of the 'V' - in the same way as aiming a rifle,

the boat can be seen to be travelling in a straight line and '*on station*'.
See picture on page 268

STEERS

The Henley programme shows the member of a ***coxless crew*** that has responsibility for steering the ***boat***.
See - STEERING.

THE STEWARDS

See - STEWARDS' CHALLENGE CUP, STEWARDS' ENCLOSURE or STEWARDS OF THE REGATTA as each is/are often referred to simply as 'the Stewards'.

THE STEWARDS' BARGE

See - FLOATING STAND

STEWARDS' BOAT DOCK

This is the area of water ***downstream*** of the ***Fixed Stage*** between the ***Berkshire*** bank and the Berkshire line of ***booms***.

Entrance to the ***Stewards' Enclosure*** from the Boat Dock

is via the gap in the rail at the downstream end of the Fixed Stage. Entry for boats into the Boat Dock is via the ***Regatta Course***.

The Boat Dock is available, with prior permission, for a limited number of small, hand propelled, boats belonging to ***Members of the Stewards' Enclosure***.

No new licences are now being granted to use this facility so, eventually, it will cease to exist.

THE STEWARDS' BOX

Situated on the ***Berkshire*** side of the ***Regatta Course*** level with the finish line, opposite the ***Judges' Box*** and ***upstream*** of the ***Floating Stand***.

The Stewards' Box, which is for the use of ***Stewards*** only, is reached by a ***catwalk*** from the ***Stewards' Lawn***

See picture on page 104

THE STEWARDS' CHALLENGE CUP

The Stewards' Challenge Cup is second in seniority to the ***Grand Challenge Cup***. The event, referred to simply as the 'Stewards', is the senior ***coxless fours*** event at the Regatta - the unrestricted entry qualifications being the same as for the ***Grand***, the ***Queen Mother***, the ***Henley Prize*** and the ***Women's Quadruple Sculls***, ie. for any club ***crew*** of international standard.

The base was added to the trophy in 1899.

The entrance fee for this event is £50 and the ***Stewards*** have limited the number of entries to 16.

The Stewards' Challenge Cup was established in 1841 for ***coxed*** fours until the infamous incident in 1868 when WB Woodgate rowing in the Brasenose College, Oxford coxed four, arranged for the ***cox***, FE Weatherly, to jump overboard at the start of the race. Woodgate had built a contraption enabling him to ***steer*** the ***boat*** from the no 3 position and Brasenose won the race easily - but were then disqualified.

As a result of Woodgate's efforts the '***Presentation Cup for Four Oars without Coxswains***' event was included in the programme for 1869 with the same entry qualifications as the Stewards'. However it was not repeated until 1872 and then there were only two entries, one of which withdrew before the race. In 1873 the Presentation Cup was discontinued and the Stewards' Challenge Cup was made coxless. In 1874 the ***Visitors'*** and ***Wyfold Challenge Cups*** followed suit.

The Woodgate/Brasenose disqualification in the Stewards' did more to influence the Regatta than just the introduction of coxless fours. Three crews went on to reach the final of the Stewards' in 1868 - London Rowing Club, University College, Oxford and Oscillators Club, Kingston (the latter as a result of the Brasenose disqualification). Unfortunately V Weston, the cox of the Oscillators Club, Kingston was also the cox of London Rowing Club. Neither wanted to release him so the Captain of ***Leander Club*** was called on to arbitrate and decided that Weston should be dropped from both crews. It later transpired that the reason Weston was in such demand was because he was a boy weighing only 4st 9lb!

So incidents in the Stewards' Challenge Cup of 1868 resulted in the introduction at Henley in 1869 of:-

· a new event for coxless fours - the '***Presentation Cup for Four Oars Without Coxswains***',

· a new rule prohibiting coxswains from 'doubling up' and steering for more than one crew in the same event

· a new rule requiring the cox to be in the boat at the Finish, even if one or more of the ***athletes*** is not in the boat,

· a sliding scale to relate the ***minimum weight*** of a cox to the average weight of the crew (dropped after 1962) (Note: The Stewards in 1869 had wanted to relate the weight of the cox to the type of crew, requiring a school crew to carry a cox weighing not less than 7st whilst requiring all other crews to carry a cox weighing not less than 8st, but this was not received favourably by oarsmen), and

· a minimum weight for coxswains below which they would be prohibited from competing in the Regatta (dropped after the 2000 Regatta).

The 1868 event had one final link with history, which might be appreciated by music lovers - the cox Frederick Edward Weatherly (1848-1929) later wrote the songs 'Danny Boy' and 'Roses of Picardy'.

See - REGATTA TROPHIES and SUBSTITUTIONS

THE STEWARDS' CHARITABLE TRUST

Following the financial success of the Regatta throughout the 1980s the ***Stewards*** established their own Charitable Trust in 1988 to receive donations from those anxious to support rowing among the young. In the first 10 years the Trust was able to disburse some £700,000 for the benefit of rowing, particularly junior rowing. Recipients have included ***Project Oarsome***, Oxford Adaptive Rowing, The British Universities Sports Association and the Rowing Foundation.

At the end of 2000 the Stewards' Charitable Trust had assets amounting to £2.2m.

Outside the Trust the Regatta has also supported other bodies that have links with Henley and the Regatta including ***Henley Rowing Club***, ***Leander Club***, the ***River and Rowing Museum*** and ***St Mary's Parish Church***.

STEWARDS' ENCLOSURE

Since the early days of the Regatta there has been an enclosure for the ***Stewards of the Regatta*** and their guests. In 1919, in order to raise funds, the Stewards established the Stewards' Enclosure Club. Members of the Club were personally elected by the ***Committee of Management*** (as ***Members of the Stewards' Enclosure*** are today) and allowed access to the Stewards' Enclosure.

The Stewards' Enclosure, often simply referred to as the Stewards', is a private Enclosure situated on the ***Berkshire*** bank at the finish of the ***Regatta Course***. Admission is generally restricted to Members and their Guests although a limited number of badges are available for purchase by ***overseas competitors***.

The Stewards of the Regatta strive to maintain the atmosphere of an English Garden Party of the Edwardian period in the Enclosure. Foremost in their efforts is the dress code. Gentlemen, as part of a long established tradition, are required to wear lounge suits or jackets or ***blazers*** with flannels (trousers - usually white), and a tie or cravat. Ladies are expected to wear dresses or suits with a hemline below the knee - and will not be admitted wearing divided skirts, culottes or, since 1980, trousers of any kind. Similarly anyone wearing shorts, jeans or denim suits or whose attire is indecent or disreputable will be refused entry.

(I am always amazed at the number of ladies, apart from those who are accompanied by press photographers for the publicity, who arrive at the Stewards' Enclosure wearing dresses that are too short. I always imagined that if there is one thing that everyone knew about Henley, thanks to the tabloid press, it had to be the dress code - even if most people do not realise that the hemline rule only applies to those entering the Stewards' Enclosure - MCNJ)

Special dispensation is made for those wearing national

costume and occasionally for competitors in track suits

There are four Bars in the Stewards' Enclosure - the ***Bridge Bar***, the ***Champagne & Pimm's Bar***, the ***Coffee & Liqueur Bar*** and the ***Fawley Bar***. The Regatta determines the opening and closing times of the bars within the 10am - 8pm period of the licence granted to ***Letherby and Christopher*** the Regatta's official caterers.

Members and their Guests are not permitted, for reasons of security, to bring parcels and other property into the Stewards' Enclosure. A tent where items can be deposited subject to availability of space is situated outside the main entrance to the Enclosure.

Babies, dogs, picnics, radios, televisions and tape recorders are not permitted in the Stewards' Enclosure and neither are children under the age of 10 (banned since 1980) and mobile phones (banned since 1996). Cameras are permitted but photographers are not allowed to use tripods.

The Regatta employs some 70 attendants and security personnel to help the Stewards and other officials maintain standards in the Enclosure.

Members are specifically warned each year that if they, or their Guests, ignore or flout the 'Codes of Behaviour' with particular regard to the dress code and mobile phones, the two areas which cause the most problems, they put their continued membership of the Stewards' Enclosure at risk.

Press, radio, television and film crews are not permitted to enter the Stewards' Enclosure unless accompanied by an Official of the Regatta.

It was possible to estimate from the responses to the 1999 ***Membership Survey*** that the attendance figures in the Stewards' Enclosure on each of the five days of the 1999 Regatta were 14,000 on Wednesday, 16,000 on Thursday,

20,000 on Friday, 16,500 on Saturday and 12,500 on Sunday.

The 1999 Survey also produced a significant number in favour of continuing the exclusion of children under the age of 10 and the maintenance of the dress regulations. There was also a small percentage that wanted the return of closed circuit television particularly so that those races on the early part of the Course can be seen in the Enclosure. This was a justifiable response as a recent review has shown that in 82% of races the competitor that is ahead at the ¼ mile ***signal*** stays ahead to win the race. The percentage increases at the ***Barrier*** where 86% of those ahead go on to win.

STEWARDS' LAWN

The Stewards' Lawn is the area between the ***Secretary's Tent*** and the river-bank, level with the finish of the ***Regatta Course***. Access is restricted to Stewards and their guests and ***Chairman's Assistants***.

Entry is through the Secretary's Tent or through a gate behind the ***Floating Stand*** or from the ***towpath*** by the ***umpire launches***.

The Stewards' Lawn is occasionally referred to as the Committee Lawn because, in the mid 20th century, the area was divided into two lawns, one for members of the ***Committee of Management***, the other for the remaining ***Stewards of the Regatta***.

STEWARDS OF THE REGATTA

In May 2001 there were 52 Stewards although the ***Constitution and Rules*** does not specify a maximum number but simply states that they 'shall constitute a council for the general control of the affairs of the Regatta'.

The Stewards meet twice a year - on the Saturday before the Regatta in ***Regatta Headquarters***, following which they attend at the Town Hall in Henley for the ***Draw***; and in December in London for the Annual General Meeting, when they appoint annually a ***Committee of Management*** to oversee the running of the Regatta. There is a provision in the Constitution for meetings to be called at other times if imperative.

The Stewards also nominate and appoint new Stewards. Nominations and voting are secret and need the support of over 75% ('one black ball in four shall exclude') of the Stewards attending the meeting to secure election.

Once elected, a Steward normally retains the appointment and his personal silver badge until death - when the badge is returned.

The Regatta has always been organised by a self-electing body of Stewards. It was not considered essential to appoint rowing men as Stewards until 1868 but since 1886, apart from the ex-officio appointment of the Mayor of Henley, although there have been occasions when the Mayor has been a rowing man, and the more recent appointment of the 'Henley Steward', the Stewards have generally been rowing men.
(Note: The Henley Steward position was created in 1973 and is the 'town nominee' who is appointed on a three-year term as a Steward and member of the Management Committee to ensure the Regatta continues to have a close link with Henley Town Council)

In December 1997 Mrs J (Di) Ellis, Chairman of the Executive Committee of the ***ARA***, became the first woman to be elected a Steward. There have been women Mayors of Henley serving as Stewards during their year of Office, but Mrs Ellis was the first to be elected a Steward in her own right.

Stewards are completely honorary appointments and they are not entitled to any income from the Regatta. In the event of a winding up of the Regatta they would be personally responsible for the Regatta's debts and, should there be a surplus of funds, for deciding which sporting events, philanthropic organisations or charities should benefit.

It is no coincidence that the body which runs the ***Olympic Games*** operates on the same oligarchic, self-perpetuating system as that of the ***Stewards of the Regatta***. Before establishing the modern Olympic Games in 1896, Baron Pierre de Coubertin (himself an oarsman) attended ***Henley Royal Regatta*** and used the Henley organisational/management structure as a role model for the International Olympic Committee.

STONES/POUNDS st lb kg equivalent

Since 1841 the ***Regatta Records Books*** have shown the weights of competitors and, since 1886, the weights have been shown in the ***Regatta Programme***. Since 1947 the average weight, excluding the weight of the cox, of ***eights***, ***fours*** and ***quads*** has also been shown in the Programme.

Despite the change to kilograms in the ***ARA*** and ***FISA*** Rules of Racing, the Regatta has continued to show competitor weights in stones and pounds in the programme. The Regatta's Constitution and Rules shows both.

The equivalents are:-

1 stone(st) = 14 pounds (lb)
1 pound = 0.4536 kilograms (kg)
1 kilogram = 2.205 pounds

See - WEIGHTS AND MEASURES

STRAIGHT COURSE

This is the Course used at the Regatta today, having been established in 1924.

See - REGATTA COURSE

STREAM

The flow of the river is referred to as the stream, ie. ***upstream***, or ***downstream***.

The ***stream*** on the ***Henley Reach*** flows from ***Marsh Lock*** through ***Henley Bridge*** towards ***Temple Island*** and on to ***Hambleden Lock***. Thus the competitors on the ***Regatta Course*** race upstream ie. against the stream.

See - ENVIRONMENT AGENCY and RIVER THAMES

STRIKING

See - RATE OF STROKE

STROKE

Stroke has two meanings.

Stroke is the name given to the ***athlete*** nearest the stern of the ***boat*** who, because his ***blade***(s) can be seen and copied by the rest of the ***crew***, sets the rhythm and the ***rating*** at which the spoons go into the water. This is referred to as stroking the boat; the athlete responsible is referred to as 'Str' in the ***Regatta Programme***.

The athlete '***rowing***' at stroke usually has his ***oar*** on the port side of the boat (port = left-hand side looking towards the ***bow***). Because of this, athletes who row with their oar on the port side of the boat are referred to as rowing on 'stroke side'.

A stroke is also the description of the ***rowing*** cycle of the spoon moving into and out of the water.

See - RATE OF STROKE

SUBSTITUTIONS

The rules specify the procedure which needs to be followed in the event of substitutions.

Generally up to half of a ***crew*** and the ***cox*** can be substituted up to eight days after the closing date for ***entries*** by sending details in writing to the Regatta ***Secretary***. After this date substitutions can be made only in exceptional circumstances and with the consent of the ***Committee of Management***, such requests having to be made at least two hours before the race concerned.

There are also special rules regarding substitutions on medical grounds which are subject to the consent of the Committee. These rules also state that any ***athlete*** for whom a substitution has been made on medical grounds is not permitted to compete in any other race at the same Regatta.

Substitutions in the ***Silver Goblets and Nickalls'*** and ***Double Sculls Challenge Cups*** require the consent of the Committee.

No substitution is permitted in the ***Diamond Challenge Sculls*** and the ***Princess Royal Challenge Cup***.

The rules of 1839, 1840 and 1841 did not prevent athletes rowing for more than one crew in the same event, usually by way of substituting in a crew after losing.

Although the rule was changed in 1843 to cover the substitution of rowers, it was not changed for ***coxswains*** until 1869. Both changes were associated with famous incidents in the history of the Regatta. In 1843 it was the ***Seven-Oar Crew*** and in 1868 it was the action of WB Woodgate of Brasenose College, Oxford, competing for the ***Stewards' Challenge Cup***, instructing his cox to jump overboard so that his crew could be coxless.

From 1886 to 1973 the names of possible substitutes for crews were listed in the ***Regatta Programme***.

SWANS

Since 1894 swans have been moved from the ***Henley Reach*** for the duration of the Regatta. A team, led by HM The

Queen's Swan Marker (David Barber since 1993), collects the swans and cygnets two weeks before the Regatta and moves them to Mrs Beeson's Swan Sanctuary at Egham. They are returned after the Regatta has finished - although occasionally a few will fly in from other reaches of the river while the Regatta is in progress.

This temporary removal of swans, usually around 50 birds is paid for by the Regatta and is as much for the safety of the swans as for the safety of competitors. An adult swan can weigh up to 15kg and fly at 30mph. Any competitor colliding with a swan will not only injure the bird but may injure himself, indeed such a collision may cause a smaller boat, eg. a ***sculling boat*** or a ***pair***, to capsize.

Swan Upping

Removal of the swans from the Henley Reach before the Regatta has nothing to do with the tradition of Swan Upping which takes place two weeks after the Regatta.

On that occasion HM The Queen's Swan Marker, (the title was Queen's Swan Keeper until 1993) accompanied by the Queen's Swan Warden, leads six 25ft ***skiffs*** of Swan Uppers

and a large number of spectator craft on a five day journey ***upstream*** from Sunbury to Abingdon. Their search for swans with cygnets usually produces up to 35 pairs of swans and around 85 cygnets.

The six boats comprise two representing the Crown, two from the Worshipful Company of Dyers and two from the Worshipful Company of Vintners, both City of London Livery Companies.

The Crown's boats are crewed by men wearing scarlet and white uniforms, the boat carrying the Queen's Swan Marker flying a white flag with the royal insignia and crown. The men in the two boats of the Dyers' Company wear navy blue and the leading boat of the Swan Marker and Bargemaster of the Dyers' Company flies a blue flag emblazoned with the Dyers' coat of arms and a swan. The Vintners boats have crews wearing dark green and the Vintners' Swan Marker occupies a boat flying a red flag showing the Vintners' coat of arms and a swan.

Each of the boats is rowed as a ***pair***, each ***rower*** having one ***oar***, except for the 'randan' of the Queen's Swan Marker which has a ***sculler*** positioned between a rower at ***bow*** and another rower at ***stroke*** although in a 'randan' it is the sculler in the middle who is supposed to set the ***rating***. In recent years the swan uppers have included Queen's Watermen and Freemen of the Company of Watermen and Lightermen as well as past Henley Royal Regatta and Doggett's Coat and Badge winners

The boats are towed upstream until swans with cygnets are spotted at which point the words 'All Up' is called. The towing ropes are then cast off and the skiffs form a ring round the brood. The birds are then lifted out of the water, an identification ring put on the left leg of the swans, and the left feet of the cygnets are tagged. (Note: Cygnets are tagged because a ring, small enough not to fall off, would be too tight when the cygnet became a swan).

The Queen's Swan Warden, a qualified veterinary surgeon, then checks on the health of the birds. He weighs them and takes various measurements to record their development . Blood samples are taken if necessary before returning them to the river. It was this welfare aspect of the ceremony that helped in identifying the lead poisoning, caused by swans ingesting anglers' lead weights, that was prevalent in the late 1980s and which was only contained after the use of lead for fishing was banned.

The tradition of upping (taking up - lifting) and then marking swans and cygnets with the name of the owner goes back to the 12th century when swans were privately owned and kept for eating. Most swans were penned, much like turkeys and geese today, but some were allowed to breed on rivers. (Note: Swans start breeding after three years and some continue for over 15 years)

At regular intervals owners would examine all breeding pairs and mark the cygnets. If a cob (male) had bred with a pen (female) belonging to someone else then the cygnets were apportioned between the two owners. The owner of the land where they had nested was also entitled to one of the cygnets. Branding was by way of a hot iron or with a knife with the owner's 'mark' being made on the bill (beak). The birds were also pinioned ie. a part of the wing would be cut off to prevent flight.

By 1793 the habit of eating swans had died out and the number of permitted owners had been reduced to the present three. Nevertheless the tradition of marking the swans and cygnets on the Thames continued and the ownership of the cygnets is still decided by apportioning the brood between the ownership of the parent birds. The Crown is deemed the owner of any parent bird that is not marked and the beneficiary where the brood cannot be divided equally.

The system of marking and branding was changed in 1878 after the RSPCA intervened but nicking the beaks, one nick for those belonging to the Dyers' Company, two for those belonging to the Vintners continued to 1997 after which the present system of ringing and tagging was adopted

See - CANADA GEESE

SWIMMING

The ***Environment Agency*** does not encourage swimming in the river and it is prohibited during the hours of racing at the Regatta between ***Henley Bridge*** and ***Temple Island***. This is for safety reasons and to prevent swimmers being an obstruction to navigation.

Whilst less polluted than in the 1970s, the river is still far from clean and river users are aware of the potentially fatal

Weil's Disease which can be contracted from a virus found in slow moving rivers and streams.

On the Saturday evening of the Regatta, when there are a great many people celebrating in the town, not all having come to watch the racing during the day, there have been occasions when revellers have jumped into the river from the parapet of Henley Bridge. Apart from the risk of landing on, or being hit by, a boat there is also the risk of being impaled on the wooden piles of an earlier bridge that protrude from the bed of the river, or simply drowning as a result of being drunk.

With regard to the ***River Thames*** generally, over the years and even taking into consideration the high risks during the times of flooding and fast streams, there are very, very few drownings, although regrettably a number of those that do happen are alcohol related. One gruesome statistic that is often quoted is that a body, once in the river and submerged, will stay down for between 10 and 14 days depending on the temperature of the water, before it rises to the surface usually at a point well ***downstream*** from where it entered.

T & V

See - HENLEY TOWN & VISITORS' REGATTA

TAMESIS

The ***River Thames*** was named Tamesis in Roman times and Temese by the Anglo-Saxons. (Note: Tamesis occasionally spelt Thamesis)

One author has suggested that, as ***Isis*** is an alternative name for the river from its source to the point ***downstream*** of Dorchester where the River Thame flows into the River Thames, it gives credence to the name Tamesis - which was the Roman name for the whole river.

A relief carving of Tamesis or 'Old Father Thames' can be seen above the centre arch on the downstream side of ***Henley Bridge*** and on some of the ***Henley Royal Regatta*** winners' ***medals***.
See - POLICE

TC

See - THAMES CONSERVANCY

TEAMS

Spectators unfamiliar with ***rowing***, and even reputable newspapers, occasionally, incorrectly, refer to a ***crew*** as a team.

Normally the only references to teams in rowing are in relation to groups of ***athletes*** selected for a particular purpose such as to represent their country at an international event eg. the Great Britain Team for the ***Olympic Games***. Even here the sport more often refers to a squad, certainly in the training stage eg. the Men's ***Heavyweight*** Squad.

TELEVISION

See - RADIO AND TELEVISION

THE TEMPLE

See - TEMPLE ISLAND or TEMPLE CHALLENGE CUP

THE TEMPLE CHALLENGE CUP

The Temple Challenge Cup, the event being referred to simply as 'The Temple', was originally known as the ***Henley Prize*** when it was established in 1990. The event replaced the ***Special Race for Schools***. The Temple is for ***eights*** from any university, college and school.

Current ***heavyweight*** and lightweight national squad oarsmen are not allowed to compete in the Temple; neither is any oarsman who has ***rowed*** 'or ***sculled***' in the ***Olympic Games*** or any similar high-ranking event. (Note: The sport generally treats rowing and sculling as separate disciplines, an athlete's status in one not influencing the other) Neither is a 'Blue (meaning he has represented Oxford or Cambridge in the Boat Race), or a 'Purple' (meaning he has rowed with distinction for London University) or one who has rowed at similar level at university in the USA, allowed to enter.

Composite crews are only permitted from secondary schools and from not more than two college boat clubs from any one university.

No ***athlete*** may compete in the Temple if he has previously won an event at the Regatta - other than the ***Princess Elizabeth*** or the ***Fawley***.

Athletes, other than ***coxswains***, competing in this event are not permitted to compete in any other eight-oared event at the same Regatta.

The Cup, made in 1835 by Charles Fox, was purchased by the Regatta and adapted by adding the silver statue of an oarsman hallmarked 1831, an engraving of the Temple, as on ***Temple Island***, and a modern base. It was first presented in 1992

The entrance fee for this event is £80 and the Stewards have limited the number of entries to 32.
See - REGATTA TROPHIES

THE TEMPLE CUP
See - ROYAL HENLEY PEACE REGATTA and TEMPLE CHALLENGE CUP

TEMPLE ISLAND

Temple Island is situated at the start of the ***Regatta Course***.

The Temple on the island, with its early 'Etruscan' style wall paintings, was designed and built in 1769/1771 by James Wyatt, surveyor of Westminster Abbey, for Sambrook Freeman the owner of the Fawley Estate. Wyatt also carried out many alterations to ***Fawley Court*** at this time.

Major alterations were carried out in 1884 by the new owner, Edward Mackenzie, and a four-roomed cottage added together with a large wooden balcony. The cottage was occupied for many years but the last tenant left in the 1950s; and the balcony had been removed before the property was taken over by the Regatta.

After the Second World War a statue of a 'naiad' (water nymph), was placed under the cupola (small rounded dome on the roof). In 1954 this statue, which had been laid on the lawn whilst repairs were carried out to the roof of the cupola, was stolen. It was later recovered, minus an arm, and returned to the Mackenzie family, but it was in a very poor condition and, rather than being replaced, was subsequently sold at auction.

Ownership of the island remained in the Mackenzie family of Fawley Court until Miss Margaret Mackenzie established two Temple Island Trusts to take over the ownership.

In December 1987, a donation of £515,001 to the Regatta from Mr Alan Burrough, CBE, a ***Steward of the Regatta***, and his late wife Rosemary, secured a 999-year lease of the island for the Regatta from the two Trusts. The annual ground rental for each lease is an 'egg', both eggs normally being presented by the ***Chairman*** of the ***Committee of Management*** of the Regatta, to the Trustees on the Saturday of the Regatta.

Since 1987 the Stewards have carried out considerable renovation work on the island and the building including restoring the wall paintings which may be the work of Biagio Rebecca and are believed to be the first example of the use of Etruscan-style decorations in England.

In 1989 a marble statue of Bacchante the Greek goddess of wine, sculptured circa 1770 (see picture on left) and thus contemporaneous with the Temple, a gift of John L Garton, CBE, ***President*** and Past Chairman of the Regatta, was placed under the cupola.

Temple Island has also been described in the past as 'The Abbot's Tower' but the reason for this isn't known.

During the Regatta, Temple Island is used by ***Sodexho Prestige*** for corporate and private hospitality, guests being

conveyed to the island by boat via the ***Fawley Meadows Hospitality Village***.

At other times of the year the Regatta allows the island to be used for private parties and wedding receptions. The Temple has luncheon and dining facilities for up to 40 guests and, by using a marquee in the grounds, the numbers can be increased to 150.

TEMPLE ISLAND ENCLOSURE

This is a Private Enclosure, on land owned by ***Remenham Farm***, ***downstream*** from the ***Barrier***, opposite ***Temple***

Island. Temple Island Enclosure has no connection with the Regatta's Official ***Hospitality*** facility on Temple Island.

TENTAGE

See - BLACK & EDGINGTON

TENTS

At Henley Offices are often referred to as Tents and vice versa

THE THAMES

See - RIVER THAMES or THAMES CHALLENGE CUP

THE THAMES CHALLENGE CUP

The Thames Challenge Cup was established in 1868 for ***eights*** with the same qualifications as the ***Grand*** except that ***athletes*** in ***crews*** entered in the Grand, ***Ladies'*** or ***Stewards'*** at the same Regatta were not eligible. Similarly any competitor who had been in a winning Grand or Stewards' crew was not permitted to enter.

Traditionally the 'Thames', the abbreviated name of this event, has attracted the ordinary rowing club crew that was not up to Grand status but was not eligible to enter the Ladies'.

The Thames has also been popular with American School and lightweight '150lb' crews, the US recognising lightweight rowing before the UK.

Since 1985 the ***Stewards of the Regatta*** have made many changes to the entry requirements for the Thames, and since 1996 student crews and certain highly qualified athletes such as those who have ***rowed*** 'and s***culled***' in the ***Olympic Games*** and other high ranking events have not been permitted to enter. (Note: The sport generally treats rowing and sculling as separate disciplines, an athlete's status in one not influencing the other)

No oarsman may compete in this event if he has previously won any event at the Regatta - other than The ***Temple***, The ***Princess Elizabeth*** and The ***Fawley Challenge Cups***.

By qualifying the entry in this way the Stewards have tried to keep this event for 'genuine' club crews below Ladies' standard.

Athletes, other than ***coxswains***, competing in this event are not permitted to compete in any other eight-oared event at the Regatta.

The entrance fee for this event is £80 and the Stewards have limited the number of entries to 32.

See - REGATTA TROPHIES

THAMES CONSERVANCY

The TC as it was often referred to (and occasionally still is), became responsible for the full length of the ***River Thames*** from Cricklade to Teddington in 1866 when it took over the work of the Thames Navigation Commission, which had been established in 1751

The TC had been constituted in 1857 following a dispute between the Crown and the City of London over ownership/control of the river from Staines to the sea.

Changes in the late 20th century and the Water Act of 1973 resulted in the work of the Thames Conservancy being taken over by the ***Thames Water Authority*** on 1 April 1974.

Responsibility for the river subsequently passed from the Thames Water Authority to the ***National Rivers Authority*** in 1989 and to the ***Environment Agency*** in 1996.

THAMES HERITAGE TRUST

Established in 1978 as a registered charity to undertake improvements to the river-side walks and riverbanks and to encourage the preservation of the ***River Thames*** and its environment as a national heritage.

THE THAMES PATH

The Thames Path National Trail is the name given to the 340km (213miles) of footpaths and ***towpaths*** along the river. Walkers are able to walk on level ground, following the 'acorn' signs, for the full length of the river from its source at Kemble near Cricklade in Gloucestershire to the Thames Barrier at Greenwich.

THAMES SALMON TRUST

The Trust, formed in 1986, is responsible for introducing salmon back into the ***River Thames***. Most ***locks*** now have salmon ladders built by the weirs, to enable the salmon to swim ***upstream*** each year - the cost of the ladders being covered by local sponsorship.

THAMES SIDE

This is the stretch of river-bank on the town (Oxfordshire) side of the river between the ***Henley Bridge*** and ***Hobbs & Sons*** on the corner of Station Road. The part of Thames Side

between the bottom of Friday Street and Hobbs is also referred to as River Terrace.

THAMES TRADITIONAL BOAT RALLY

This annual gathering of boats was established by the ***River Thames Society*** in 1978 and takes place in July, based on ***Fawley Meadows***. The TTBR is now an independent organisation and brings together members of the Thames Vintage Boat Club, the Thames Traditional Boat Society, the Steam Boat Association of Great Britain and the Association of Dunkirk Little Ships, together with a range of launches, ***skiffs***, motorised, and non-motorised ***punts***, Edwardian day boats, steam boats, ***canoes*** and dinghies.

THAMES WATER AUTHORITY

The Thames Water Authority was established under the 1973 Water Act and took over responsibility for the ***River Thames*** from the ***Thames Conservancy*** on 1 April 1974

As a result of the Water Act of 1989 and following a further reorganisation, the Thames Water Authority passed over the responsibility for the river to the ***National Rivers Authority*** in 1989. What was left under the control of the TWA was then privatised as part of the Conservative Government privatisation of the water industry. Thames Water was established as a private company in 1990 and deals with all water and sewage matters in the Henley area.

Responsibility for the river subsequently passed from the ***National Rivers Authority*** to the ***Environment Agency*** in 1996.

THAMESFIELD

Thamesfield Nursing Home, is situated on the ***Berkshire*** bank of the river, 200m ***upstream*** from ***Regatta Headquarters*** and next to the ***Eyot Boat Centre***.

Built in 1860 as a private residence, Thamesfield for many years was the home of the Edwards-Moss family. The building was used in the 1960s and 1970s as the Henley Youth Centre before it was sold and became a private nursing home.
See - RAILWAY

THIRD BRIDGE

This refers to the need for an additional bridge to relieve the pressure on Henley and Sonning Bridges. The possibility of a third bridge at Reading at the end of the A329(M) road, crossing the river and the proposed 'Redgrave Pinsent Rowing Course', a 2000m training facility being planned at Caversham, has been considered for many years. This solution however is vehemently opposed by most residents of the villages that would be on the ***Oxfordshire*** side of such a bridgehead.

TICKETS

Regatta literature normally differentiates between ***badges***, ***labels***, ***passes*** and tickets.

At Henley tickets are generally issued in instances where they will be handed in when used eg. tickets for Luncheon and Tea in the ***Luncheon Tent*** in the ***Stewards' Enclosure***, tickets received in exchange for items left in the ***Left Luggage Tent*** outside the Stewards' Enclosure and for items left in the cloakrooms.

TIMEKEEPER

See - RACE REPORTS

TOWN & COUNTY

See - SODEXHO PRESTIGE

THE TOWN CUP

The Town Cup, made by Makepeace & Co of Lincoln's Inn, London, was one of the two trophies competed for at the first Henley Regatta in 1839 - the other trophy from 1839 being the ***Grand Challenge Cup***.

The Town Cup was offered as the prize for ***coxed fours*** to ***crews*** of ***amateurs*** from within five miles of Henley. The radius was extended in 1852 to include all clubs on the Thames between Oxford and Windsor but excluding Oxford University.

Picture courtesy of Henley Stewards

The popularity of this event declined over the years and in 1884 the ***Stewards*** offered the trophy to the Henley Town Regatta (subsequently renamed the ***Henley Town & Visitors' Regatta***) where it is held in trust and competed for each year by ***coxless fours***.

When not on display at the Town & Visitors' Regatta at the end of July or at that Regatta's Annual Dinner in November, or in the ***Prize Tent*** during the Royal Regatta, the Cup is on display in ***Regatta Headquarters***.

TOWPATH

Towpaths exist along most stretches of the river and are so called because they were, and occasionally still are, used by horses and men towing boats along the river.

Readers may recall the three men in Jerome K Jerome's novel 'Three Men In A Boat', written in 1889, who ***sculled*** and towed their boat ***upstream*** from Kingston

The path along the full length of the ***Berkshire*** bank from ***Henley Bridge*** to ***Hambleden lock*** is the towpath. In 1950 the Regatta laid tarmac on the towpath from the ***Barrier*** to the Start, and extended this in 1952 to a point opposite Greenlands (the ***Henley Management College***).

Pedestrians generally have a right to use the towpath when it crosses private land. In 1956 Berkshire County Council contended that the towpath on Regatta land was an unrestricted right of way. In June 1957 this claim was contested by the Regatta at the Berkshire Quarter Sessions claiming that it had always been closed for the Regatta certainly within living memory. 1892 was mentioned because this was the living memory of Lieut.-Colonel CD Burnell, DSO, OBE, a ***Steward of the Regatta***, who gave evidence to the Court. This resulted in a declaration granting that the right of way was conditional upon the right of the Stewards to close it for Regattas sponsored by them - which it does each year for the Royal and ***Town & Visitors'*** Regattas.

Coaches cycling along the towpath are requested to keep to the right-hand side.

The Regatta closes the towpath at 4pm on the Tuesday before the Regatta from the upstream end of the Stewards' Enclosure to the ***downstream*** end of the ***Regatta Enclosure***. The towpath then stays closed until the Regatta finishes on the Sunday. The rest of the towpath in front of the Boat Tent, upstream from the ***Enclosures***, to the point where the ***Boat Tent Area*** meets the ***Leander*** Wall, is then closed on the Wednesday morning and also stays closed until the Regatta has finished.

The towpath is still used on occasions for towing boats. Until the early 1990s, the ***Environment Agency*** would employ a tugboat to remain on standby during the Regatta just in case a boat wished to be towed along the ***Henley Reach*** and encountered problems as a result of the special navigation rules, the crowds and the towpath being closed.

Most of the towpaths along the river are now part of the ***Thames Path***.

TRAFFIC LIGHTS

The name of the indicator lights used by the ***Start Judge*** to advise the ***Umpire*** when the competitors are being aligned (red light) and then when they are level (green light).
See - STARTING A RACE AT HENLEY

TRAINS

See - RAILWAY

TROPHIES

See - REGATTA TROPHIES

TS GUARDIAN

The *TS Guardian* 179 Sea Cadets Corp, (TS = Training Ship)

established in Henley in 1942, is situated on the ***Berkshire*** bank of the river ***upstream*** of ***Henley Bridge*** next to the ***Eyot Boat Centre***.

ULYSSES

Ulysses is one of the three 50ft ***umpire launches*** owned by the Regatta. The other two are ***Argonaut*** and ***Ariadne***. *Ulysses* was built by The Steam & Electric Launch Company of Ludham, Norfolk, using the mould taken from the lines of the hull of the umpire launch *Amaryllis*.

Ulysses, together with the umpire launch *Argonaut*, was launched on 7th May 1993 by the ***Chairman*** of the ***Committee of Management*** Mike Sweeney and the two past Chairmen, John Garton CBE, and Peter Coni, OBE, QC.

UMPIRES

All Umpires at the Royal Regatta are ***Stewards of the Regatta*** and licensed ***ARA*** umpires, and most are qualified to umpire at ***FISA*** events eg. the ***Olympic Games*** and World Rowing Championships. The retirement age for umpires at the Regatta is 65.

See - UMPIRING A RACE AT HENLEY

UMPIRES' LAUNCH BAY

The name of the area of water surrounded by the ***Press Box***

catwalk, the catwalk to the ***Stewards' Box*** and the river-bank immediately in front of the ***Bridge Bar Lawn***.

The Umpires' Launch Bay is for umpire launches and official boats only.

UMPIRE LAUNCHES

The Regatta uses five umpire launches on the first two days of the Regatta and on Friday morning, after which the number is reduced to four. An additional launch is kept in reserve throughout the Regatta.

The launches used are ***Amaryllis***, ***Argonaut***, ***Ariadne***, ***Bosporos***, ***Enchantress*** and ***Ulysses*** - all 50ft open launches known affectionately in the rowing world as 'Hobbs launches' because they are all similar to the launches built by ***Hobbs and Sons*** of Henley in the 1920s for use at the Regatta. The advantage of these large launches is that they provide a stable base for the ***Umpire*** and other officials. They are also a means by which supporters of the competitors can follow a race and in the past have occasionally carried around twenty five to thirty people,

In recent years there have been complaints to the Environment Agency from other river users and spectators at regattas, including spectators on the river at the Royal Regatta, about the wash from these launches following races, ironically the very races these people have come to watch! So the ***Environment Agency*** have imposed stringent speed restrictions on these launches when umpiring.

Because of the high standard of most competitors at Henley the speeds attained by the umpire launches are higher than at most regattas. So when approaching the Enclosures they will usually slow down to reduce the wash - unless the race is close and/or there is a risk of a collision between the competitors in which case a launch driver will keep up with the competitors to the finish of the ***Regatta Course***.

Sadly, because of the rules imposed by the Environment Agency, many regattas have changed to smaller, and in many cases far less stable, launches for umpires. Others have dispensed with umpire launches altogether and arrange for races to be umpired by positioning umpires along the river-bank. The overall result is that the traditional Hobbs 50ft umpire launches, which were used at many regattas the length of the Thames during the 20th century, are now only used at events on the ***Henley Reach*** and at Reading Town Regatta ***upstream*** of Teddington. They continue to be used at some Tideway regattas and for the ***University Boat Race*** and the three launches owned by the Regatta, *Amaryllis*, *Argonaut* and *Ariadne*, are driven down the river each March especially for this.

In addition, for safety reasons, the ***Environment Agency*** has determined that each of the 50ft umpire launches should carry no more than 12 passengers in addition to the driver. At the Royal Regatta the complement of each launch usually comprises:-

- the Umpire, who is officially in charge of the launch,
- the Timekeeper,
- the Race Recorder,
- the Race Reporter, who is a member of the ***commentary*** team,
- two guests of the Umpire, and
- six other passengers - these places usually being allocated to guests of the Timekeeper and Race Recorder, television and radio reporters, the press, VIPs and other Regatta Guests, and supporters of those in the race.

JD Bishop of ***Leander Club*** umpired at the first Henley Regatta in 1839 on horseback. In 1840 the Umpire took to the water and umpired races from an eight-oared cutter (a high-sided boat with a flat stern usually associated with naval boats) rowed by professional London watermen. By 1867 the manually propelled umpire's boat had difficulty keeping up with races. This may have been because there was only one boat and a limited number of watermen who had to follow every race. Amateur oarsmen were used together with professional ***crews*** in 1868.

The outcome was the introduction in 1869 of the first steam-powered umpire launch to be used at Henley - probably the *Ariel.* A steam launch, built specifically for the purpose by Thornycroft, was used between 1871 and 1876 and then, from 1877, the Regatta hired a steam launch from Messrs DesVignes, possibly the *Aramis*, which was used in 1891. In 1893 a steam launch was hired from the Kingdom Company and in 1897 two steam launches were used although one created wash problems and was not used after the first morning

Other steam launches used for umpiring at the Regatta in the late 19th century included the 45ft, *Eva* and the 50ft, *Consuta. Eva* was built in Chiswick by Thornycroft in 1874 and used at the Regatta in 1874, 1875 and 1876 following which she underwent a major refit before being sold by the Regatta. *Eva* is now on display in the Henley Gallery of the ***River and Rowing Museum***. *Consuta* was built in 1898 by Sam Saunders at Goring to Royal Regatta specifications, and used for many years at the Regatta; and is now undergoing restoration at the Kew Steam Museum.

Petrol-driven launches were introduced in the early 20th century and many of the steam-powered launches were converted.

Launches used for umpiring at Henley during the 20th century, mainly 40ft launches, include, *Magnolia* (subsequently renamed *Majestic*), *Matrona* (now named *Panache*) and *Clivanda* (now named *Pommery*) all now owned by Chas. Newens of Putney. *Consuta*, having been converted from steam-power, was used together with *Hibernia* and later *Maritana.*

Magician, built in 1921 and owned by Hobbs and Sons until sold in 1996, was used from 1921 to 1994 and in particular for the visit to the Regatta of HRH The Prince of Wales in 1921. In 1927 *Magician* was used in London for the first live outside radio broadcast of the Oxford and Cambridge University Boat Race. *Arethusa*, built by Hobbs & Sons in 1921 and now owned by Miss Charlotte Every, has been used on occasions at the Regatta since 1986.

The Regatta was able to cope with one umpire launch until 1902 when, with the increase in entries, it was again necessary to engage two launches, two having been tried unsuccessfully in 1897. The number of launches was increased to three in 1922 and four in 1933 and by the end of the 20th century the Regatta was regularly using five umpire launches.

Umpire launches at Henley fly a white ***flag*** with the word UMPIRE in blue in letters from the stern flagpole.

On Wednesday, Thursday and Friday, when there is often more than one race on the Course at the same time, umpire launches proceed to the Start via the ***navigation*** channel which is entered through the 'sliding boom' gap in the ***booms*** on the ***Buckinghamshire*** side of the Course ***downstream*** from the ***Progress Board***. On Saturday and Sunday the umpire launches sometimes proceed to the Start down the Course as far as the crossing point at the $1^1/_8$miles signal and then down the channel between the booms and the bank on the ***Berkshire*** side of the river. In view of the amount of traffic on the river an umpire's launch normally leaves the ***Umpires' Launch Bay*** 20 minutes before the start of the race to which it has been allocated.

During the Regatta the umpire launches are kept in the Umpires' Launch Bay at the upstream end of the ***Stewards' Enclosure***.

Although the 50ft Hobbs launches have been used at the Regatta for over 80 years it was not until the early 1970s that the system for turning them round at the end of races, which had been by means of using a barge pole, was changed to the driver pointing the bows of the launch towards the ***Photographers' Box*** and then reversing into the Umpires' Launch Bay to the appropriate landing stage.

UMPIRING A RACE AT HENLEY

Apart from the first Regatta in 1839, when the ***Umpire*** officiated on horseback, umpires at Henley have always followed races in boats (***umpire launches***).

Contrary to any impression that might be gained from the following information regarding fouls, interferences, etc, most races proceed without incident.

The rules require that competitors keep on their proper course, which is such - *as will enable him to reach the winning post in the shortest possible time provided that he allows ample water for his opponent to steer his own proper course on the side on which that opponent started.* In the event of a dispute the Umpire, who will follow the race in the centre of the ***Regatta Course***, is the sole judge of a competitors proper course.

If the Umpire wishes to warn a competitor for possible interference or if there is a risk of a clash, he will raise a white ***flag***, name the offending competitor and indicate with the flag the direction the competitor should take. If both competitors are in danger of clashing in the centre of the Course the Umpire will raise the white flag and instruct both competitors to 'move apart'.

The Umpire may disqualify a competitor who leaves his proper course and interferes with his opponent's progress; or in the event of a foul. In this regard a competitor has fouled his opponent in a race if he comes into contact by his ***oar***, ***scull***, ***boat*** or person with the oar, scull, boat or person of his opponent.

The Umpire may only warn a competitor if there is a likelihood of a foul, or if the competitor is in danger of interfering with his opponent or if there is an obstruction ahead of him. With regard to the latter, the ***booms***, ***buoys*** or ***piles*** along the side of the Course, while in place, are not considered to be 'obstructions' even though some competitors are inclined to collide with them.

If the Umpire wishes to stop a race he will raise a red flag and give the order 'Stop'. (Note: Umpires officiating at regattas held under ***FISA*** and ***ARA*** Rules also ring a bell when stopping a race). If the Umpire wishes to stop one of the competitors but not the race he will raise a white flag, name the competitor and give the order 'Stop'.

The Umpire may restart the race or order it to be re-rowed at a later time if a competitor is interfered with by an outside agency eg. a boat, log or loose boom on the Course.

In the event of a foul, a competitor may claim that his opponent be disqualified, such a claim must be made to the Umpire or a Judge by the competitor himself before getting out of his boat. In the event of a foul the Umpire may:-

- disqualify the offending competitor,
- restart the race, or
- order it to be re-rowed at a later time.

If the Umpire reserves his decision he will normally give it soon after the race has finished.

Nevertheless the Umpire need not wait for a competitor to make a claim for his opponent to be disqualified for a foul or interference and is permitted to take the decision immediately if:-

· he considers the competitor to have 'wilfully encroached on the proper course of his opponent', or

· the foul or interference is of such a nature as to clearly influence the race.

The Umpire may also disqualify a competitor who receives any extraneous assistance during a race such as being given steering advice from a boat following the race or any form of advice from the bank. The use of megaphones by supporters, as well as any radio communication with the competitors, is forbidden.

Henley Rule 38(q) specifies that 'The Umpire's jurisdiction shall extend over the whole race from the time that it is specified to start until its end, and his decisions shall be final and without appeal'.

See - STARTING A RACE AT HENLEY and FINISHING A RACE AT HENLEY

UNIVERSITY BOAT RACE

This annual race is held on the tidal Thames in London between Oxford and Cambridge Universities.

The first race was held at 7.56pm on Wednesday 10th June 1829 at Henley, 10 years before the first ***Henley Regatta***, and was won by Oxford. This race, like that in 2001, was restarted as a result of a clash. In 1829 the ***crews*** were clashing blades as soon as they left the start at ***Hambleden*** which, it was claimed, was all part of the fun. Oxford, rowing on the ***Buckinghamshire*** side of the river, decided to row on the ***Berkshire*** side of ***Temple Island***. In crossing over they collided with Cambridge. On that occasion each university had its own ***umpire***. The Oxford Umpire decided that Oxford should be disqualified but the Cambridge Umpire refused to take a decision claiming that Cambridge had not made an appeal for a foul. The race was restarted and this time Oxford moved sufficiently ahead to be able to cross over safely and won the race 'by several lengths'. The ***boat*** used by Oxford in 1829 is on display in the Rowing Gallery of the River and Rowing Museum.

All the subsequent races have taken place in London. There were races at Henley between the two universities in 1940 and 1945 but these were not 'Official' races, the participants were not awarded blues for representing their university and the results do not count in the Boat Race records.
See - HENLEY BOAT RACES

UNIVERSITY COLLEGE BARGE

This was built in 1880 and used at Oxford as a clubhouse and headquarters for University College oarsmen. In the 19th and early 20th century most Oxford colleges had their own college barge.

The University College Barge is now privately owned and, having been fully restored in 1988, is towed from its base in the Thames and Kennet Marina at Sonning Eye/Caversham to Henley each year where it is used for entertaining during the Regatta.

UPPER THAMES FOURS AND SMALL BOATS HEAD

Established in 1982 this ***head of the river race*** takes place each October, river conditions permitting, and is based at ***Upper Thames Rowing Club***. Competitors race over a course 3,000m (1.86 miles) ***upstream*** from '***Pink Cottage***' (***Ferry Cottage***) to the finish of the Royal ***Regatta Course***.

UPPER THAMES ROWING CLUB

Established in 1963, UTRC is situated on the ***Berkshire*** bank of the river next to, and immediately ***downstream*** from, ***Remenham Club***. UTRC consists of two buildings (see picture), the clubhouse on the left and the boathouse on the right,

the latter being the old ***Boom Shed***.

Upper Thames RC was founded as a base for senior oarsmen from local 'up river' clubs. It now has a wide range of men and women members from juniors to veterans and is also part of ***Project Oarsome***, a scheme for attracting young persons to rowing.

UPSTREAM

The ***stream*** on the ***Henley Reach*** flows from ***Marsh Lock*** through ***Henley Bridge*** towards ***Temple Island*** and on to ***Hambleden Lock***. Thus competitors on the ***Regatta Course*** race upstream ie. against the stream.

It is acceptable to refer to a place that is upstream of another as being 'above' it eg. ***Henley Bridge*** is above the finish of the Regatta Course.

See - DOWNSTREAM and RIVER THAMES

THE VISITORS' CHALLENGE CUP

The Visitors' is open to any coxless four that is below ***Stewards' Challenge Cup*** standard (ie. not a ***heavyweight***, lightweight or ***FISA*** Senior B [under 23] national crew).

Because of the initial popularity of the ***Town Cup*** in 1839, another event for 'local' ***coxed fours*** was established in 1840 known as the ***District Challenge Cup***. This event wasn't a resounding success and in 1847 another event was established in place of the District Cup, this being for 'any' coxed four. The District Challenge Cup was renamed the Visitors' Challenge Cup and the event, usually referred to simply as the 'Visitors', was subsequently given the same entry qualifications as the ***Ladies'***.

The Visitors' remained an event for coxed fours until 1874 when, like the ***Stewards***' and ***Wyfold Challenge Cups***, it became a ***coxless fours*** event. The entry requirements for the Visitors' did not change significantly between 1874 and 2000 other than to allow overseas entries and in 1878 it was the first event to be won by an overseas crew.

The base was added to the trophy in 1897.

The entrance fee for this event is £50 and the Stewards have limited the number of entries to 16.

See - OVERSEAS ENTRIES and REGATTA TROPHIES

WAR YEARS

The 1914 Regatta took place after the assassination at Savajevo on 28 June of Archduke Francis Ferdinand and before his funeral, - and a month before Great Britain, in support of Serbia, Russia, and France, declared war on Germany and Austria-Hungary.

Henley Royal Regatta did not take place in the years 1915 to 1918 during the Great War. On Saturday 5 July 1919, the ***Royal Henley Peace Regatta*** was held.

The 1939 Regatta took place two months before war was again declared against Germany.

No Regattas took place between 1940 and 1944 and the ***Royal Henley Regatta*** took place on Saturday 7 July 1945. This Regatta, taking place only two months after the cessation of hostilities in Europe, was, of necessity, a smaller event than that of 1919.

These 11 years, 1915 -1919 and 1940 - 1945 inclusive, were the only occasions since 1839 that the full Regatta did not take place.

Regatta land was used as a timber depository during both World Wars.

The booms, used in the construction of the ***Regatta Course*** remained stored in the wooden ***Boom Shed*** for the duration of the Second World War together with ***boats*** belonging to ***Henley Rowing Club***, it being thought that the boats would be at less risk from bomb damage than in the Club's boathouse in Henley. In the event neither building was damaged but a German incendiary bomb dropped in February 1941 close to the Boom Shed might well have caused post war problems for the Regatta and Club had it been a direct hit.

The sesquicentennial (150th) anniversary of the Regatta was celebrated in 1989 but, because of the nine Regattas missed because of the two world wars, and the Royal Henley Peace Regatta of 1919 and the Royal Henley Regatta of 1945, which were not full Regattas hence their different titles, the 150th Regatta did not take place until 1999.

THE WARGRAVE CLUB

This Club was the runner up in the first race for ***fours*** for the ***Wyfold Challenge Cup*** in 1855. It received a special mention in the Henley history books because it was the only club to have competed at the Regatta without the names of the crew being recorded in the books.

THE WARGRAVE MANOR CUP

See - ROYAL HENLEY PEACE REGATTA

WARM UP AREA

This is the 600m stretch of water, also known as the Practice

Area, that is reserved for competitors immediately ***down-stream*** of the start of the ***Regatta Course***

See - BUOYS and ERGO ROOM

WATERLINES

This is the name of the news sheet published by the Regatta Press Office on each day of the Regatta during the 1990s for journalists. It gave details of the previous days events on and off the water.

WEATHER

See - REGATTA WEATHER

WEIGHING-IN

Since 1841 the weights of ***athletes*** at Henley have been recorded in the records - although in the early days not all scullers' weights were shown. Since 1886 the weights of athletes have been recorded in the ***Regatta Programme***.

Other than in the ***Henley Prize***, ***coxswains*** must weigh not less than 55kg (8st 9lb), the ***minimum weight*** requirement for the Henley Prize is 50kg (7st 12lb). ***Crews*** are required to carry ***dead-weight*** if necessary to bring the weight (of the cox) up to the specified minimum.

Coxswains are weighed-in in vest and shorts. Any additional clothing, life-jacket or any equipment normally carried by the cox is not included when calculating the additional weight to be carried.

From 1869 to 1962 the minimum weight of the cox was related to the average weight of the crew on a sliding scale so that heavier crews carried a heavier cox. This required the Official in charge of weighing calculating the average weight of a crew immediately after they had weighed-in, so that when the cox was weighed the amount of dead-weight, if any, that would need to be carried could be calculated.

Until 1970 the dead-weight was slabs of lead but since then sealed packets of sand have been used. These must be carried as close to the cox as possible and are checked into and out of the ***boat*** by an Official before and after each of the races involving the carrying of dead-weight.

Henley Rules require all athletes, including coxswains, to register their 'racing weight' on the ***entry*** form and to 'weigh-in' as early as possible before the Regatta so that the weights shown on the entry form can be verified. In addition, as the entry form may have been submitted many weeks before the Regatta, the opportunity is taken, when weighing-in, to check the final order of rowing and the names and initials of those on the form. Accurate information can then be given to the Press Office, recorded in the Regatta Programme and subsequently, in the case of a few, engraved on the trophy and recorded in the ***Books of Honour***.

The Officials responsible for weighing competitors are based in the Crews' Enquiries Office in the ***Boat Tent Area***.

See - STEWARDS' CHALLENGE CUP

WEIGHTS

See - WEIGHING-IN and WEIGHTS AND MEASURES

WEIGHTS AND MEASURES

Weights

One kilogram (kg) is approximately 2.205 pounds.
One pound (lb) is approximately 0.454 kg.
One stone (st) = 14lbs.
One pound = 16 ounces (oz).

Measurements

One kilometre (km) or (1,000 metres) is
approximately 0.6214 mile or 1,093.66 yards.
One metre (m) is approximately 39.37 inches.
One mile (1,760 yards) = 1,609.344m.
One yard (3 feet or 36 inches) = 0.9144m.
One nautical mile is approximately 1.15 mile or
6,080ft or 1,853.18m.

See - KNOT

WEIL'S DISEASE

A potentially fatal disease, also known as leptospirosis, which can be contracted by contact with infected water (water infected by bacteria carried in rats' urine). Symptoms, which occur within three to nineteen days of making contact, include a high temperature, an influenza type illness, loss of appetite, nausea, nose bleeds and joint and muscle pains particularly in the calf muscles.

Athletes are advised always to wash or take a shower after boating, to cover any abrasions with a waterproof plaster, to use footwear to avoid cutting feet and to contact a doctor immediately should they experience any of the symptoms, advising the possibility of Weil's disease.

WHEELCHAIR VISITORS IN THE STEWARDS' ENCLOSURE

There is a special viewing area on the river-bank in front of the ***Fawley Stand*** for Members and Guests who visit the ***Stewards' Enclosure*** in wheelchairs.

WHITE HILL

The A4130 road enters Henley over ***Henley Bridge*** after passing down White Hill.

WILDLIFE

There is wide range of wildlife on the ***Henley Reach*** and most exist quite happily during the Regatta.

During the Regatta, for their own safety as much as for the safety of competitors, ducks are enticed off the ***Regatta Course*** by feeding them and ***Canada geese*** are encouraged to move off the Course by a 'goose patrol boat'. The ***swans*** are removed from the Reach for the period of the Regatta and kept in the swan sanctuary at Egham.

See - BIRDS and FISH

WOKINGHAM DISTRICT COUNCIL

Wokingham District Council is the unitary authority responsible for the whole of the ***Berkshire*** bank from ***Marsh Lock*** to ***Hambleden Lock***. The Berkshire County Council was abolished in 1998.

WOMEN

Women did not compete at Henley until 1975 when women ***coxswains*** were allowed to be included in male ***crews***.

However some influential newspapers and magazines have mistakenly reported the ***Ladies' Challenge Plate*** as a race for women.

In 1981, as an experiment to assess the feasibility of including races over a shortened course during the normal Regatta programme, the Regatta held two invitation events for women. Four ***coxed fours*** and four ***double sculls*** were invited to race over a course using the Start by the ***Barrier*** as used for the ***Special Race for Schools***. The winners received Regatta medals.

The experiment was repeated in 1982 over an even shorter course starting at Fawley, and an Invitation event for four Women ***single scullers*** was added. The winners also received Regatta medals.

It was not repeated in 1983 the main reason being that to include events for women at that time would have necessitated restricting or withdrawing some existing event(s). Following this the ***Henley Women's Regatta*** was established in 1988 and now takes place two weeks before the Royal Regatta and uses the first part of the Royal ***Regatta Course***.

After 10 years, consideration was again given to including a women's event at the Royal Regatta and a special event for Women's ***Single Sculls*** was established in 1993 as part of the ***FISA*** World Cup, now called the ***Princess Royal Challenge Cup***.

In 1998 the ***Stewards*** invited the National Women's ***Eights*** from Australia, Canada, United States and Great Britain, to race at the Regatta. In 1999 ***Women's eights*** were invited from Poland and the USA in addition to two of the best Great Britain eights. Such was the success that, in 2000, the Women's Eights event for the ***Henley Prize*** was established with the same entry requirements as the ***Grand Challenge Cup***. At the Stewards' meeting in December 2000 a third event for women was established - the ***Women's Quadruple Sculls***.

Today one third of ***rowing athletes*** throughout the country are women.

Off the water, women have been eligible for membership of the ***Stewards' Enclosure*** since December 1946 and now comprise 8.5% of the total membership.

In December 1997, the year women were admitted to membership of ***Leander Club***, Mrs J (Di) Ellis, Chairman of the Executive Committee of the ***ARA***, became the first woman to be elected a ***Steward*** of the Regatta. There had been a few women Mayors of Henley who had served as Stewards during their year of office, but Mrs Ellis was the first to be elected in her own right.

WOMEN'S EIGHTS

Invitation races for women's ***eights*** took place in 1998 and 1999. In 2000 it became an established event for women's eights, competing for the ***Henley Prize*** with the same ***Qualification Rules*** as the ***Grand Challenge Cup*** except that the number of entries is limited to eight.

At present there is no trophy for this event.

THE WOMEN'S QUADRUPLE SCULLS

The decision to establish the ***Women***'s ***Quadruple Sculls*** event was taken at a meeting of the ***Stewards*** in December 2000. This followed the success of the Great Britain Women's Quad who won the silver medal at the Sydney ***Olympic Games*** in 2000. This was the first Olympic rowing medal of any sort won by Great Britain women since women's ***rowing*** and ***sculling*** was first included in the Games in 1976.

The unrestricted entry qualifications are the same as for the ***Grand***, the ***Stewards'***, the ***Queen Mother*** and the ***Henley Prize***, being for any club crew of international standard.

The entrance fee for this event is £50 and the ***Stewards***

have limited the number of entries to eight. At present there is no trophy for the Women's Quadruple Sculls.
See - REGATTA TROPHIES

WOMEN'S SINGLE SCULLS
See - PRINCESS ROYAL CHALLENGE CUP

THE WYFOLD CHALLENGE CUP
The Wyfold Challenge Cup was presented to the Regatta in 1847 by Mr Donkin of Wyfold Court. At that time, eights would race against each other (the races were called 'trial heats') to decide who should '***challenge***' the previous year's winner of the ***Grand*** Challenge Cup - the Wyfold Challenge Cup being presented to the winning challenger.

In 1855 the trophy was presented for ***coxed fours*** and, in 1874, like the ***Stewards*** and the ***Visitors***, the event, often referred to as the 'Wyfolds', became a ***coxless fours*** event.

Since 1996 the entry requirements have been similar to the ***Thames*** with the exclusion of student ***crews*** and certain highly qualified ***athletes*** such as those who have ***rowed*** 'or ***sculled***' in the ***Olympic Games*** and other high ranking events. (Note: The sport generally treats rowing and sculling as separate disciplines, an athlete's status in one not influencing the other) In addition no oarsman may compete in this event if he has previously won any event at the Regatta - other than the ***Temple***, the ***Princess Elizabeth*** and the ***Fawley***. By qualifying the entry in this way the ***Stewards*** have tried to keep this event for 'genuine' club crews below Stewards' standard.

The entrance fee for this event is £50 and the Stewards have limited the number of entries to 32.
See - REGATTA TROPHIES

Recommended reading

The Book of Henley-on-Thames by GHJ(Harry) Tomalin
The Brilliants - A History of the Leander Club by Richard Burnell and Geoffrey Page
British Rowing Almanack published by the Amateur Rowing Association
The Henley-on-Thames Branch by Paul Karau
Henley Races 1903 to 1914 by Sir Theodore Cook
Henley Records 1919 to 1938 by CT Steward.
Henley Royal Regatta by Christopher Dodd
Henley Royal Regatta 150th Magazine published by the Stewards in 1989 to celebrate the Regatta's Sesquicentennial (150th) Anniversary
Henley Royal Regatta 1938 to 1969 published by the Stewards of the Regatta
Henley Royal Regatta - A celebration of 150 years by Richard Burnell
A History of Rowing by Hylton Cleaver
The Hostelries of Henley by Ann Cottingham
Records of Henley Royal Regatta 1839 to 1902 by HT Steward
Regatta Magazine published by the Amateur Rowing Association
Regatta Records 1969 to 1999 published by the Stewards of the Regatta
The River Thames Book by Chris Cove-Smith
The Thames Locks by John Kemplay

AUTHOR

Michael Jones has spent a lifetime in rowing. He has been involved with Henley Royal Regatta for 50 years following in the tradition of his father, grandfather and great grandfather; a labour of love he has now passed on to his son Simon.

As a Chairman's Assistant he has been involved from the outset with the Regatta's successful move into hospitality services on Fawley Meadows, a venture which is still responsible for introducing hundreds of people each year to the Regatta and to rowing.

He is Secretary of the Henley Town & Visitors' Regatta (Henley's second Regatta!), a Committee member and past Captain of Henley Rowing Club, Secretary of the ARA's National Umpires Commission and a member of the Thames Rowing Council. He is Archivist and a past Committee member of Leander Club and was also actively involved in the formative years of the River and Rowing Museum at Henley. He represents much of Henley rowing on the local River Users Group and rowing in general on the Environment Agency's Thames Navigation Working Group.

Although he now lives outside the town, Michael Jones grew up in Henley, his family's involvement in the town stretching back over ten generations to the 17th century.

He owns a sculling boat and a speedboat although, apart from occasionally rowing just to keep fit, has little opportunity these days to mess about on the river - other than as a licensed rowing umpire.

After a career in banking, which took him to the four corners of the world Michael Jones turned to writing and his first book, **Michael Jones Guide to Rowing**, was published early in 2001.

This book is his second venture into the world of non-fiction writing and he hopes to follow it with his Guide to **Memorable Henley Races**.